# Exam Ref AZ-800
# Administering Windows
# Server Hybrid Core
# Infrastructure

Orin Thomas

T0321317

# Exam Ref AZ-800 Administering Windows Server Hybrid Core Infrastructure

Published with the authorization of Microsoft Corporation by:
Pearson Education, Inc.

ISBN-13: 978-0-13-772926-5
ISBN-10: 0-13-772926-X

Library of Congress Control Number: 2022938820

ScoutAutomatedPrintCode

## TRADEMARKS

## WARNING AND DISCLAIMER

## SPECIAL SALES

For information about buying this title in bulk quantities, or for special sales opportunities (which may include electronic versions; custom cover designs; and content particular to your business, training goals, marketing focus, or branding interests), please contact our corporate sales department at corpsales@pearsoned.com or (800) 382-3419.

For government sales inquiries, please contact governmentsales@pearsoned.com.

For questions about sales outside the U.S., please contact intlcs@pearson.com.

**EDITOR-IN-CHIEF**
Brett Bartow

**EXECUTIVE EDITOR**
Loretta Yates

**SPONSORING EDITOR**
Charvi Arora

**DEVELOPMENT EDITOR**
Songlin Qiu

**TECHNICAL EDITOR**
Andrew Warren

**MANAGING EDITOR**
Sandra Schroeder

**SENIOR PROJECT EDITOR**
Tracey Croom

**COPY EDITOR**
Elizabeth Welch

**INDEXER**
Tim Wright

**PROOFREADER**
Barbara Mack

**EDITORIAL ASSISTANT**
Cindy Teeters

**COVER DESIGNER**
Twist Creative, Seattle

**COMPOSITOR**
codeMantra

# Pearson's Commitment to Diversity, Equity, and Inclusion

Pearson is dedicated to creating bias-free content that reflects the diversity of all learners. We embrace the many dimensions of diversity, including but not limited to race, ethnicity, gender, socioeconomic status, ability, age, sexual orientation, and religious or political beliefs.

Education is a powerful force for equity and change in our world. It has the potential to deliver opportunities that improve lives and enable economic mobility. As we work with authors to create content for every product and service, we acknowledge our responsibility to demonstrate inclusivity and incorporate diverse scholarship so that everyone can achieve their potential through learning. As the world's leading learning company, we have a duty to help drive change and live up to our purpose to help more people create a better life for themselves and to create a better world.

Our ambition is to purposefully contribute to a world where

- Everyone has an equitable and lifelong opportunity to succeed through learning
- Our educational products and services are inclusive and represent the rich diversity of learners
- Our educational content accurately reflects the histories and experiences of the learners we serve
- Our educational content prompts deeper discussions with learners and motivates them to expand their own learning (and worldview)

While we work hard to present unbiased content, we want to hear from you about any concerns or needs with this Pearson product so that we can investigate and address them.

Please contact us with concerns about any potential bias at https://www.pearson.com/report-bias.html.

# Contents at a glance

# Contents

## Chapter 3  Manage virtual machines and containers  127

**Chapter 5    Manage storage and file services                 233**

# Introduction

The AZ-800 exam deals with advanced topics that require candidates to have an excellent working knowledge of Windows Server and Azure Hybrid functionality. Some of the exam comprises topics that even experienced Windows Server Hybrid administrators may rarely encounter unless they are consultants who manage hybrid cloud workloads on a regular basis. To be successful in taking this exam, not only do candidates need to understand how to deploy and manage AD DS, hybrid identity, Windows Servers, virtual machines, containers, hybrid networks, and storage services, but they also need to know how to perform these tasks with on-premises and Azure IaaS instances of Windows Server.

Candidates for this exam are information technology (IT) professionals who want to validate their advanced Windows Server Hybrid administration skills and knowledge. To pass, candidates require a thorough theoretical understanding as well as meaningful practical experience implementing the technologies involved.

This edition of this book covers Windows Server and the AZ-800 exam objectives as of mid-2022. As Windows Server hybrid technologies evolve, so do the AZ-800 exam objectives, so you should check carefully if any changes have occurred since this edition of the book was authored and study accordingly.

This book covers every major topic area found on the exam, but it does not cover every exam question. Only the Microsoft exam team has access to the exam questions, and Microsoft regularly adds new questions to the exam, making it impossible to cover specific questions. You should consider this book a supplement to your relevant real-world experience and other study materials. If you encounter a topic in this book that you do not feel completely comfortable with, use the "Need more review?" links you'll find in the text to find more information and take the time to research and study the topic. Great information is available on Microsoft Docs, Microsoft Learn, and in blogs and forums.

## Organization of this book

This book is organized by the "Skills measured" list published for the exam. The "Skills measured" list is available for each exam on Microsoft Learn: *https://microsoft.com/learn*. Each chapter in this book corresponds to a major topic area in the list, and the technical tasks in each topic area determine a chapter's organization. If an exam covers six major topic areas, for example, the book will contain six chapters.

# Microsoft certifications

Microsoft certifications distinguish you by proving your command of a broad set of skills and experience with current Microsoft products and technologies. The exams and corresponding certifications are developed to validate your mastery of critical competencies as you design and develop, or implement and support, solutions with Microsoft products and technologies both on-premises and in the cloud. Certification brings a variety of benefits to the individual and to employers and organizations.

> **NEED MORE REVIEW    ALL MICROSOFT CERTIFICATIONS**
>
> For information about Microsoft certifications, including a full list of available certifications, go to *http://www.microsoft.com/learn.com/learn*.

Check back often to see what is new!

# Quick access to online references

Throughout this book are addresses to webpages that the author has recommended you visit for more information. Some of these addresses (also known as URLs) can be painstaking to type into a web browser, so we've compiled all of them into a single list that readers of the print edition can refer to while they read.

Download the list at

*MicrosoftPressStore.com/ExamRefAZ800/downloads*

The URLs are organized by chapter and heading. Every time you come across a URL in the book, find the hyperlink in the list to go directly to the webpage.

# Errata, updates, & book support

We've made every effort to ensure the accuracy of this book and its companion content. You can access updates to this book—in the form of a list of submitted errata and their related corrections—at:

*MicrosoftPressStore.com/ExamRefAZ800/errata*

If you discover an error that is not already listed, please submit it to us at the same page.

For additional book support and information, please visit *http://www.MicrosoftPressStore.com/Support*.

Please note that product support for Microsoft software and hardware is not offered through the previous addresses. For help with Microsoft software or hardware, go to *http://support.microsoft.com*.

## Stay in touch

Let's keep the conversation going! We're on Twitter: *http://twitter.com/MicrosoftPress*.

# About the author

ORIN THOMAS is a Principal Cloud Advocate at Microsoft and has written more than 3 dozen books for Microsoft Press on such topics as Windows Server, Windows Client, Azure, Office 365, System Center, Exchange Server, Security, and SQL Server. He has authored Azure Architecture courses at Pluralsight and has authored multiple Microsoft Official Curriculum and EdX courses on a variety of IT Pro topics. You can follow him on Twitter at *http://twitter.com/orinthomas*.

# CHAPTER 1

# Deploy and manage Active Directory Domain Services in on-premises and cloud environments

Identity is the keystone of a successful hybrid cloud deployment. Users want to be able to access resources across on-premises and cloud estates using the same set of credentials. For more than two decades, Active Directory Domain Services (AD DS) has been the foundation of the on-premises Microsoft ecosystem and is still used by hundreds of thousands of customers today. Being able to manage and maintain AD DS is a skill that will be critical for many organizations for decades to come. The identity keystone of Microsoft Azure is Azure Active Directory (Azure AD). In this chapter you'll learn how to manage and maintain the complex elements of an on-premises identity infrastructure and how you can build a bridge so that on-premises identities can be used to access resources and workloads in Azure.

## Skills covered in this chapter:

- Skill 1.1: Deploy and manage AD DS domain controllers
- Skill 1.2: Configure and manage multi-site, multi-domain, and multi-forest environments
- Skill 1.3: Create and manage AD DS security principals
- Skill 1.4: Implement and manage hybrid identities
- Skill 1.5: Manage Windows Server by using domain-based Group Policies

## Skill 1.1: Deploy and manage AD DS domain controllers

Domain controllers are the pillars that hold AD DS together and are perhaps the most important servers in your on-premises network. Without domain controllers there is no centralized identity, and with no centralized identity, access to disparate resources becomes at best complicated and at worst logistically impossible. The domain controller server role processes authentication requests, hosts the AD DS database, and maintains all the background processes that keep Microsoft's on-premises identity infrastructure functioning.

---

**This skill covers how to:**

- Deploy and manage domain controllers on-premises
- Deploy and manage domain controllers in Azure
- Deploy Read-Only Domain Controllers (RODCs)
- Troubleshoot flexible single master operations (FSMO) roles

---

# Deploy and manage domain controllers on-premises

Active Directory, the identity glue that binds on-premises Microsoft networks, is at the center of almost all on-premises networks. Although each computer can have its own unique individual user and service accounts, Active Directory provides a central user, computer, and service account store.

But Active Directory is more than an identity store; it can also be used to store data for Active Directory–aware applications. One example of this is Microsoft Exchange Server, which stores server configuration information in Active Directory. Other applications, such as Configuration Manager, are also highly dependent on Active Directory.

## Managing Active Directory

You should perform Active Directory management tasks remotely using Windows Admin Center, management consoles, or PowerShell rather than signing on to the domain controller directly using RDP. If you're doing all your administrative tasks remotely using Windows Admin Center, management consoles, or PowerShell, it won't make any difference to you that you've deployed the domain controller in the more secure Server Core configuration. Using remote administration tools also reduces the chance of malware being introduced to the domain controller. There are countless stories of organizations having their security compromised because an administrator signed in to a server using Remote Desktop, went to download a utility from the internet using the built-in web browser, and ended up with more than they bargained for in terms of malware because they weren't careful about their browsing destinations.

A general rule about consoles is that if you need to perform a task only a couple of times, you should use Windows Admin Center or a console. If you are new to a task, you're less likely to mess it up if you use a GUI tool. This is because a GUI tool holds your hand and assists you through the task. If you must repeatedly perform the same task, and it's a task that you are familiar with, you should automate it using tools such as PowerShell. One caveat is that you should avoid spending days automating a task that takes only a couple of minutes to perform manually unless, over enough time, you'd get those days back because of the amount of time the automation would save you.

There are a number of consoles that you can use to perform Active Directory administrative tasks. These include the following:

- Active Directory Administrative Center
- Active Directory Users and Computers
- Active Directory Sites and Services
- Active Directory Domains and Trusts

As of this writing, Windows Admin Center provides some Active Directory administrative functionality but not nearly enough that AD administrators could use it as their primary tool for managing AD DS. Microsoft's intention is that Windows Admin Center will eventually be the primary tool to manage AD DS. As a part of your AZ-800 studies, you should experiment with what is possible using Windows Admin Center in your own practice lab environment.

### ACTIVE DIRECTORY ADMINISTRATIVE CENTER

Active Directory Administrative Center (ADAC) was introduced with Windows Server 2012, but it never caught on as the primary method of managing AD DS for most administrators. ADAC allows you to manage users, computers, and service accounts to perform tasks with the Active Directory, such as Recycle Bin, and to manage functionality, such as Dynamic Access Control.

ADAC is a newer console that has better search functionality than the other consoles listed in this chapter, which haven't substantively changed since the release of Windows 2000.

You can use ADAC to manage the following:

- User, computer, and service accounts
- Domain and forest functional level
- Fine-grained password policies
- Active Directory Recycle Bin GUI
- Authentication policies
- Dynamic Access Control

ADAC is built on PowerShell, meaning that it provides a graphical interface to build and enact PowerShell cmdlets. You can use the PowerShell History Viewer to see which cmdlets were used to carry out a task that you configured in the GUI. This simplifies the process of automating tasks because you can copy code straight out of the PowerShell history and then paste it into tools such as PowerShell ISE or Visual Studio Code.

One of the most useful elements of ADAC is the search functionality. You can use this functionality to locate accounts that might require further attention, such as users who haven't signed in for a certain period of time, users configured with passwords that never expire, or users with locked accounts. Using the **Add criteria** option in the **Global Search** node of the ADAC, you can search based on the following criteria:

- Users with disabled/enabled accounts
- Users with an expired password
- Users whose password has an expiration date/no expiration date

- Users with enabled but locked accounts
- Users with enabled accounts who haven't logged on for more than a given number of days
- Users with a password expiring in a given number of days
- Computers running as a given domain controller type
- Last modified between given dates
- Object type is user/inetOrgPerson/computer/group/organizational unit
- Directly applied password settings for a specific user
- Directly applied password settings for a specific global security group
- Resultant password settings for a specific user
- Objects with a given last known parent
- Resource property lists containing a given resource property
- Name
- Description
- City
- Department
- Employee ID
- First name
- Job title
- Last name
- SamAccountName
- State/province
- Telephone number
- UPN
- Zip/postal code
- Phonetic company name
- Phonetic department
- Phonetic display name
- Phonetic first name
- Phonetic last name

There are several tasks that you can't do with ADAC or with PowerShell, such as running the Delegation Of Control Wizard. Generally speaking, when managing Active Directory using a console on Windows Server, you should use ADAC as your first option and fall back to Active Directory Users and Computers if you can't accomplish what you need to in ADAC.

## ACTIVE DIRECTORY USERS AND COMPUTERS CONSOLE

The Active Directory Users and Computers console is the one that many system administrators use to perform basic AD-related tasks. They use this console primarily out of habit because almost all functionality present in this console is also present in Active Directory Administrative Center. Active Directory Users and Computers has been around since the days of Windows 2000 Server.

Active Directory Users and Computers allows you to perform a number of tasks, including:

- Running the Delegation of Control Wizard
- Administering different domains within the forest
- Selecting which domain controller or LDAP port the tool connects to
- Finding objects within the domain
- Raising the domain functional level
- Managing the RID Master, PDC Emulator, and Infrastructure Master FSMO role locations
- Creating and editing the properties of
  - Computer accounts
  - User accounts
  - Contacts
  - Groups
  - InetOrgPerson
  - msDS-ShadowPrincipalContainers
  - msImaging-PSPs
  - MSMQ Queue Alias
  - Organizational units
- Printers
- Shared folders
- Resultant Set of Policy planning

The View Advanced Features function allows you to see more details of the Active Directory environment. You enable this from the View menu of Active Directory Users and Computers. Enabling this view allows you to see containers that aren't visible in the standard view. If you've ever read a set of instructions that tell you to locate a specific object using Active Directory Users and Computers, and you haven't been able to find that object, chances are that you haven't enabled the View Advanced Features option.

The Delegation of Control Wizard is only available in Active Directory Users and Computers. This wizard allows you to delegate control over the domain and organizational units (OUs). For example, you use this wizard to delegate the ability for a specific group to reset user passwords in an OU. This wizard is useful when you want to delegate some privileges to a group of IT operations staff but you don't want to grant them all the privileges that they'd inherit if you made them a member of the Domain Admins group.

### ACTIVE DIRECTORY SITES AND SERVICES CONSOLE

You use the Active Directory Sites and Services console to manage Active Directory sites, which indirectly allows you to control a number of things, including replication traffic and which server a client connects to when using products such as Exchange Server. Sites are configured for the forest, with each domain in the forest sharing the same set of sites. You'll learn more about configuring and managing replication and sites later in the chapter.

### ACTIVE DIRECTORY DOMAINS AND TRUSTS CONSOLE

You use the Active Directory Domains and Trusts console to configure and manage trust relationships. By default, all domains in a forest trust each other. Your primary use of this console is to create trust relationships between:

- Domains in separate forests
- Separate forests
- Kerberos V5 realms

When creating a trust, you can choose among the following types:

- **One-Way: Incoming**   In this trust relationship, your local domain or forest is trusted by a remote domain or forest.
- **One-Way: Outgoing**   In this trust relationship, your local domain or forest trusts a remote domain or forest.
- **Two-Way**   In this trust relationship, your local domain or forest trusts (and is trusted by) a remote domain or forest.

When configuring a trust, you can determine whether you want to configure selective authentication. By default, the trust works for all users in the source or destination forest or domain. When you configure selective authentication, you can limit which security principals are allowed access and which resources they can access. You do this by configuring those users with the Allowed To Authenticate permission on each resource computer in the trusting domain or forest. Trusts are discussed in more detail later in the chapter.

## Deploying Domain Controllers

Domain controllers (DCs) are the heart of AD DS. Their primary role is to host the AD DS database, stored in the ntds.dit file. Deploying an AD DS domain controller involves first installing the AD DS binaries and then promoting the domain controller. You can perform this process using the Server Manager console or PowerShell. When you promote the domain controller, you choose whether you want to:

- Add a domain controller to an existing domain
- Add a new domain to an existing forest
- Add a new forest

If you are adding a domain controller to an existing domain, ensure the computer is domain joined before promoting it. When you add a new domain to an existing forest, choose between adding a child domain or a tree domain. When you add a tree domain, you create a new namespace within an existing forest. For example, you can create the Adatum.com domain in the existing contoso.com forest. contoso.com remains the root domain of the forest.

Microsoft's recommendation is that you use a registered root domain name, such as contoso.com for the domain name, rather than a nonexternally resolvable domain name like contoso.internal. Having a registered externally resolvable domain name simplifies the process when you're configuring synchronization with Azure AD Connect.

If you choose to use a publicly registered domain name, understand that Windows Server 2022 and Azure DNS both support split DNS. This means that you can configure zones so that a subset of records is resolvable for clients on external networks and that internal records will only be resolvable by internal clients. Many organizations still use nonresolvable domain names, and you should take the Microsoft advice into account only if you are deploying a new forest or reconfiguring a domain in preparation for synchronizing with Azure Active Directory.

When you add a new child domain to an existing forest, you specify the parent domain. For example, you could add the australia.contoso.com child domain to the contoso.com domain. After you've done that, you can add the victoria.australia.contoso.com child domain to the australia.contoso.com parent domain. Adding a child domain requires Enterprise Administrator credentials in the forest.

When deploying a domain controller in an environment with multiple sites configured, you can select which site you want the domain controller to belong to. You can change this after deployment using the Active Directory Sites and Services console.

## Directory Services Restore Mode passwords

Directory Services Restore Mode (DSRM) allows you to perform an authoritative restore of deleted objects from the AD DS database. You must perform an authoritative restore of deleted items because if you don't, the restored item is deleted the next time the AD database synchronizes with other domain controllers where the item is marked as deleted. Authoritative restores are covered later in this chapter. You configure the Directory Services Restore Mode password on the Domain Controller Options page of the Active Directory Domain Services Configuration Wizard, as shown in Figure 1-1. Note that even though a computer running Windows Server 2022 is being configured as a domain controller, the maximum forest and domain functional levels are Windows Server 2016. This is because there is no Windows Server 2019 or Windows Server 2022 domain or forest functional level.

In the event that you forget the DSRM password, which, in theory, should be unique for each domain controller in your organization, you can reset it by running ntdsutil.exe from an elevated command prompt and entering the following commands at the ntdsutil.exe prompt, at which point you are prompted to enter a new DSRM password:

```
set dsrm password
Reset password on server null
```

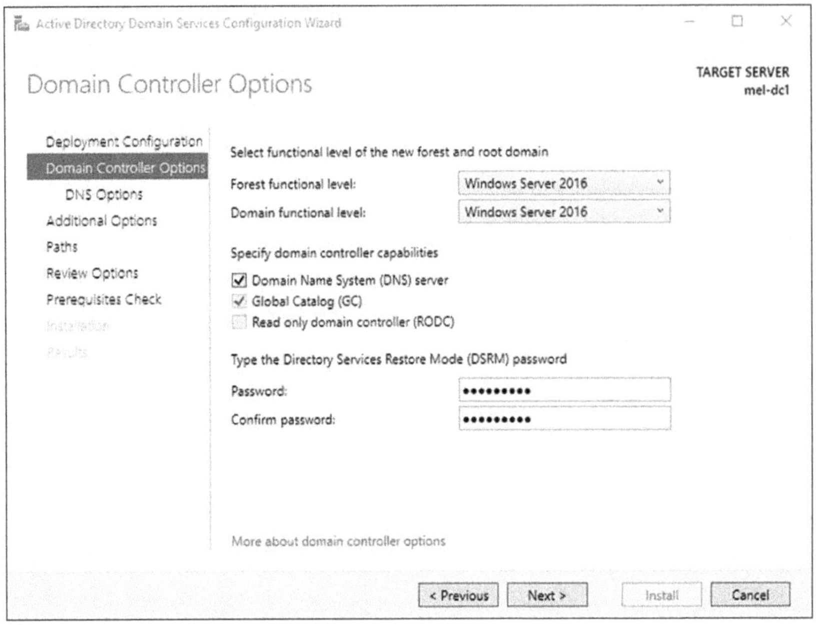

**FIGURE 1-1** Configuring Domain Controller Options.

## Advanced installation options

One of the advanced installation options for domain controllers is to install from media. Installing from media gives you the option of prepopulating the AD DS database for a new DC from a backup of an existing DC's AD DS database, rather than having that database populated through synchronization from other domain controllers in your organization. This is very useful when you need to deploy a DC at a remote location that has limited wide area network (WAN) connectivity and you don't want to flood the WAN link with AD DS database synchronization traffic during domain controller deployment. Instead, you ship a backup of the AD DS database to the remote site, and that backup is used to perform initial AD DS database population. After the newly installed DC connects to other domain controllers, it performs a synchronization, bringing the database up to date with a much smaller synchronization than what would be required when synchronizing from scratch.

## Server Core

Because the reduced attack surface area of Server Core deployments makes it more secure, domain controllers that don't have a GUI dependency are one of several perfect workloads for Server Core deployments. Microsoft recommends deploying domain controllers using the Server Core deployment option and managing those servers remotely.

To configure a computer running Server Core as a domain controller, you can:

1.   Remotely connect to the server using the **Server Manager** console.

2. Run the **Add Roles and Features Wizard** to remotely install the Active Directory binaries on the server.

3. Run the **Active Directory Domain Services Configuration Wizard** to promote the computer to a domain controller.

You can also use Windows Admin Center to deploy the AD DS feature, but the amount of AD DS configuration you can perform remotely using Windows Admin Center isn't yet at parity with the older Server Manager or Microsoft Management Console tools. As an alternative to using the wizard or console, you can run the following PowerShell commands, either locally or remotely, to install the AD DS binaries and promote the server to domain controller:

```
Install-WindowsFeature AD-Domain-Services -IncludeManagementTools
Install-ADDSDomainController -DomainName contoso.internal -InstallDNS:$True -credential
(Get-Credential)
```

In addition to running this set of commands, you need to specify a Directory Service Restore Mode password before the computer running Server Core completes the domain controller promotion process. You'll need to use the `Install-ADDSForest` cmdlet if you are installing the first domain in a new forest, as shown here:

```
Install-ADDSForest -DomainName contoso.internal -InstallDNS
```

## Virtualized domain controllers

Domain controllers can be run on supported virtualization platforms, including the latest version of VMware and Hyper-V. With the Production Checkpoints feature available in Windows Server 2022 Hyper-V, domain controllers can be restored from a checkpoint without causing problems. Microsoft recommends that you run virtualized domain controllers as shielded virtual machines (VMs) on a guarded virtualization fabric or on Azure Stack HCI because this will minimize the chance that a nefarious or compromised virtualization administrator account could be used to access the contents of the DC VM.

## Global catalog servers

Global catalog servers host a full copy of all objects stored in its host directory and a partial, read-only copy of all other objects in other domains in the same forest. They are used when it's necessary to perform a check of other objects in the forest, such as when a check is performed of a universal group's membership, which could contain members from other domains in the forest.

You can use the Active Directory Sites and Services console to configure a server to function as a global catalog server by right-clicking the NTDS settings of the server. Alternatively, you can run the `Set-ADObject` cmdlet. For example, to configure the DC MEL-DC1 in the Melbourne-Site site as a global catalog server, you'd run the following command:

```
Set-ADObject "CN=NTDS Settings,CN=MEL-DC1,CN=Servers,CN=Melbourne-Site,CN=Sites,
CN=Configuration,DC=Contoso,DC=Internal" -Replace @{options='1'}
```

Consider the following when choosing to deploy Global Catalog servers:

- For optimal performance, make every domain controller a Global Catalog server in a single domain forest.
- In multi-domain forests, deploy at least one Global Catalog server to each site that has more than 100 users.

The drawback to deploying Global Catalog servers in multi-domain environments (and the reason why this role isn't enabled by default) is replication. In multi-domain forests in which universal groups are in use, Global Catalog servers can be responsible for a substantial amount of replication traffic across branch-office WAN links. If a site has fewer than 100 users, you can enable universal group membership caching to achieve a similar result without the bandwidth utilization that deploying a Global Catalog server incurs.

Universal group membership caching (UGMC) performs a function similar to the one that a Global Catalog server performs. UGMC is suitable for small sites that don't have enough users to justify deploying a Global Catalog server. You enable UGMC at the site level instead of the Global Catalog server level by configuring NTDS Site Settings properties.

## Active Directory backup

AD DS is backed up when you perform a backup of the server's system state. This occurs when you back up all critical volumes on a domain controller. The primary tool you use for backing up this data is Windows Server Backup, which is not installed by default on computers running Windows Server. You can install Windows Server Backup using the following PowerShell command:

```
Install-WindowsFeature -IncludeAllSubFeature -IncludeManagementTools Windows-
Server-Backup
```

The majority of restore operations occur because Active Directory objects were accidentally (rather than deliberately) deleted. You can configure objects to be protected from accidental deletion by editing the object properties. When you attempt to delete an object that is protected from accidental deletion, a dialog box will inform you that the object can't be deleted because it is protected from accidental deletion. This protection option must be removed before you or anyone else can delete the object.

## Restoring deleted items

Sometimes an Active Directory account, such as a user account or even an entire OU, is accidentally or, on occasion, maliciously deleted. Rather than go through the process of re-creating the deleted item or items, it's possible to restore the items. Deleted items are retained within the AD DS database for a period of time specified as the *tombstone lifetime*. You can recover a deleted item without having to restore the item from a backup of Active Directory as long as the item was deleted in the Tombstone Lifetime window.

The default tombstone lifetime for an Active Directory environment at the Windows Server 2008 forest functional level or higher is 180 days. You can check the value of the tombstone lifetime by issuing the following command from an elevated command prompt (substituting dc=Contoso,dc=Internal for the suffix of your organization's forest root domain):

```
Dsquery * "cn=Directory Service,cn=Windows NT,cn=Services,cn=Configuration,dc=Contoso,dc
=Internal" -scope base -attr tombstonelifetime
```

For most organizations the 180-day default is fine, but some administrators might want to increase or decrease this value to give them a greater or lesser window for easily restoring deleted items. You can change the default tombstone lifetime by performing the following steps:

1. From an elevated command prompt or PowerShell session, type **ADSIEdit.msc**.

2. From the Action menu, select **Connect To**. In the **Connection Settings** dialog box, ensure that **Configuration** is selected under **Select a well known Naming Context**, as shown in Figure 1-2, and then select **OK**.

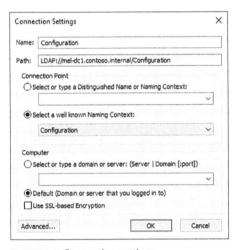

**FIGURE 1-2** Connection settings.

3. Navigate to, and then right-click the CN=Services, CN=Windows NT, CN=Directory Service node and select Properties.

4. In the list of attributes, select **tombstoneLifetime**, as shown in Figure 1-3, and select Edit.

5. Enter the new value, and then select **OK** twice.

**FIGURE 1-3** Tombstone lifetime.

### ACTIVE DIRECTORY RECYCLE BIN

Active Directory Recycle Bin allows you to restore items that have been deleted from Active Directory but that are still present within the database because the tombstone lifetime has not been exceeded. Active Directory Recycle Bin requires that the domain functional level be set to Windows Server 2008 R2 or higher. You can't use the Active Directory Recycle Bin to restore items that were deleted before you enabled Active Directory Recycle Bin.

Once it's activated, you can't deactivate the Active Directory Recycle Bin. There isn't any great reason to want to deactivate AD Recycle Bin once it's activated. You don't have to use it to restore deleted items should you still prefer to go through the authoritative restore process.

To activate the Active Directory Recycle Bin, perform the following steps:

1.  Open the **Active Directory Administrative Center** and select the domain that you want to enable.

2.  In the **Tasks** pane, select **Enable Recycle Bin**, as shown in Figure 1-4.

After you have enabled the AD Recycle Bin, you can restore an object from the newly available **Deleted Objects** container. This is, of course, assuming that the object was deleted after the Recycle Bin was enabled and assuming that the tombstone lifetime value has not been exceeded. To recover the object, select the object in the Deleted Objects container and then select **Restore** or **Restore To**. Figure 1-5 shows a deleted item being selected that can then be restored to its original location. The Restore To option allows you to restore the object to another available location, such as another OU.

**FIGURE 1-4** Enable Recycle Bin.

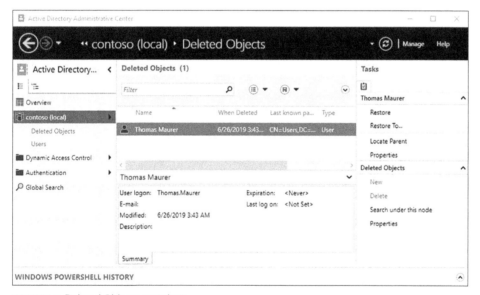

**FIGURE 1-5** Deleted Objects container.

## AUTHORITATIVE RESTORE

An *authoritative restore* is performed when you want the items you are recovering to overwrite items that are in the current Active Directory database. If you don't perform an authoritative restore, Active Directory assumes that the restored data is simply out of date and overwrites it when it is synchronized from another domain controller. If you perform a normal Restore on an item that was backed up last Tuesday when it was deleted the following Thursday, the item is deleted the next time the Active Directory database is synchronized. You do not need to perform an authoritative restore if you only have one domain controller (DC) in your organization because there is no other domain controller that can overwrite the changes.

Authoritative Restore is useful in the following scenarios:

- You haven't enabled Active Directory Recycle Bin.

- You have enabled Active Directory Recycle Bin, but the object you want to restore was deleted before you enabled Active Directory Recycle Bin.

- You need to restore items that are older than the tombstone lifetime of the AD DS database.

To perform an authoritative restore, you need to reboot a DC into Directory Services Restore Mode. If you want to restore an item that is older than the tombstone lifetime of the AD DS database, you also need to restore the AD DS database. You can do this by restoring the system state data on the server. You'll likely need to take the DC temporarily off the network to perform this operation simply because if you restore a computer with old system state data and the DC synchronizes, all the data that you wish to recover will be deleted when the domain controller synchronizes.

You can configure a server to boot into Directory Services Restore Mode from the System Configuration utility. To do this, select **Active Directory repair** on the **Boot** tab, as shown in Figure 1-6. After you've finished with Directory Services Restore Mode, use the same utility to restore normal boot functionality.

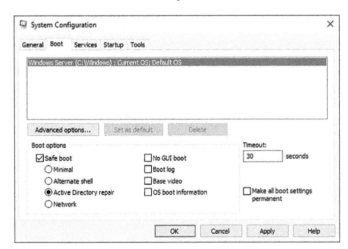

**FIGURE 1-6** System Configuration.

To enter Directory Services Restore Mode, you need to enter the Directory Services Restore Mode password.

To perform an authoritative restore, perform the following general steps:

1. Choose a computer that functions as a Global Catalog server. This DC functions as your restore server.

2.  Locate the most recent system state backup that contains the objects that you want to restore.

3.  Restart the restore server in DSRM mode. Enter the DSRM password.

4.  Restore the system state data.

5.  Use the following command to restore items (where `Mercury` is the object name, `Planets` is the OU that it is contained in, and `contoso.com` is the host domain):

```
Ntdsutil "authoritative restore" "restore object cn=Mercury,ou=Planets,dc=contoso,
dc=com" q q
```

6.  If an entire OU is deleted, you can use the Restore Subtree option. For example, if you deleted the Planets OU and all the accounts that it held in the contoso.com domain, you could use the following command to restore it and all the items it contained:

```
Ntdsutil "authoritative restore" "restore subtree OU=Planets,DC=contoso,DC=com" q q
```

### NONAUTHORITATIVE RESTORE

When you perform a nonauthoritative restore, you restore a backup of Active Directory that's in a good known state. When rebooted, the domain controller contacts replication partners and overwrites the contents of the nonauthoritative restore with all updates that have occurred to the database since the backup was taken. Nonauthoritative restores are appropriate when the Active Directory database on a database has been corrupted and needs to be recovered. You don't use a nonauthoritative restore to recover deleted items, since any deleted items that are restored when performing the nonauthoritative restore will be overwritten when changes replicate from other DCs.

Performing a full system recovery on a DC functions in a similar way to performing a non-authoritative restore. When the recovered DC boots, all changes that have occurred in Active Directory since the backup was taken overwrite existing information in the database.

### OTHER METHODS OF RECOVERING DELETED ITEMS

Although the recommended way of ensuring that deleted Active Directory objects are recoverable is to enable the Active Directory Recycle Bin or to perform an authoritative restore using DSRM, you can also use tombstone reanimation to recover a deleted object. Tombstone reanimation involves using the ldp.exe utility to modify the attributes of the deleted object so that it no longer has the deleted attribute. Because it may lead to unpredictable results, you should use tombstone reanimation only if no backups of the system state data exist and you haven't enabled the Active Directory Recycle Bin.

Although Active Directory snapshots do represent copies of the Active Directory database at a particular point in time, you should use mounted snapshots to determine which backup contains the items you want to authoritatively restore. It is possible to export objects from snapshots and to reimport them into Active Directory using tools such as LDIFDE (LDAP Data Interchange Format Data Exchange), but this can lead to unpredictable results.

## Virtual domain controller cloning

All versions of Windows Server since Windows Server 2012 support virtual domain controller cloning. Rather than redeploying DCs from scratch each time you need one, domain controller cloning allows you to take an existing virtual machine (VM), make a copy of it, and deploy that copy.

Virtual domain controller cloning has the following prerequisites:

- The hypervisor must support VM-GenerationID. The version of Hyper-V included with Windows Server 2012 and later supports this technology, as do the most recent versions of VMware.

- The source domain controller needs to be running Windows Server 2012 or later.

- The domain controller that hosts the PDC Emulator role must be online and contactable by the cloned DC. The computer that hosts the PDC Emulator role must also be running Windows Server 2012 or later.

- The source DC must be a member of the Cloneable Domain Controllers group.

You also need to create the DCCloneConfig.xml file. You can do this by using the New-ADDCCloneConfig cmdlet in PowerShell. When running this cmdlet, you must specify the cloned DC's IPv4 address information and the site the cloned DC is deployed into.

For example, to create the clone configuration file for a clone DC that has the IP address 10.10.10.42 with the subnet mask 255.255.255.0, a default gateway of 10.10.10.1, a DNS server address of 10.10.10.10, and a site name of MEL-SITE, issue this command:

```
New-ADDCCloneConfigFile -IPv4Address 10.10.10.402 -IPv4DefaultGateway 10.10.10.1
-IPv4SubnetMask 255.255.255.0 -IPv4DNSResolver 10.10.10.10 -Static -SiteName MEL-SITE
```

After the clone configuration file is created, you import the VM using this file and specify a copy of the source DC's exported virtual hard disk.

> **NEED MORE REVIEW?**   **INSTALL ACTIVE DIRECTORY DOMAIN SERVICES**
>
> You can learn more about topic at *https://docs.microsoft.com/windows-server/identity/ad-ds/ deploy/install-active-directory-domain-services--level-100-/.*

## AD DS Structure

AD DS is made up of forests and domains. A forest is a collection of AD DS domains that share a schema and some security principals. The majority of organizations in the world have a single forest domain. Multiple domain forests are generally used by larger, geographically dispersed organizations.

### DOMAINS

For the majority of organizations in the world, a single domain would be sufficient. There are two general reasons for having multiple domains in a forest. The first is that your organization is geographically dispersed, and there are issues around domain replication traffic. The second is that your organization is very large. A single domain can hold a staggering number of objects. Unless your organization has tens of thousands of users, a single domain is usually more than enough.

A domain tree is a collection of domains that share a namespace in a parent-child relationship. For example, the domains australia.contoso.com and tonga.contoso.com would be child domains of the contoso.com domain.

You should always deploy at least two DCs per domain for redundancy purposes. Make sure that if you have a multi-domain forest, you are making regular backups of the domain controllers in the root domain. There has been more than one organization with a multi-domain forest that has had the root domain AD DS domain controllers fail irreparably, making it necessary to redeploy the entire forest from scratch.

### MULTI-DOMAIN ACTIVE DIRECTORY ENVIRONMENTS

The majority of current AD DS deployments in small and medium-sized enterprises have a single domain. This hasn't always been the case because earlier versions of the Windows Server operating system, such as Windows NT4, supported far fewer accounts. Supporting a smaller number of accounts often necessitated the use of multiple domains, and it wasn't unusual to see medium-sized organizations that used complicated domain structures.

Each Windows Server domain controller can create approximately 2.15 billion objects during its lifetime, and each domain supports the creation of up to approximately 2.15 billion relative identifiers (RIDs). Given this, however, few administrators implement multiple-domain forests because they need to support a large number of users.

There are many reasons why organizations implement multi-domain forests. These can include but are not limited to:

- **Historical domain structure**  Even though newer versions of the Windows Server operating system handle large numbers of objects more efficiently, some organizations have retained the forest structure that was established when the organization first adopted AD DS.

- **Organizational or political reasons**  Some organizations are conglomerates, and they might be composed of separate companies that share a common administrative and management core. An example of this is a university faculty in Europe or Australia, such as a Faculty of Science, that consists of different departments or schools, such as the School of Physics and the Department of Botany. For political or organizational reasons, it might have been decided that each department or school should have its own domain that is a part of the overall faculty forest. AD DS gives organizations the ability to create domain namespaces that meet their needs, even if those needs might not directly map to the most efficient way of accomplishing a goal from a strict technical perspective.

- **Security reasons**   Domains enable you to create authentication and authorization boundaries. You can also use domains to partition administrative privileges so that you can have one set of administrators who are able to manage computers and users in their own domain, but who are not able to manage computers and users in a separate domain. Although it's possible to accomplish a similar goal by delegating privileges, many organizations prefer to use separate domains to accomplish this goal.

## DOMAIN TREES

A *domain tree* is a set of names that share a common root domain name. For example, contoso.com can have pacific.contoso.com and atlantic.contoso.com as child domains, and these domains can have child domains themselves. A forest can have multiple domain trees. When you create a new tree in a forest, the root of the new tree is a child domain of the original root domain. In Figure 1-7, adatum.com is the root of a new domain tree in the contoso.com forest.

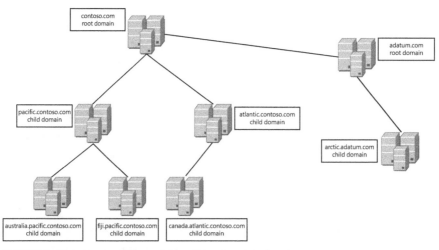

**FIGURE 1-7**  Contoso.com as the root domain in a two-tree forest.

The depth of a domain tree is limited by a domain having maximum fully qualified domain name (FQDN) length for a host of 64 characters.

## INTRA-FOREST AUTHENTICATION

All domains within the same forest automatically trust one another. This means that in the environment shown earlier in Figure 1-7, you can assign a user in the Australia.pacific.contoso.com permissions to a resource in the arctic.adatum.com domain without performing any extra configuration.

Because of the built-in automatic trust relationships, a single forest implementation is not appropriate for separate organizations, even when they are in partnership with one another. A single forest makes it possible for one or more users to have administrative control. Most organizations aren't comfortable even with trusted partners having administrative control over their IT environments. When you do need to allow users from partner organizations to have access to resources, you can configure trust relationships or federation.

## DOMAIN FUNCTIONAL LEVELS

The domain functional level determines which AD DS features are available and which operating systems can participate as domain controllers within the domain. The domain functional level determines the minimum domain controller operating system. For example, if the domain functional level is set to Windows Server 2012, DCs must run Windows Server 2012 or later. This rule does not apply to member servers. You can have a domain running at the Windows Server 2016 functional level that still has servers running the Windows Server 2012 R2 operating system. Unlike previous versions of the Windows Server operating system, which introduced new domain functional levels, there is no Windows Server 2019 or Windows Server 2022 domain functional level and Windows Server 2016 is as far as you can go.

You can configure or verify the current domain functional level from the Active Directory Administrative Center console by selecting the domain and selecting Raise Domain Functional Level. You can also perform this task from the Active Directory Domains and Trusts console and the Active Directory Users and Computers console. You can also configure the domain functional level using the `Set-ADDomainMode` PowerShell cmdlet.

Windows Server 2022 DCs support the following functional levels:

- Windows Server 2008
- Windows Server 2008 R2
- Windows Server 2012
- Windows Server 2012 R2
- Windows Server 2016

You can introduce a DC running Windows Server 2022 to a domain at the Windows Server 2008 functional level as long as all the appropriate updates are installed and the domain is configured to use Distributed File Service (DFS) rather than File Replication System (FRS) for replication. You can raise the functional level after you've retired existing DCs running older versions of the Windows Server operating system. If all your DCs are running Windows Server 2022, you should update your domain functional level to the Windows Server 2016 functional level.

Even when older Windows Server DCs have long been removed, it's not unusual for people to have forgotten to elevate the functional level. Because you get greater functionality by raising functional levels and there is no downside to doing so beyond not being able to introduce a domain controller running an operating system below that of the functional level, you should raise functional levels as high as possible. Because you should be running only Windows Server 2022 domain controllers to have the best possible security, your organization's domain functional level should be Windows Server 2016.

## FORESTS

A *forest* is a collection of domains that share a schema and a Global Catalog. There are automatic trust relationships between all domains in a forest. Accounts in one domain in a forest can be granted rights to resources in other domains. As mentioned earlier in this chapter, forests don't need to have a contiguous namespace. For example, a forest can contain both the contoso.com and adatum.com domains.

There are several reasons why an organization might have multiple forests with trust relationships configured between those forests. The most common is that one organization has acquired another and multiple forests exist until such a time that the users and resources hosted in the forest of the acquired organization are moved to the forest of the acquiring organization. A less common one is that an organization is splitting off a part of itself and users need to be migrated out of the existing forest and into a new forest prior to the split occurring.

Forest functional levels are determined by the minimum domain functional level in the forest. After you've raised the domain functional levels in the forest, you can raise the forest functional level. Unlike in previous versions of AD DS, it is possible to lower both the forest and domain functional levels after they have been raised. An important caveat with this is that the forest functional level must be lowered so that it is never higher than the lowest intended domain functional level.

You can raise the forest functional level from the Active Directory Administrative Center console by selecting the forest root domain and selecting Raise Forest Functional Level. You can also perform this task from the Active Directory Domains and Trusts console. You can also configure the domain functional level using the Set-ADForestMode PowerShell cmdlet.

### ACCOUNT AND RESOURCE FORESTS

Some organizations with strict security requirements deploy Enhanced Security Administrative Environment (ESAE) forests. In an ESAE forest design, all of the accounts used for administrative tasks in the production forest are hosted in a second forest known as the ESAE, bastion, or administrative forest. The ESAE forest is configured with one-way trust relationships with the production forest.

In their native administrative forest, the accounts used for administrative tasks in the production forest are traditional unprivileged user accounts. These accounts and the groups that they are members of in the administrative forest are delegated privileges in the production forest.

The advantage of this approach is that should one of these accounts become compromised, it can't be used to alter any permissions or settings in the administrative forest because the account only has privileges in the production forest.

## Active Directory database optimization

There are several steps you can take to optimize your Active Directory database, including defragmenting the database, performing a file integrity check, and performing a semantic integrity check.

When you defragment the Active Directory database, a new copy of the database file, Ntds. dit, is created. You can defragment the Active Directory database or perform other operations only if the database is offline. You can take the Active Directory database offline by stopping the AD DS service, which you can do from the Update Services console or by issuing the following command from an elevated PowerShell prompt:

```
Stop-Service NTDS -force
```

You use the ntdsutil.exe utility to perform the fragmentation using the following command:

```
ntdsutil.exe "activate instance ntds" files "compact to c:\\" quit quit
```

After the defragmentation has completed, copy the defragmented database over the original located in C:\windows\NTDS\ntds.dit and delete all log files in the C:\windows\NTDS folder.

You can check the integrity of the file that stores the database using the ntdsutil.exe by issuing the following command from an elevated prompt when the AD DS service is stopped:

```
ntdsutil.exe "activate instance ntds" files integrity quit quit
```

To verify that the AD DS database is internally consistent, you can run a semantic consistency check. The semantic check can also repair the database if problems are detected. You can perform a semantic check using ntdsutil.exe by issuing the following command:

```
ntdsutil.exe "activate instance ntds" "semantic database analysis" "verbose on" "go fixup" quit quit
```

## Active Directory metadata cleanup

The graceful way to remove a domain controller is to run the Active Directory Domain Services Configuration Wizard to remove AD DS. You can also remove the domain controller gracefully by using the `Uninstall-ADDSDomainController` cmdlet. When you do this, the domain controller is removed, all references to the domain controller in Active Directory are also removed, and any FSMO roles that the domain controller hosted are transferred to other DCs in the domain.

Active Directory metadata cleanup is necessary if a domain controller has been forcibly removed from Active Directory. Here's an example: An existing domain controller catches fire or is accidentally thrown out of a window by a systems administrator having a bad day. When this happens, references to the domain controller within Active Directory remain. These references, especially if the domain controller hosted FSMO roles, can cause problems if not removed. Metadata cleanup is the process of removing these references.

If you use the Active Directory Users and Computers or Active Directory Sites and Services console to delete the computer account of a domain controller, the metadata associated with the domain controller are cleaned up. The console will prompt you when you try to delete the account of a domain controller that can't be contacted. You confirm that you can't contact the domain controller. When you do this, metadata cleanup occurs automatically.

To remove server metadata using ntdsutil, issue the following command, where <ServerName> is the distinguished name of the domain controller whose metadata you want to remove from Active Directory:

```
Ntdsutil "metadata cleanup" "remove selected server <ServerName>"
```

## Active Directory snapshots

You can use ntdsutil.exe to create snapshots of the Active Directory database. A *snapshot* is a point-in-time copy of the database. You can use tools to examine the contents of the database as it existed at that point in time. It is also possible to transfer objects from the snapshot of the Active Directory database back into the version currently used with your domain's domain controllers. The AD DS service must be running to create a snapshot.

To create a snapshot, execute the following command:

```
Ntdsutil snapshot "Activate Instance NTDS" create quit quit
```

Each snapshot is identified by a GUID. You can create a scheduled task to create snapshots on a regular basis. You can view a list of all current snapshots on a domain controller by running the following command:

```
Ntdsutil snapshot "list all" quit quit
```

To mount a snapshot, make a note of the GUID of the snapshot that you want to mount and then issue the following command:

```
Ntdsutil "activate instance ntds" snapshot "mount {GUID}" quit quit
```

When mounting snapshots, you must use the {} braces with the GUID. You can also use the snapshot number associated with the GUID when mounting the snapshot with the ntdsutil.exe command. This number is always an odd number.

When the snapshot mounts, take a note of the path associated with the snapshot. You use this path when mounting the snapshot with dsamain. For example, to use dsamain with the snapshot mounted as c:\$SNAP_201212291630_VOLUMEc$\, issue this command:

```
Dsamain /dbpath 'c:\$SNAP_201212291630_VOLUMEC$\Windows\NTDS\ntds.dit' /ldapport 50000
```

You can choose to mount the snapshot using any available TCP port number; 50000 is just easy to remember. Leave the PowerShell windows open when performing this action. After the snapshot is mounted, you can access it using Active Directory Users and Computers. To do this, perform the following steps:

1. Open **Active Directory Users and Computers**.
2. Right-click the root node, and select **Change Domain Controller**.
3. In the **Change Directory Server** dialog box, enter the name of the domain controller and the port, and select **OK**. You can then view the contents of the snapshot using Active Directory Users and Computers in the same way that you would the contents of the current directory.

You can dismount the snapshot by using Ctrl+C to close dsamain, and then executing the following command to dismount the snapshot:

```
Ntdsutil.exe "activate instance ntds" snapshot "unmount {GUID}" quit quit
```

# Deploy and manage domain controllers in Azure

Many organizations deploy Windows Server Active Directory Domain Controllers as VMs in Azure, and join other VMs on the same virtual network to the domains hosted on these domain controllers. These domain controllers can be configured as:

- **A standalone forest**   In this configuration, the domain controllers function as the domain root in their own forest. Many organizations deploy this simple type of domain when migrating on-premises applications that have a dependency on AD DS and NTLM authentication to Azure. You can configure a trust relationship to an on-premises AD DS forest if a VPN or ExpressRoute connection to that on-premises forest is appropriately configured.

- **A domain in an existing forest**   These domain controllers are in a child domain of an on-premises forest and connect to that on-premises forest through appropriately configured VPN or ExpressRoute connections. The Azure Virtual Network that hosts these domain controllers is configured as a separate Active Directory Site.

- **A site in an existing on-premises domain**   It's possible to configure AD DS domain controllers connected through a site-to-site VPN or ExpressRoute connection as simply another site in an existing on-premises domain.

Most organizations that want to use on-premises security principals with resources hosted on Azure infrastructure-as-a-service (IaaS) VMs should configure a forest trust relationship. This allows those security principals to be used to access those resources without the complications of trying to extend an on-premises forest to Azure.

When deploying a Windows Server VM that will function as an AD DS domain controller in Azure, consider the following configuration options:

- Configure a separate virtual data disk for the VM to store the Active Directory database, logs, and sysvol folder.

- Configure Host Cache Preference to None for this data disk. By default, data disks attached to an IaaS VM use write through caching, and this can cause errors in some circumstances with AD DS.

- Ensure that you deploy two VMs in the domain controller role and add them to an availability set.

- Configure the VM network interface with a static private IP address.

- Configure the virtual network DNS settings to point VMs on the virtual network to the IP addresses of the newly deployed AD DS domain controllers. You can't configure DNS settings within an Azure IaaS VM as this operation must be performed using the Azure management tools.

- As you would with on-premises domain controllers, prevent the VMs hosting this role from direct inbound or outbound communication with any host on the internet. Restrict communication using a Network Security Group to known authorized services. Make remote connections either through Windows Admin Center in the Azure Portal or through a VPN or ExpressRoute connection from an on-premises network.

# Deploy read-only domain controllers (RODCs)

Read-only domain controllers (RODCs) are a special type of domain controller. They host a read-only copy of the AD DS database. Rather than storing the passwords for all users in the domain, RODCs only store the passwords of a specific set of accounts that you configure. The first domain controller in a new domain or forest cannot be an RODC.

The justification for RODCs is that DCs sometimes need to be located in places where servers have poor physical security and might be stolen. For example, many organizations had branch offices where servers were kept under someone's desk. A good rule of thumb is that you should consider a location insecure if it is accessible to anyone other than IT staff. If a janitor can pull out a computer's power cord to plug in a vacuum cleaner, the computer isn't in a secure location.

If a server that hosts a domain controller is stolen, the best practice is to reset the account passwords that might have been compromised because it's possible, with the correct tools, to extract passwords from the AD DS database if you have direct access to it. If an ordinary DC is stolen, you would, in theory, need to reset the passwords of every account in the domain because you could never be sure that someone hadn't gained access to the AD DS database and found a way to extract the passwords of people in your organization.

With shielded VMs and shielded fabrics, it's possible to run a DC in a manner where the VM itself is protected by encryption. In the event that the host server is stolen, the AD DS database cannot be recovered because the contents of the virtualization server's storage are encrypted using BitLocker.

Concerns about the physical security of a DC are the primary reason to deploy an RODC, so it is extremely unlikely that you would have both an RODC and a writable DC at the same site. RODCs are for sites where the domain controller once was placed in a location that wasn't secure. However, if you do have concerns about the security of a location, it's probably not a great idea to deploy a domain controller at that location!

## RODC password replication

One of the most important steps in configuring an RODC is limiting which passwords can be replicated down to the server from a writable domain controller. The default configuration of an RODC has it store almost everything from AD DS except for user and computer account passwords. In the event that a user or computer account needs to be authenticated against AD DS, the RODC acts as a proxy for a writable Windows Server DC. The authentication occurs but depends on the WAN link to be functional because if you could host a writable DC locally, you wouldn't need the RODC.

Although you can configure an RODC to not cache any passwords locally, you can configure an RODC to cache the passwords of select staff working at a branch office to speed their login. Caching passwords also allows branch office users to log in if the WAN link fails. If the WAN link fails and the user's credentials are not cached, the user is simply unable to log in to the domain.

You configure which accounts can authenticate using the RODC by using the Password Replication Policy, as shown in Figure 1-8. By default, only members of the Allowed RODC Password Replication group can use the RODC to authenticate. This is only the case if the user account is not a member of the Account Operators, Administrators, Backup Operators, Server Operators, or Denied RODC Password Replication Group groups.

**FIGURE 1-8** Password Replication Policy.

## RODC partial attribute set

You can configure Active Directory so that only specific attributes on AD DS objects are replicated to an RODC. You would do this because some applications are configured to store sensitive data such as passwords or encryption keys as attributes for an object. If you add these sensitive attributes to the filtered attributes set, you can ensure that this information will not be replicated and stored on an RODC.

It is not possible to add system-critical attributes to the RODC filtered attribute set. Attributes that cannot be added to the filtered attribute set are those required for AD DS, the Local Security Authority (LSA), Security Accounts Manager (SAM), and Microsoft-specific security services providers to be able to function correctly. You mark an attribute as confidential by removing the Read permission for that attribute for the Authenticated Users group.

## RODC local administrators

Because you deploy RODCs as a security measure, they are almost always placed at branch office sites. Resources at branch office sites are often sparse, so it is also likely that you'll co-locate other services on the server hosting the RODC role. For example, a server that functions as an RODC can also function as a file server, DNS server, DHCP server, and local intranet server. You can allow a user without Domain Admin privileges to deploy an RODC if you have pre-created an RODC account and added it to the appropriate Active Directory Domain Services site and the user is a member of the local Administrators group on the computer. You can perform this task in PowerShell or Active Directory Administrative Center.

If the computer hosting the RODC role also needs to host other roles, you might need to grant administrator access to a user who works at the branch office (but who is not a member of your organization's usual IT staff) in case your normal remote administration techniques don't work. RODCs differ from normal domain controllers in that you can grant local administrator access without having to make the user a member of the Domain Admins group.

To configure a user to function as a local administrator on the computer that hosts the RODC role, edit the properties of the RODC's computer account and configure a security group for the Managed By setting.

## Decommissioning an RODC

If you suspect that an RODC has been compromised, you can delete the RODC's account from the Domain Controllers container in Active Directory Users and Computers. When you do this, you get the option of resetting all passwords for user and computer accounts that were cached on the RODC, as well as the option of exporting a list of all potentially compromised accounts.

> **NEED MORE REVIEW?** **READ-ONLY DOMAIN CONTROLLERS**
>
> You can learn more about topic at *https://docs.microsoft.com/windows-server/identity/ ad-ds/deploy/rodc/install-a-windows-server-2012-active-directory-read-only-domain- controller--rodc---level-200-.*

# Troubleshoot flexible single master operations (FSMO) roles

The FSMO roles are five special roles present on domain controllers. Two of these roles, the schema master and the domain naming master, are unique within each forest. The other three roles, PDC emulator, infrastructure master, and RID master, must be present within each domain in the forest. For example, in a three-domain forest there is only one schema master and domain naming master, but each domain in the forest has its own PDC emulator, infrastructure master, and RID master.

By default, FSMO roles are allocated to the first domain controller in a domain. After you have more than one domain controller in each domain, you should manually start to move FSMO roles to other domain controllers. This protects you from a situation where the first domain controller deployed in each domain goes offline and all FSMO roles become unavailable. When you do need to take a domain controller offline for an extended period of time, ensure that you transition any FSMO roles that it hosts to another domain controller in the same domain.

## Schema master

The schema master is the single server in the forest that is able to process updates to the AD DS schema. The AD DS schema defines the functionality of AD DS. For example, by modifying the schema, you can increase the available attributes for existing objects as well as enable AD DS to store new objects. Products such as Exchange Server and Configuration Manager require that the default AD DS schema be extended prior to product installation so that each product can store important data in AD DS.

The domain controllers that host the schema master role should be located in the root domain of the forest. If you need to extend the schema before installing products such as Exchange Server, do so either on the computer that hosts the schema master role or on a computer in the same site. The account used to extend the schema needs to be a member of the Schema Admins security group. If you're unable to extend the schema, the computer that hosts this FSMO role may not be available.

You can determine which computer hosts the schema master role by running the following PowerShell command:

```
Get-ADForest example.internal | FT SchemaMaster
```

## Domain naming master

The domain naming master is a forest-level role that is responsible for managing the addition and removal of domains from the forest. The domain naming master also manages references to domains in trusted forests. In a multi-domain environment, the domain controller that hosts this forest-level role should be deployed in the root forest. The domain naming master is also contacted when new instances of AD DS application directory partitions are added, such as when you configure a limited directory partition replication scope for an AD DS integrated DNS zone. If you can't add new domains or partitions, the computer hosting this FSMO role may not be available.

You can determine which server hosts the domain naming master role by running the following PowerShell command:

```
Get-ADForest example.internal | FT DomainNamingMaster
```

## PDC emulator

The PDC (Primary Domain Controller) emulator role is a domain-level FSMO role that is responsible for handling both changes to account passwords as well as domain time synchronization. Account Lockout is also processed by the PDC emulator. PDC emulators in child domains synchronize time against the PDC emulator in the forest root domain. You should ensure that the PDC emulator in the forest root domain synchronizes against a reliable external time source. If users are unable to change passwords or accounts aren't able to be unlocked, the PDC emulator may have failed.

To determine which domain controller in a specific domain hosts the PDC emulator role, run the following PowerShell command:

```
Get-ADDomain example.internal | FT PDCEmulator
```

## Infrastructure master

The computer that hosts the infrastructure master role keeps track of changes that occur in other domains in the forest as they apply to objects in the local domain. The infrastructure master FSMO role holder updates an object's SID (Security Identifier) and distinguished name in a cross-domain object reference. If group names or memberships for groups hosted in other domains don't appear current in the local domain, it may be that the infrastructure master has failed.

You should avoid having the infrastructure master role co-located with a domain controller that hosts the Global Catalog server role unless all DCs in the domain are configured as Global Catalog servers. You can determine which computer in a domain hosts the infrastructure master role by running the following PowerShell command:

```
Get-ADDomain example.internal | FT InfrastructureMaster
```

## RID master

The RID (Relative ID) master processes relative ID requests from domain controllers in a specific domain. Relative IDs and domain Security IDs are combined to create a unique Security ID (SID) for the object. There is a RID master in each domain in the forest. When a new security principal object like a group or user account is created, a unique SID is attached to that object. SIDs consist of:

- Domain SID that will be the same for all SIDs created in the host domain
- A RID that is unique to each security principal SID created in a domain

Each AD DS DC has a pool of RIDs that it can allocate to security principals it creates. When this pool becomes exhausted, the DC will query the RID master for additional RIDs to add to this pool. If the RID master is not available, the pool cannot be replenished and new accounts cannot be created. You can use the following PowerShell command to determine which computer hosts the RID Master role:

```
Get-ADDomain example.internal | FT RidMaster
```

## Seizing FSMO roles

In some cases, a domain controller hosting an FSMO role fails and you need to seize the FSMO role to move it to another domain controller. For example, to move the RID Master, Infrastructure Master, and Domain Naming Master roles to a domain controller named MEL-DC2, run the following command:

```
Move-ADDirectoryServerOperationMasterRole -Identity MEL-DC2 -OperationMasterRole
RIDMaster,InfrastructureMaster,DomainNamingMaster -Force
```

> **NEED MORE REVIEW? FSMO ROLES**
>
> You can learn more about troubleshooting FSMO roles at *https://docs.microsoft.com/troubleshoot/windows-server/identity/fsmo-roles*.

**EXAM TIP**

Remember the symptoms associated with the failure of each FSMO role.

# Skill 1.2: Configure and manage multi-site, multi-domain, and multi-forest environments

Trust relationships allow security principals in one Active Directory environment to access resources in another Active Directory environment. In hybrid environments, trusts might be configured between an Azure AD DS forest and an on-premises forest or between domains hosted in different cloud providers and domains hosted in Azure. Sites are the way that server proximity is defined within Active Directory, with site topology determining how AD DS domain controllers in one location communicate with AD DS domain controllers in another.

> **This skill covers how to:**
> - Configure and manage forest and domain trusts
> - Configure and manage AD DS sites
> - Configure and manage AD DS replication

## Configure and manage forest and domain trusts

Trusts make it possible for users in one domain to be authenticated by domain controllers in a separate domain. For example, if there is a bidirectional trust relationship between the domains contoso.local and adatum.remote, users with accounts in the contoso.local domain are able to authenticate in the adatum.remote domain. By configuring a trust relationship, it's possible to allow users in one domain to access resources in another, such as being able to use shared folders and printers or being able to sign on locally to machines that are members of a different domain than the one that holds the user's account.

Some trusts are created automatically. For example, domains in the same forest automatically trust each other. Other trusts, such as external trusts, realm trusts, shortcut trusts, and forest trusts, must be created manually. Trusts use the Kerberos V5 authentication protocol by default, and they revert to NTLM if Kerberos V5 is not supported. You configure and manage trusts using the Active Directory Domains and Trusts console or the netdom.exe command-line utility with the /trust switch.

Although trusts themselves are relatively easy to come to terms with, the terminology around trusts tends to confuse many people. It's important that you understand the difference between a trusting and a trusted domain and how trust direction, incoming or outgoing, relates to which security principals are able to authenticate.

To understand trusts, you have to understand the difference between a trusting domain or forest and a trusted domain or forest. The trusting domain or forest contains the resources to which you want to grant security principals from the trusted domain or forest access. The trusted domain or forest hosts the security principals that you want to allow to access resources in the trusting forest. For example, if you want to grant users in the adatum.remote domain access to resources in the contoso.local domain, the adatum.remote domain is the trusted domain and the contoso.local domain is the trusting domain. In bidirectional trust relationships, a domain or forest is both trusting and trusted.

## Trust transitivity

A transitive trust is one that extends beyond the original trusting domains. For example, if you have a trust between two domain forests and that trust is transitive, all of the domains in each of the forests trust each other. Forest trusts are transitive by default. External trusts are not transitive by default. When you create a trust, keep in mind that there may be domains beyond the one you are establishing the relationship with that may be included. You might trust the administrator of adatum.remote not to allow access by nefarious users, but do you trust the administrator of subdomain.adatum.remote?

## Trust direction

When you create a new trust, you specify a trust direction. You can choose a two-way (or bidirectional) trust or a unidirectional trust, which is either one-way incoming or one-way outgoing.

When you configure a one-way incoming trust, users in the local domain are authenticated in the remote domain, realm, or forest. Remember that if you are configuring a one-way incoming trust between the single domain forests contoso.local and adatum.remote, users with accounts in contoso.local are able to access resources in adatum.remote. Similarly, if you are configuring a one-way outgoing trust between the single-domain forests contoso.local and adatum.remote, users with accounts in adatum.remote are able to access resources hosted in contoso.local.

The terminology around trusts can be a little confusing. The key thing to remember is that the direction of trust is the opposite of the direction of access, as shown in Figure 1-9. An outgoing trust allows incoming access, and an incoming trust allows outgoing access.

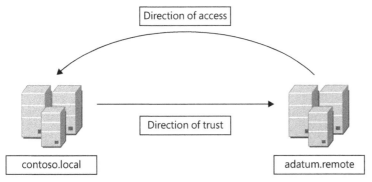

**FIGURE 1-9** The direction of trust and direction of access.

## Forest trusts

When you configure a forest trust, one AD DS forest trusts the other one. Forest trusts are transitive. When you configure a forest trust, you can allow any domain in the trusting forest to be accessible to any security principal in the trusted forest. Forest trusts require that each forest be configured to run at the Windows Server 2003 forest functional level or higher. Forest trusts can be bi- or unidirectional. You are most likely to configure forest trusts if your organization has two or more AD DS forests. You can configure a trust between a forest hosted in Azure and one hosted on-premises.

You can configure one of two authentication scopes when you configure a forest trust. The type of authentication scope that you configure depends on your security requirements. The options are:

- **Forest-wide authentication**   When you choose forest-wide authentication, users from the trusted forest are automatically authenticated for all resources in the local forest. You should use this option when both the trusted and trusting forests are part of the same organization.

- **Selective authentication**   When you configure this option, Windows does not automatically authenticate users from the trusted forest. You can then configure specific servers and domains within the forest to allow users from the trusted forest to authenticate. Use this option when the two forests are from different organizations, or you have more stringent security requirements.

## Configuring selective authentication

Configuring selective authentication means granting specific security principals in the trusted forest the **Allowed to authenticate** (allow) permission on the computer that hosts the resource to which you want to grant access. For example, assume you had configured a forest trust with selective authentication. You want to grant users in the Research universal group from the trusted forest access to a Remote Desktop Services (RDS) server in the trusting forest. To accomplish this goal, you can configure the properties of the RDS server's computer account in Active Directory Users and Computers and grant the Research universal group from the trusted forest the **Allowed to authenticate** permission. Doing this only allows users from this group to authenticate; you still have to grant them access to RDS by adding them to the appropriate local group on the RDS server.

## External trusts

External trusts enable you to configure one domain in one forest to trust a domain in another forest without enabling a transitive trust. For example, you configure an external trust if you want to allow the auckland.fabrikam.com domain to have a trust relationship with the wellington.adatum.com domain without allowing any other domains in the fabrikam.com or adatum.com forests to have a security relationship with each other.

You can use external trusts to configure trust relationships with domains running unsupported Windows Server operating systems, such as Windows 2000 Server and Windows NT 4.0, because these operating systems do not support forest trusts. Even though these operating systems are well beyond their supported lifespan, there are still organizations out there with servers, and even domains, running these operating systems. It's possible, though unlikely, that you might need to configure a trust relationship between a domain running these operating systems and one running Windows Server 2022 domain controllers.

## Shortcut trusts

Shortcut trusts enable you to speed up authentication between domains in a forest that might be in separate branches or even separate trees. For example, in the hypothetical forest shown in Figure 1-10, if a user in the canada.atlantic.contoso.com domain wants to access a resource in the arctic.adatum.com domain, authentication needs to travel up through the atlantic.contoso.com and contoso.com domains before passing across to the adatum.com domain and finally back to the arctic.adatum.com domain. If you implement a shortcut trust between the canada.atlantic.contoso.com and arctic.adatum.com domains, authentication traffic instead travels directly between these two domains without having to traverse the two domain trees in the forest.

You configure a shortcut trust using the Active Directory Domains and Trusts console by editing the properties of one domain and triggering the New Trust Wizard on the Trusts tab. Shortcut trusts can be uni- or bidirectional. As is the case with the creation of other trusts, ensure that you have name resolution working properly between the trusting and the trusted domains either by having the DNS zones propagate through the forest, by configuring conditional forwarders, or by configuring stub zones.

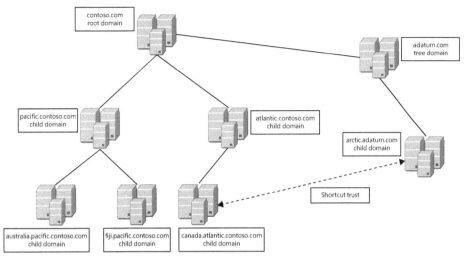

**FIGURE 1-10** Shortcut trust.

## Realm trusts

You use a realm trust to create a relationship between an Active Directory Domain Services domain and a Kerberos V5 realm that uses a third-party directory service. Realm trusts can be transitive or nontransitive. They can also be uni- or bidirectional. You're most likely to configure a realm trust when you need to allow users who use a UNIX directory service to access resources in an AD DS domain or users in an AD DS domain to access resources in a UNIX Kerberos V5 realm.

You can configure a realm trust from the Active Directory Domains and Trust console. You do this by selecting the **Realm trust** option, as shown in Figure 1-11. When configuring a realm trust, you specify a realm trust password that you use when configuring the other side of the trust in the Kerberos V5 realm.

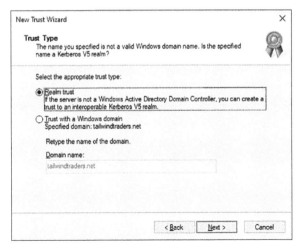

**FIGURE 1-11** Configure the realm trust.

## Netdom.exe

You use netdom.exe with the /trust switch to create and manage forest, shortcut, and realm trusts from the command line. When using netdom.exe, you specify the trusting domain name and the trusted domain name.

The syntax of netdom.exe with the /trust switch is shown in Figure 1-12.

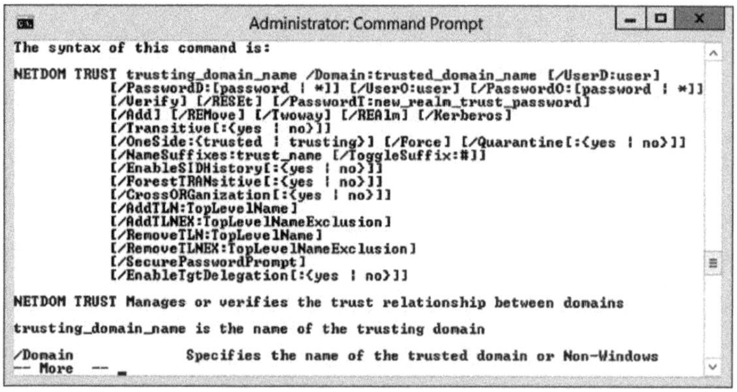

```
The syntax of this command is:

NETDOM TRUST trusting_domain_name /Domain:trusted_domain_name [/UserD:user]
            [/PasswordD:[password | *]] [/UserO:user] [/PasswordO:[password | *]]
            [/Verify] [/RESEt] [/PasswordT:new_realm_trust_password]
            [/Add] [/REMove] [/Twoway] [/REAlm] [/Kerberos]
            [/Transitive[:<yes | no>]]
            [/OneSide:<trusted | trusting>] [/Force] [/Quarantine[:<yes | no>]]
            [/NameSuffixes:trust_name [/ToggleSuffix:#]]
            [/EnableSIDHistory[:<yes | no>]]
            [/ForestTRANsitive[:<yes | no>]]
            [/CrossORGanization[:<yes | no>]]
            [/AddTLN:TopLevelName]
            [/AddTLNEX:TopLevelNameExclusion]
            [/RemoveTLN:TopLevelName]
            [/RemoveTLNEX:TopLevelNameExclusion]
            [/SecurePasswordPrompt]
            [/EnableTgtDelegation[:<yes | no>]]

NETDOM TRUST Manages or verifies the trust relationship between domains

trusting_domain_name is the name of the trusting domain

/Domain            Specifies the name of the trusted domain or Non-Windows
-- More --  _
```

FIGURE 1-12  The command syntax for netdom.exe.

PowerShell does not include much in the way of cmdlets for creating and managing trust relationships beyond the Get-ADTrust cmdlet, which allows you to view the properties of an existing trust.

## SID filtering

In a trusted domain, it's possible, though extremely difficult, for you to configure an account in your domain to have SIDs that are identical to those used by privileged accounts in a trusting domain. If you use this configuration, then the accounts from trusted domains gain the privileges of the accounts in the trusting domain. For example, you can configure the SIDs of an account in a trusted domain so that it has domain administrator privileges in the trusting domain.

To block this type of configuration, Windows Server 2022 enables *SID filtering*, also known as *domain quarantine*, on all external trusts. SID filtering blocks users in a trusted forest or domain from being able to grant themselves elevated user rights in the trusting forest domain by discarding all SIDs that do not have the domain SID of the trusting domain.

It's possible to verify SID filtering settings on a trust using the Get-ADTrust cmdlet in a PowerShell session run by a user with administrative privileges. For example, to verify that SID filtering is enabled on the trust with the margiestravel.com forest, issue the command

```
Get-ADTrust tailwindtraders.com | fl *SID*
```

To disable SID filtering for the trusting forest, use the netdom trust command with the following option:

```
/enablesidhistory:Yes
```

Enabling SID history allows you to use SIDs that don't have the domain SID of the trusting domain. You enable or disable SID filtering on the trusting side of the trust. For example, if you are an administrator in the contoso.com domain and you want to disable SID filtering, you can issue the following command from an elevated command prompt:

```
Netdom trust contoso.com /domain:tailwindtraders.com /enablesidhistory:Yes
```

In the same scenario, if you want to reenable SID filtering, you can issue the following command:

```
Netdom trust contoso.com /domain:tailwindtraders.com /enablesidhistory:Yes
```

The default configuration, where SID filtering is enforced by default on trusts, is something that you should probably leave as it is. In the past it was necessary to allow SID history when trusts were created with forests running Windows 2000 Server domain controllers. Since Windows 2000 is no longer supported by Microsoft, and SID history is not necessary for trust relationships with Windows Server 2003 or later domain controllers, you probably won't need to disable it.

### Name suffix routing

Name suffix routing enables you to configure how authentication requests are routed when you configure a forest trust between two AD DS forests. When you create a forest trust, all unique name suffixes are routed. Name suffix routing assists when users sign on with a UPN, such as rick_claus@contoso.com. Depending on the UPNs that are configured, you might want to allow or disallow the use of specific UPN suffixes. You do this by configuring name suffix routing on the **Name Suffix Routing** tab of the trust's properties.

> ***NEED MORE REVIEW?*** **FOREST TRUSTS**
>
> You can learn more about topic at *https://docs.microsoft.com/azure/active-directory-domain-services/tutorial-create-forest-trust*.

## Configure and manage AD DS sites

AD DS sites enable you to configure AD DS so that it understands which network locations have a fast local network connection. Generally this means the computers are in the same building, although if your organization has a group of buildings in the same area that are connected by a high-speed network, you use a single AD DS site configuration.

An Active Directory site is a collection of TCP/IP subnets. Sites allow you to define geographic locations for Active Directory on the basis of TCP/IP subnets. You can have multiple TCP/IP subnets in a site. You should put subnets together in a site where the hosts in that site have a high-bandwidth connection to each other. Usually, this means being in the same building, but it could also mean multiple buildings with very-low-latency gigabit links between them.

For example, imagine that your organization has its head office in Melbourne and a branch office in Sydney. You can set up two sites: one site for Melbourne and the other for Sydney. This ensures that computers in the Melbourne location interact as much as possible with resources located in Melbourne, and computers in the Sydney location interact as much as possible with resources located in Sydney.

You associate the TCP/IP subnets in the head office with the Melbourne site and the TCP/IP subnets in the branch office with the Sydney site. After you do this, functionality such as replication topology is automatically configured.

You configure sites by associating them with IP address ranges. For example, you might associate the subnet 192.168.10.0 /24 with the AD DS Site BNE-Site. Any computers that have an IP address in this range would be located in that site. You can configure network addresses using IPv4 or IPv6 networks. When you install AD DS for the first time, a default site, named Default-First-Site-Name, is created. You configure sites using the Active Directory Sites and Services console, shown in Figure 1-13.

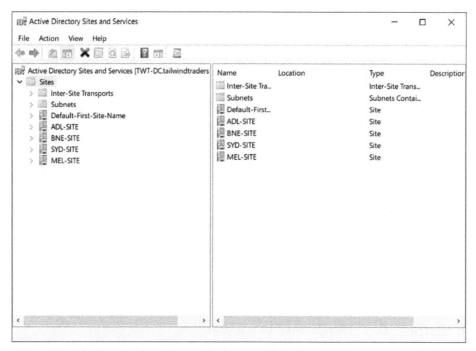

**FIGURE 1-13** The Active Directory Sites and Services console.

It's important that you add sites for each separate location in your organization. If you don't, AD DS assumes that all computers are located on the same fast network, and this might cause problems with other products as well as with AD DS. Microsoft products such as Exchange Server use AD DS site information when generating network topologies.

Sites enable you to do the following:

- **Separate different locations that are connected by a slow WAN or expensive WAN link**   For example, if your organization has a branch office in Sydney and another branch office in Melbourne, and these branch offices are connected by a WAN link that is rated at 512 kilobits per second (Kbps), you configure the Sydney and Melbourne branch offices as separate sites.

- **Control which domain controllers are used for authentication**   When users log on to the network, they perform authentication against an available domain controller located in their AD DS site. Although users are still able to sign on and authenticate against a DC in another site if one isn't available in their local site, you should strongly consider placing a domain controller at any site with a sufficient number of users. What counts as "a sufficient number of users" varies depending on the speed and reliability of the site's connection to the rest of the organization's network. In some cases you might deploy an RODC to aid authentication at some branch office sites.

- **Control service localization**   As mentioned earlier, many Microsoft products such as Exchange Server and technologies such as BranchCache and DFS use AD DS sites as a way of determining network topology. To ensure that these products and technologies work well, you should ensure that each AD DS site is configured properly.

- **Control AD DS replication**   You can use AD DS sites to manage domain controller replication. The default settings make it possible for replication to occur 24 hours a day, 7 days a week. You can use AD DS site configuration to instead configure replication to occur according to a specific schedule.

## Creating sites

To add a new Active Directory site, right-click the Sites node in the Active Directory Sites and Services console and select New Site. Specify the site name and select a site link object, and then select OK twice.

A site link object represents a connection between two sites. The default site link object is named DEFAULTIPSITELINK. You can change the site link object later. Figure 1-14 shows the creation of a site named *Sydney*.

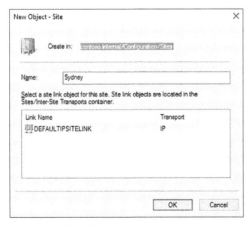

**FIGURE 1-14**  Creating a new site.

You can use the `New-ADReplicationSite` PowerShell cmdlet to create a new site. For example, to create a new site named HBA-SITE that is associated with the default IP site link, issue this command:

```
New-ADReplicationSite HBA-SITE
```

After you've created a site, you need to associate it with IP address ranges. You can't do that until you've added IP address ranges as subnets. When you create a subnet, you specify an IPv4 or IPv6 network prefix. For an IPv4 network. you specify the network address and the subnet in CIDR notation. For example, you specify network 192.168.15.0 with a subnet mask of 255.255.255.0 as 192.168.15.0 /24.

## Creating subnets

To add a subnet, right-click the Subnets node in Active Directory Sites and Services and then select New Subnet. You can specify the new subnet in IPv4 or IPv6 format. After you've specified the subnet, you have to specify which site the subnet is associated with. Figure 1-15 shows the 10.10.10.0/24 subnet associated with the Melbourne site.

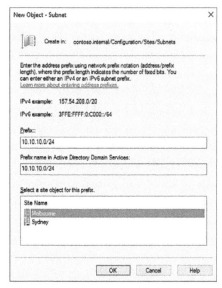

**FIGURE 1-15** New subnet.

You can create a new subnet from PowerShell with the `New-ADReplicationSubnet` cmdlet. For example, to create a new subnet that has the address 192.168.16.0/24 and associate it with the HBA-SITE site, issue the command:

```
New-ADReplicationSubnet -Name "192.168.16.0/24" -Site HBA-SITE
```

You can verify which subnets are associated with a particular AD DS site by viewing the properties of that site. You can't change which subnets are associated with a site by editing the site properties; you can only do so by editing the subnet properties. You can associate multiple subnets with an AD DS site, but you can't associate multiple AD DS sites with a specific subnet.

# Creating site links

Site links enable you to specify how different AD DS sites are connected to each other. When you add a site, you're asked to specify the site link, and the DEFAULTIPSITELINK site link is the default option even if another site link is available. Sites that are connected to the same site link are able to replicate with each other directly. For example, if all the sites in Figure 1-16 are associated with the DEFAULTIPSITELINK site link, each site assumes that it could replicate directly with the others. When troubleshooting replication, determine whether you want all sites connected to DEFAULTIPSITELINK or if you want them to use separate site links for alternative replication paths. For example, a domain controller in the Melbourne site attempts to replicate directly with a domain controller in the Canberra site. With this topology, you instead configure site links for Melbourne-Sydney, Adelaide-Sydney, and Canberra-Sydney. This way, domain controllers in Canberra, Melbourne, and Adelaide only replicate with the Sydney site rather than attempting to directly replicate with each other.

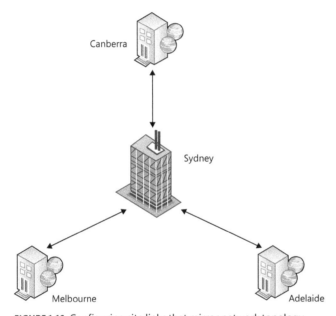

**FIGURE 1-16** Configuring site links that mirror network topology.

You can create a new IP site link using the Active Directory Sites and Services console. When you create a site link, you specify the sites that use the link. You can configure the cost and replication schedule of a site link after it is created by editing the Site Link properties. The default Cost is 100, and site links that have lower costs are preferred for replication over site links that have a higher cost. Replication occurs every 180 minutes by default, 24 hours a day. You can modify when replication occurs by configuring a replication schedule.

If you want replication to occur as quickly as possible, you can enable the **Use notify** replication option by modifying a site link's options attribute. You can perform this task by using the **Attribute Editor** tab in the site link's properties.

You can create a site link using the `New-ADReplicationSiteLink` cmdlet. For example, to create a new site link named ADL-CBR that links the ADL-SITE and CBR-SITE sites, issue this command:

```
New-ADReplicationSiteLink "ADL-CBR" -SitesIncluded ADL-SITE, CBR-SITE
```

Members of the Enterprise Admins security group can create and modify site links. Members of the Domain Admins security group in the forest root domain can also perform site link management tasks. User accounts that are only members of child domain but not the forest root domain's Domain Admins security group are unable to manage site links.

## Creating site link bridges

Site link bridges create transitive links between site links. Each site link in a bridge must have a site in common with another site link in the bridge. It's only necessary to create a site link bridge with complex network topologies as site link bridges are automatically created based on the topology created when you configure site links. You are likely to need to create a site link bridge if:

- Your IP network is not fully routed. If you disable the **Bridge all site links** option, all site links will be treated as nontransitive. You can then use your own site link bridges to reflect the manner in which traffic is routed across your network.

- You need to control replication flow between sites. By disabling the **Bridge all site links** for the site link IP transport and creating a site link bridge, you can create a disjointed network. This ensures that site links within the bridge can route AD DS traffic transitively but that they will not route traffic outside of the site link bridge.

## Moving domain controllers

When you deploy a new domain controller, the domain controller promotion process performs a lookup to determine which AD DS site the domain controller should be a member of based on its IP address. If you haven't created a subnet in the Active Directory Sites and Services console that maps to the IP address of the server that you are promoting to the domain controller, the domain controller is instead assigned to the first AD DS site, which is Default-First-Site-Name unless you have changed it.

The domain controller does not automatically reassign itself to a new site if you create the subnet and site objects in the Active Directory Sites and Services console if it has already been added to the Default-First-Site-Name site. In this instance, you need to manually move the domain controller to the new site. You can move the domain controller using the Active Directory Sites and Services console by right-clicking the domain controller that you want to move, selecting **Move**, and selecting the destination site in the **Move Server** dialog box.

You can also move a domain controller to a different site using the `Move-ADDirectoryServer` PowerShell cmdlet. For example, to move the server PERTH-DC to the Perth-Site AD DS site, execute the following command:

```
Move-ADDirectoryServer -Identity "PERTH-DC" -Site "Perth-Site"
```

# Configure and manage AD DS replication

Replication makes it possible for changes that are made on one AD DS domain controller to be replicated to other domain controllers in the domain and, in some cases, to other domain controllers in the forest. Rather than replicating the AD DS database in its entirety, the replication process is made more efficient by splitting the database into logical partitions. Replication occurs at the partition level, with some partitions only replicating to domain controllers within the local domain, some partitions replicating only to enrolled domain controllers, and some partitions replicating to all domain controllers in the forest. AD DS includes the following default partitions:

- **Configuration partition**   This partition stores forest-wide AD DS structure information, including domain, site, and domain controller location data. The configuration partition also holds information about DHCP server authorization and Active Directory Certificate Services certificate templates. The configuration partition replicates to all domain controllers in the forest.

- **Schema partition**   The schema partition stores definitions of all objects and attributes as well as the rules for creating and manipulating those objects. There are a default set of classes and attributes that cannot be changed, but it's possible to extend the schema and add new attributes and classes. Only the domain controller that holds the Schema Master FSMO role is able to extend the schema. The schema partition replicates to all domain controllers in the forest.

- **Domain partition**   The domain partition holds information about domain-specific objects such as organizational units, domain-related settings, user, group, and computer accounts. A new domain partition is created each time you add a new domain to the forest. The domain partition replicates to all domain controllers in a domain. All objects in every domain partition are stored in the Global Catalog, but these objects are stored only with some, not all, of their attribute values.

- **Application partition**   Application partitions store application-specific information for applications that store information in AD DS. There can be multiple application partitions, each of which is used by different applications. You can configure application partitions so that they replicate only to some domain controllers in a forest. For example, you can create specific application partitions to be used for DNS replication so that DNS zones replicate to some, but not all, domain controllers in the forest.

Domains running at the Windows Server 2008 and higher functional level support attribute-level replication. Rather than replicate the entire object when a change is made to an attribute on that object, such as when group membership changes for a user account, only the attribute that changes is replicated to other domain controllers. Attribute-level replication substantially reduces the amount of data that needs to be transmitted when objects stored in AD DS are modified.

## Understanding multi-master replication

AD DS uses multi-master replication. This means that any writable domain controller is able to make modifications of the AD DS database and to have those modifications propagate to the other domain controllers in the domain. Domain controllers use *pull replication* to acquire changes from other domain controllers. A domain controller may pull changes after being notified by replication partners that changes are available. A domain controller notifies its first replication partner that a change has occurred within 15 seconds and additional replication partners every 3 seconds after the previous notification. Domain controllers also periodically poll replication partners to determine whether changes are available so that those changes can be pulled and applied to the local copy of the relevant partition. By default, polling occurs once every 60 minutes. You can alter this schedule by editing the properties of the connection object in the Active Directory Sites and Services console.

## Knowledge Consistency Checker (KCC)

The Knowledge Consistency Checker (KCC) runs on each domain controller. The KCC is responsible for creating and optimizing the replication paths between domain controllers located at a specific site. In the event that a domain controller is added or removed from a site, the KCC automatically reconfigures the site's replication topology. The KCC topology organization process occurs every 15 minutes by default. Although you can change this value by editing the registry, you can also trigger an update using the repadmin command-line tool with the kcc switch.

## Store and forward replication

AD DS supports store and forward replication. For example, the Canberra and Melbourne branch offices are enrolled in a custom application partition. These branch offices aren't connected to each other, but they are connected to the Sydney head office. In this case, changes made to objects stored in the application partition at Canberra can be pulled by the domain controller in Sydney. The Melbourne domain controller can then pull those changes from the domain controller in Sydney, as shown in Figure 1-17.

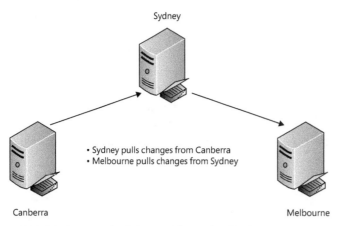

**FIGURE 1-17** An example of store and forward replication.

## Conflict resolution

In an environment that supports multi-master replication, it's possible that updates may be made to the same object at the same time in two or more different places. Active Directory includes sophisticated technologies that minimize the chance that these conflicts will cause problems, even when conflicting updates occur in locations that are distant from each other.

Each domain controller tracks updates by using *update sequence numbers (USNs)*. Each time a domain controller updates, either by processing an update performed locally or by processing an update acquired through replication, it increments the USN and associates the new value with the update. USNs are unique to each domain controller as each domain controller processes a different number of updates to every other domain controller.

When this happens, the domain controller that wrote the most recent change, known as the last writer, wins. Because each domain controller's clock might not be precisely synchronized with every other domain controller's clock, last write isn't simply determined by a comparison of time stamps. Similarly, because USNs are unique to each domain controller, a direct comparison of USNs is not made. Instead the conflict resolution algorithm looks at the attribute version number. This is a number that indicates how many times the attribute has changed and is calculated using USNs. When the same attribute has been changed on different domain controllers, the attribute with the higher attribute version number wins. If the attribute version number is the same, the attribute modification time stamps are compared, with the most recent change being deemed authoritative.

If you add or move an object to a container that was deleted on another domain controller at the same time, the object is moved to the LostAndFound container. You can view this container when you enable the **Advanced Features** option in the Active Directory Users and Computers console.

## RODC replication

The key difference between an RODC and a writable domain controller is that RODCs aren't able to update the Active Directory database and that they only host password information for a subset of security principals. When a client in a site that only has RODCs needs to make a change to the Active Directory database, that change is forwarded to a writable domain controller in another site. When considering replication, remember that all RODC-related replication is incoming and that other domain controllers do not pull updates from the AD DS database hosted on an RODC.

RODCs use the usual replication schedule to pull updates from writable domain controllers except in certain cases, RODCs perform inbound replication using a replicate-single-object (RSO) operation. These cases include:

- The password of a user whose account password is stored on the RODC is changed.
- A DNS record update occurs where the DNS client performing the update attempts to use the RODC to process the update and is then redirected by the RODC to a writable DC that hosts the appropriate Active Directory Integrated DNS zone.

- Client attributes, including client name, DnsHostName, OsName, OsVersionInfo, supported encryption types, and LastLogonTimeStamp, are updated.

These updates occur outside the usual replication schedule as they involve objects and attributes that are important to security. An example is when a user at a site that uses RODCs calls the service desk to have their password reset. The service desk staff member, located in another site, resets the password using a writable domain controller. If a special RSO operation isn't performed, it is necessary to wait for the change to replicate to the site before the user is able to sign on with the newly reset password.

## Monitor and manage replication

You can use the Active Directory Sites and Services console to trigger replication. You can trigger replication on a specific domain controller by right-clicking the connection object and selecting **Replicate Now**. When you do this, the domain controller replicates with all of its replication partners.

You can also monitor replication as it occurs using DirectoryServices performance counters in Performance Monitor. Through Performance Monitor, you can view inbound and outbound replication, including the number of inbound objects in the queue and pending synchronizations.

## Repadmin

You can use the repadmin command-line tool to manage and monitor replication. This tool is especially useful at enabling you to diagnose where there are problems in a replication topology. For example, you can use repadmin with the following switches:

- **replsummary** Generates information showing when replication between partners has failed. You can also use this switch to view information about the largest intermission between replication events.
- **showrepl** Views specific inbound replication traffic, including objects that were replicated and the date stamps associated with that traffic.
- **prp** Determines which user account passwords are being stored on an RODC.
- **kcc** Forces the KCC to recalculate a domain controller's inbound replication topology.
- **queue** Enables you to display inbound replication requests that a domain controller must make to reach a state of convergence with source replication partners.
- **replicate** Forces replication of a specific directory partition to a specific destination domain controller.
- **replsingleobj** Use this switch when you need to replicate a single object between two domain controllers.
- **rodcpwdrepl** Enables you to populate RODCs with the passwords of specific users.
- **showutdvec** Displays the highest USN value recorded for committed replication operations on a specific DC.

**EXAM TIP**

Remember how to control traffic flow between sites using site links and site link bridges. Also remember how traffic might flow given a specific set of site link and site link bridge configurations.

# Skill 1.3: Create and manage AD DS security principals

Security principals include user and group accounts, as well as special accounts such as computer accounts and group managed service accounts. Knowing how each of these accounts functions and how to configure these accounts is a critical part of AD DS administration.

> **This skill covers how to:**
> - Create and manage AD DS users and groups
> - Manage users and groups in multi-domain and multi-forest scenarios
> - Implement group managed service accounts (gMSAs)
> - Join Windows Servers to AD DS, Azure AD DS, and Azure AD

## Create and manage AD DS users and groups

Accounts represent the identities of security principals in an Active Directory environment. The most common type of account is a user account, which represents a person as they interact with the Windows environment. IT operations personnel also need to regularly deal with computer accounts, group accounts, and service accounts.

### User accounts

User accounts almost always represent real people in an Active Directory environment, with the caveat that some user accounts are used for services rather than traditional users signing on to their desktop computers.

In many organizations, a user account is nothing more than a username, a password, and a collection of group memberships. User accounts can contain substantial additional information, including:

- First name
- Last name
- Middle initial
- Full name
- Office information
- Email address

- Web page
- Job title
- Department
- Company
- Manager
- Phone numbers (main, home, mobile, fax, pager, IP phone)
- Address
- User profile location
- Logon script
- Home folder
- Remote desktop service profile
- Dial-in permissions
- Published certificates
- Remote Desktop Sessions settings
- Remote Control settings

You should configure important accounts to be protected from deletion by enabling the **Protect from accidental deletion** option, as shown in Figure 1-18. Unless you disable this option, the account cannot be deleted. This setting doesn't stop an account from being removed deliberately, but it does stop the account from being deleted accidentally.

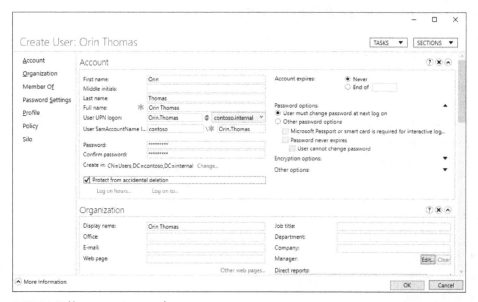

FIGURE 1-18 User account properties.

## Computer accounts

Computer accounts represent a domain-joined computer within Active Directory. You often move computer accounts to specific OUs and then apply Group Policies to those OUs as a way of configuring the computer. When you manually join a computer to the domain, the computer account is automatically placed in the default Computers container. You can only join a computer to a domain if it can locate the appropriate domain SRV records in DNS.

If you can't sign on to a computer using a domain account, it may be because the computer has become desynchronized from the domain. If a computer account becomes desynchronized from the domain of which it is a member and loses its trust relationship, you can repair the relationship by signing in with the local Administrator account and running the following PowerShell command:

```
Test-ComputerSecureChannel -Credential Domain\<AdminAccount> -Repair
```

If you don't know the local Administrator account password but suspect that cached domain administrator credentials might be present, disconnect the computer from the network, by either physically removing the Ethernet connection or disconnecting the virtual network adapter; sign in using those credentials; and then run the PowerShell command previously mentioned.

# Manage users and groups in multi-domain and multi-forest scenarios

Active Directory supports three different types of group account scopes: domain local, global (the default), and universal. It also supports two group types: Security and Distribution. You use security groups to control access to resources, delegate permissions, and for email distribution. Distribution groups can only be used for email distribution. If your organization uses Exchange Server, you manage distribution groups through Exchange. Best practice is to place users within global groups, add those global groups to domain local groups, and assign permissions and rights directly to the domain local groups. By default, members of the Account Operators, Domain Admins, or Enterprise Admins groups can modify the membership of groups.

## Universal

A universal group can hold accounts and groups from the same forest. Universal groups are stored in the Global Catalog. If you change the membership of a universal group, this change replicates to all Global Catalog servers in the forest. Universal groups are great in single-forest environments where replication traffic isn't an issue or where there are few changes to universal group membership. Universal groups can be nested within other universal groups, or they can be added to domain local groups.

### Global

Global groups can contain user accounts from its home domain. Global groups can also contain other global groups from its home domain. Global groups can be members of universal groups and domain local groups.

### Domain local

Domain local groups can have universal groups, global groups, and domain local groups as members. Domain local groups can host accounts from any domain in the forest and accounts from domains in trusted forests. Domain local groups can only be added to domain local groups within its own domain. A domain local group can only be assigned rights and permissions within its own domain. Domain local groups cannot be added to global or universal groups.

## Implement group managed service accounts (GMSAs)

Service accounts are functionally user accounts used by services to interact with the operating system and resources on the network. By assigning rights to the service account, you can limit what the service can or cannot do. One of the key things to remember about a service account is that it should not have the right to log on locally to a computer but should have the logon as a service right. This is important because administrators in many organizations have bad habits where they grant service accounts unnecessary rights and even go as far as to give all service accounts the same nonexpiring password. Sophisticated attackers know this and use it to compromise service accounts and use them as a way to gain privileged access.

### Local System

The Local System (NT AUTHORITY\SYSTEM) account is a built-in account. It has privileges equivalent to a local administrator account on the local computer. It acts with the computer account's credentials when interacting on the network. This is the most powerful service account, and generally you should be reluctant to assign this service account manually to a service given its extensive privileges.

### Local Service

The Local Service (NT AUTHORITY\LocalService) account has the same level of privilege as user accounts that are members of the local Users group on a computer. This account has fewer local privileges than the Local System account. Any services assigned to this account access network resources as a null session without credentials. Use this account when the service doesn't require network access or can access network resources as an anonymous user and requires only minimal privileges on the computer it is being used on.

## Network Service

The Network Service (NT AUTHORITY\NetworkService) account is similar to the Local Service account in that it has privileges on the local computer equivalent to those assigned to a member of the local Users group. The primary difference is that this account interacts with the computer account's credentials with resources on the network.

## GMSA

A group managed service account (GMSA) is a service account that is managed by the domain. This means that rather than having to update the service account's password manually, Active Directory updates the password in line with the domain password policy. Many organizations that use regular user accounts as service accounts tend to set a static password for these accounts, which is often simple rather than complex.

Group managed service accounts require the forest functional level to be Windows Server 2012 or higher. Forests at the Windows Server 2008 level support a version of a GMSA called an MSA, but this is more limited than a GMSA, with each MSA only being able to be installed on a single machine.

Before using GMSAs, you need to create a Key Distribution Services (KDS) root key. You can do so with the following command:

```
Add-KdsRootKey -EffectiveTime ((get-date).addhours(-10))
```

You manage GMSAs using PowerShell. To create a GMSA, specify the name of the account, a DNS hostname associated with the account, and the name of the security principals allowed to use the account. For example, to create a GMSA named MEL-SQL-GMSA for the contoso. internal domain that can be used by servers in the MEL-SQL-Servers security group, enact the following command:

```
New-ADServiceAccount MEL-SQL-GMSA -DNSHostname MEL-SQL-GMSA.contso.internal
-PrincipalsAllowedToRetrieveManagedPassword MEL-SQL-Servers
```

To install the account on a specific server so that you can use it, run the Install-ADServiceAccount cmdlet. For example, to install the MEL-SQL-GMSA account on a server so that you can assign the account to services, issue this command:

```
Install-ADServiceAccount MEL-SQL-GMSA
```

Before running this command, you may need to install the RSAT ADDS Tools on the local server. You can do so by running this command:

```
Install-WindowsFeature RSAT-ADDS-Tools
```

When assigning the account to a service, you should clear the **Password** and **Confirm password** options. You'll need to append add $ to the account name when configuring it, as shown in Figure 1-19. When you do this, Windows Server 2022 recognizes that the account is a GMSA and manages the password settings.

**FIGURE 1-19** GMSA configuration.

## Virtual account

A virtual account is the local equivalent of a group managed service account. Virtual accounts are supported by products such as SQL Server as an alternative to the default built-in accounts. You can create virtual service accounts by editing the property of a service and setting the account name to NT Service\<*ServiceName*>.

> **NEED MORE REVIEW?** **GROUP MANAGED SERVICE ACCOUNTS**
>
> You can learn more about group managed service accounts at *https://docs.microsoft.com/ windows-server/security/group-managed-service-accounts/group-managed-service-accounts-overview.*

## Kerberos delegation

Kerberos constrained delegation restricts how and where application services can act on a user's behalf. You can configure accounts so that they can be used only for specific tasks. For example, Figure 1-20 shows configuring delegation of the account for computer SYD-B, for delegation through Kerberos, for the time service on computer SYD-A. Windows Server 2012 and later enable constrained delegation to be performed where the front-end service and the resource service are located in separate domains. You can configure Kerberos delegation using the Set-ADComputer, Set-ADServiceAccount, and Set-ADUser cmdlets with the Principal-sAllowedToDelegateAccount parameter.

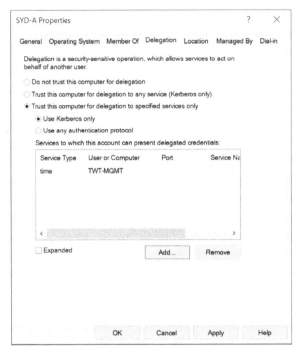

**FIGURE 1-20** Kerberos delegation.

## Kerberos policies

Kerberos policies determine how the service and user tickets are used in the Authentication function in an Active Directory domain. Like password and account lockout policy, Kerberos policy is applied at the domain level. Kerberos policies applied at the site and organizational level have no effect on resultant Kerberos policy. Kerberos policies are located in the Computer Configuration\Policies\Windows Settings\Security Settings\Account Policies\Kerberos Policy node.

You can configure the following Kerberos policies:

- **Enforce User Logon Restrictions** Ensures that Kerberos checks every request for a session ticket, also known as a service ticket.

- **Maximum Lifetime For Service Ticket** Configures the maximum lifetime of a service ticket, which is also known as a session ticket. The default value for this policy is 10 hours. The value of this policy must be less than or equal to the value specified in the Maximum Lifetime For User Ticket policy.

- **Maximum Lifetime For User Ticket** Determines the maximum lifetime of a user ticket, also known as a ticket-granting ticket (TGT). The default value of this policy is 10 hours.

- **Maximum Lifetime For User Ticket Renewal** Specifies the maximum TGT renewal period. The default is 7 days.

- **Maximum Tolerance For Computer Clock Synchronization** Specifies how much drift there can be in domain controller clocks before ticket errors occur. The default setting is 5 minutes.

### Service principal name management

Kerberos clients use a service principal name (SPN) to identify a unique instance of a service on a given computer. If there are multiple instances of the same service hosted on computers in a domain or forest, each service requires a unique SPN. Service instances can be configured with multiple SPNs, as long as those SPNs are unique.

You can use the SetSPN command-line utility to configure SPNs for computers running Windows Server. SetSPN uses this syntax: `setspn serviceclass/host:portnumber servicename`. You can use SetSPN `/?` to see a list of all SPN switches. For example, to register the HTTP service using the standard port on a computer named MEL-DC in the contoso.com domain using a GMSA named SYD-SRVC, issue this command:

```
setpspn -s http/MEL-DC.contoso.com CONTOSO\SYD-SRVC
```

# Join Windows Servers to AD DS, Azure AD DS, and Azure AD

When you deploy Windows Server for the first time, it is in workgroup or standalone configuration, with only the local Administrator account and its password, which you configured during installation, available for sign-on. When you join a Windows Server computer to an Active Directory instance, be that AD DS, Azure AD DS, or Azure AD, you'll be able to sign on to that computer using accounts in the appropriate directory instance. The security settings of the domain, such as which domain accounts have administrative privileges, will also apply to the Windows Server computer.

To be able to perform a domain-join operation, the Windows Server computer must have DNS configured so that it can contact the appropriate directory service. For on-premises AD DS, this means a DNS server that hosts the domain DNS zone, which is usually hosted on a domain controller. For Azure AD DS, this will mean ensuring that the DNS server settings for the virtual network the IaaS VM is hosted on are configured appropriately.

Once the DNS server settings are appropriately configured, you can perform the domain-join operation from within the Windows Server, either by changing the domain membership on the **Computer Name** tab of the **System Properties** dialog box or by using the Add-Computer PowerShell cmdlet with the DomainName parameter.

You can also sign on to a Windows Server IaaS VM hosted in Azure using an Azure AD account without configuring Azure AD DS. In this configuration, the Window Server IaaS VM is not traditionally domain-joined, even though it does have a security relationship with the Azure AD tenancy associated with the host subscription. To enable Azure AD login for a Windows Server IaaS VM when deploying the virtual machine through the Azure portal, on the **Management** tab of the deployment wizard, enable the **Login with Azure AD** option, as shown in Figure 1-21.

*[Screenshot of Azure portal: Create a virtual machine — Management tab]*

Home > Create a resource >

## Create a virtual machine   ...

Basics   Disks   Networking   **Management**   Advanced   Tags   Review + create

Configure monitoring and management options for your VM.

**Azure Security Center**

Azure Security Center provides unified security management and advanced threat protection across hybrid cloud workloads. Learn more

✓  Your subscription is protected by Azure Security Center standard plan.

**Monitoring**

Boot diagnostics ○            ● Enable with managed storage account (recommended)
                             ○ Enable with custom storage account
                             ○ Disable

Enable OS guest diagnostics ○   ☐

**Identity**

System assigned managed identity ○   ▢

                             ❶  System managed identity must be on to login with Azure AD credentials.
                                 Learn more

**Azure AD**

Login with Azure AD ○         ☑

                             ❶  RBAC role assignment of Virtual Machine Administrator Login or Virtual Machine
                                 User Login is required when using Azure AD login. Learn more

**FIGURE 1-21** Azure AD Login.

When the VM is deployed in this configuration, you can configure which Azure AD accounts can access the VM by assigning them the following Azure roles:

- **Virtual Machine Administrator Login**   Azure AD users assigned this role will be able to sign on to the Windows Server IaaS VM using Remote Desktop or Remote PowerShell (if configured) and will have local administrator privileges.
- **Virtual Machine User Login**   Azure AD users assigned this role will be able to sign on to the Windows Server IaaS VM using Remote Desktop or Remote PowerShell (if configured) and will have nonadministrator privileges.

You can use Azure Resource Manager (ARM) templates to simplify the process of deploying large numbers of Windows Server IaaS VMs to Azure. ARM templates configured with the domainToJoin, domainUsername, domainPassword, and ouPath parameters can automatically join Windows Server IaaS VMs to AD DS domains.

---

**EXAM TIP**

Remember how to configure and manage group managed service accounts.

---

# Skill 1.4: Implement and manage hybrid identities

In a hybrid environment you need to know how to manage users and groups on-premises as well as how to replicate those security principals so that they can be present in the cloud and people in your organization can access resources without having to reauthenticate using a new set of credentials. Using an on-premises identity to access resources in Azure can occur through identity synchronization or an appropriately configured forest trust relationship.

> **This skill covers how to:**
> - Implement Azure AD Connect
> - Manage Azure AD Connect Synchronization
> - Implement Azure AD Connect cloud sync
> - Manage Azure AD DS
> - Integrate Azure AD, AD DS, and Azure AD DS
> - Manage Azure AD Connect Health
> - Manage authentication in on-premises and hybrid environments
> - Configure and manage AD DS passwords

## Implement Azure AD Connect

Azure AD Connect allows you to connect your on-premises Active Directory accounts with an Azure AD instance. Not only is this useful for applications running in Azure, but it allows you to implement single sign-on if your organization is using Microsoft 365 or Office 365. Single sign-on allows you to use one identity to access on-premises and cloud resources. In many scenarios, the user won't even be required to reauthenticate.

Azure AD Connect is designed to streamline the process of configuring connections between on-premises deployment and an Azure AD instance. The Azure Active Directory Connect tool is designed to make the process of configuring synchronization between an on-premises Active Directory deployment and Azure Active Directory as frictionless as possible.

Azure Active Directory Connect can automatically configure and install simple password synchronization or Federation/single sign-on, depending on your organizational needs. When you choose the **Federation with AD FS** option, Active Directory Federation Services is installed and configured, along with a web application proxy server to facilitate communication between the on-premises AD FS deployment and Microsoft Azure Active Directory.

The Azure Active Directory Connect tool supports the following optional features, as shown in Figure 1-22:

- **Exchange hybrid deployment** This option is suitable for organizations that have an Office 365 deployment in which there are mailboxes hosted both on-premises and in the cloud.

- **Exchange Mail Public Folders** This feature allows organizations to synchronize mail-enabled public folder objects from an on-premises Active Directory environment to Microsoft 365.

- **Azure AD app and attribute filtering** Selecting this option gives you the ability to be more selective about which attributes are synchronized between the on-premises environment and Azure AD.

- **Password synchronization** This option synchronizes a hash of the user's on-premises password with Azure AD. When the user authenticates to Azure AD, the submitted password is hashed using the same process, and if the hashes match, the user is authenticated. Each time the user updates their password on-premises, the updated password hash synchronizes to Azure AD.

- **Password writeback** This option allows users to change their passwords in the cloud and have the changed password written back to the on-premises Active Directory instance.

- **Group writeback** With this option, changes made to groups in Azure AD are written back to the on-premises AD instance.

- **Device writeback** With this option, information about devices registered by the user in Azure AD is written back to the on-premises AD instance.

- **Directory extension attribute sync** This option allows you to extend the Azure AD schema based on extensions made to your organization's on-premises Active Directory instance.

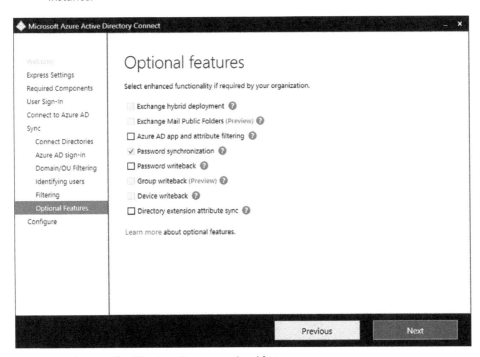

**FIGURE 1-22** Azure Active Directory Connect optional features .

## Azure AD Connect Server requirements

Azure AD Connect is software that you install on a computer that manages the process of synchronizing objects between the on-premises Active Directory and the Azure Active Directory instance. You can install Azure AD Connect on computers running the Windows Server 2012 or later operating systems.

Azure AD Connect has the following requirements:

- It must be installed on a Windows Server instance that has the GUI version of the operating system installed. You cannot install Azure AD Connect on a computer running the Server Core operating system.

- You can deploy Azure AD Connect on a computer that is either a domain controller (although not recommended) or a member server or, if you use the custom options, a standalone server can be used.

- The server hosting Azure AD Connect requires .NET Framework 4.5.1 or later.

- The server hosting Azure AD Connect requires Microsoft PowerShell 3.0 or later.

- The server hosting Azure AD Connect must not have PowerShell Transcription enabled through Group Policy.

- If you are deploying Azure AD Connect with Active Directory Federation Services, you must use Windows Server 2012 R2 or later for the Web Application Proxy, and Windows remote management must be enabled on the servers that will host AD FS roles.

- If global administrators will have multifactor authentication enabled (MFA), then the URL *https://secure.aadcdn.microsoftonline-p.com* must be configured as a trusted site.

## Connectivity requirements

The computer with Azure AD Connect installed must be a member of a domain in the forest that you want to synchronize, and it must have connectivity to a writable domain controller in each domain of the forest you wish to synchronize on the following ports:

- DNS TCP/UDP Port 53
- Kerberos TCP/UDP Port 88
- RPC TCP Port 135
- LDAP TCP/UDP Port 389
- SSL TCP Port 443
- SMB TCP 445

The computer with Azure AD Connect installed must be able to establish communication with the Microsoft Azure servers on the Internet over TCP port 443. The computer with Azure AD Connect installed can be located on an internal network as long as it can initiate communication on TCP port 443. The computer hosting Azure AD Connect does not need a publicly routable IP address. The computer hosting Azure AD Connect always initiates synchronization communication to Microsoft Azure. Microsoft Azure Active Directory does not initiate synchronization communication to the computer hosting Azure AD Connect on the on-premises network.

Microsoft recommends that you do not install Azure AD Connect on a domain controller. If you are going to be replicating more than 50,000 objects, Microsoft recommends that you deploy SQL Server on a computer that is separate from the computer that will host Azure AD Connect. If you plan to host the SQL Server instance on a separate computer, ensure that communication is possible between the computer hosting Azure AD Connect and the computer hosting the SQL Instance on TCP port 1433.

If you are going to use a separate SQL Server instance, ensure that the account used to install and configure Azure AD Connect has systems administrator rights on the SQL instance and that the service account used for Azure AD Connect has public permissions on the Azure AD Connect database.

## SQL Server requirements

When you deploy Azure AD Connect, you have the option of having Azure AD Connect install an SQL Server Express instance, or you can choose to have Azure AD Connect leverage a full instance of SQL Server. SQL Server Express is limited to a maximum database size of 10 GB. In terms of Azure AD Connect, this means that Azure AD Connect is only able to manage 100,000 objects. This is likely to be adequate for all but the largest environments.

For environments that require Azure AD Connect to manage more than 100,000 objects, you'll need to have Azure AD Connect leverage a full instance of SQL Server. Azure AD Connect can use all versions of Microsoft SQL Server, from Microsoft SQL Server 2012 with the most recent service pack to SQL Server 2022. It is important to note that SQL Azure is not supported as a database for Azure AD Connect. If deploying a full instance of SQL Server to support Azure AD Connect, ensure that the following prerequisites are met:

- **Use a case-insensitive SQL collation**   Case-insensitive collations have the _CI_ identifier included in their names. Case-sensitive collations (those that use the _CS_ designation) are not supported for use with Azure AD Connect.
- **You can use only one sync engine per SQL instance**   If you have an additional Azure AD Connect sync engine or if you are using Microsoft Identity Manager in your environment, each sync engine requires its own separate SQL instance.

## Requirements for deployment accounts

You use two accounts when configuring Azure AD Connect. One account must have specific Azure AD permissions; the other account must have specific on-premises Active Directory permissions. The accounts that you use to install and configure Azure AD Connect have the following requirements:

- The account used to configure Azure AD Connect must have Global Administrator privileges in the Azure AD tenancy. You should create a separate account for this task and configure the account with a complex password that does not expire. This account is used for the synchronization process between on-premises AD and Azure AD.

- The account used to install and configure Azure AD Connect must have Enterprise Administrator permissions within the on-premises Active Directory forest if you will be using Express installation settings. This account is only required during installation and configuration. After Azure AD Connect is installed and configured, this account no longer needs Enterprise Administrator permissions. The best practice is to create a separate account for Azure AD Connect installation and configuration and to temporarily add this account to the Enterprise Admins group during the installation and configuration process. After Azure AD Connect is installed and configured, this account can be removed from the Enterprise Admins group. You should not attempt to change the account used after Azure AD Connect is set up and configured because Azure AD Connect always attempts to run using the original account.

- The account used to install and configure Azure AD Connect must be a member of the local Administrators group on the computer on which Azure AD Connect is installed.

## Installing Azure AD Connect

Installing Azure AD Connect with Express settings is appropriate if your organization has a single Active Directory forest and you wish to use password synchronization for authentication. The Azure AD Connect Express settings are appropriate for most organizations. You can download the Azure AD Connect installation files from Microsoft's download center website.

To install Azure AD Connect with Express settings, perform the following steps:

1. Double-click the AzureADConnect.msi file that you've downloaded from the Microsoft Download Center. You'll be prompted with a security warning. After you select Run, Azure AD Connect will be installed on your computer. When the installation is complete, you'll be presented with the splash screen detailing license terms and displaying a privacy notice. You must agree to these terms before selecting **Continue**.

2. If your organization has an internal nonroutable domain, it will be necessary for you to use custom settings. The best practice is to use domain synchronization when your on-premises Active Directory instance and your Azure Active Directory instance use the same routable domain name. Click **Continue**.

3. On the **Install required components** page, shown in Figure 1-23, choose between the following options:

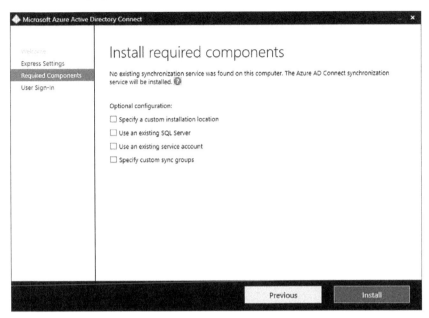

**FIGURE 1-23** Install Required Components.

- **Specify a custom installation location**   Choose this option if you want to install Azure AD Connect in a separate location, such as on another volume.
- **Specify an existing SQL Server**   Choose this option if you want to specify an alternate SQL server instance. By default, Azure AD Connect will install an SQL Server Express instance.
- **Use an existing service account**   You can configure Azure AD Connect to use an existing service account. By default, Azure AD Connect will create a service account. You can configure Azure AD Connect to use a Group Managed Service account. You'll need to use an existing service account if you are using Azure AD Connect with a remote SQL Server instance or if communication with Azure will occur through a proxy server that requires authentication.
- **Specify custom sync groups**   When you deploy Azure AD Connect, it will create four local groups on the server that hosts the Azure AD Connect Instance. These groups are the Administrators group, Operators group, Password Reset group, and the Browse group. If you want to use your own set of groups, you can specify them here. These groups must be local to the host server and not a member of the domain.

4. Once you have specified which custom options you require—and you can select none if you want—select **Install**.

5. On the **User Sign-In** page, shown in Figure 1-24, specify what type of sign-on you want to allow. You can choose between the following options, the details of which were covered earlier in this chapter. Most organizations will choose **Password Hash Synchronization** because this is the most straightforward option:

- **Password Hash Synchronization**
- **Pass-through authentication**
- **Federation with AD FS**
- **Federation with PingFederate**
- **Do not configure**
- **Enable single sign-on**

**FIGURE 1-24** User Sign-In options.

6. On the **Connect to Azure AD** page, provide the credentials of an account with Global Administrator privileges in Azure AD. Microsoft recommends you use an account in the default onmicrosoft.com domain associated with the Azure AD instance to which you will be connecting. If you choose the **Federation with AD FS** option, ensure that you do not sign in using an account in a domain that you will enable for federation.

7. After Azure AD Connect has connected to Azure AD, you will be able to specify the directory type to synchronize as well as the forest. Select **Add Directory** to add a specify forest. When you add a forest by selecting Add Directory, you will need to specify the credentials of an account that will perform periodic synchronization. Unless you are certain that you have applied the minimum necessary privileges to an account, you should provide Enterprise Administrator credentials and allow Azure AD Connect to create the account, as shown in Figure 1-25. This will ensure that the account is assigned only the privileges necessary to perform synchronization tasks.

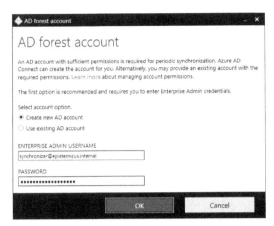

**FIGURE 1-25** AD forest account.

8. After the credentials have been verified, select **Next**.

9. On the **Azure AD sign-in configuration** page, shown in Figure 1-26, review the UPN suffix and then inspect the on-premises attribute to use as the Azure AD username. You'll need to ensure that accounts use a routable Azure AD username.

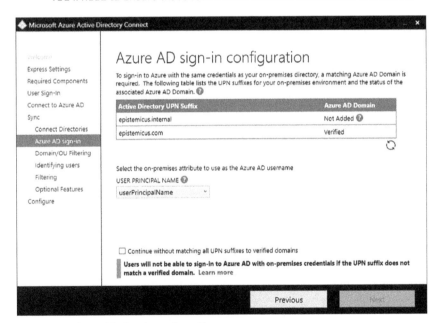

**FIGURE 1-26** Azure AD sign-in configuration.

10. On the **Domain and OU Filtering** page, select whether you want to sync all objects or just objects in specific domains and OUs.

11. On the **Uniquely identifying your users** page, shown in Figure 1-27, specify how users are to be identified. By default, users should only have one representation across all

directories. In the event that users exist in multiple directories, you can have matches identified by a specific Active Directory attribute, with the default being the **Mail attribute**.

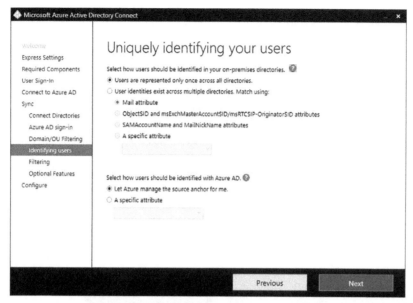

**FIGURE 1-27** Uniquely identifying your users.

12. On the **Filter users and devices** page, specify whether you want to synchronize all users and devices or only members of a specific group. Figure 1-28 shows members of the Microsoft 365-Pilot-Users group being configured so that their accounts will be synchronized with Azure.

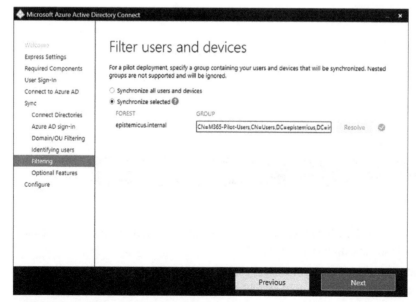

**FIGURE 1-28** Filter users and devices.

13. On the **Optional Features** page, select any optional features that you want to configure. These features include:

- **Exchange Hybrid Deployment**   This option is suitable for organizations that have an Office 365 deployment and where there are mailboxes hosted both on-premises and in the cloud.

- **Exchange Mail Public Folders**   This feature allows organizations to synchronize mail-enabled public folder objects from an on-premises Active Directory environment to Microsoft 365.

- **Azure AD App and Attribute Filtering**   Selecting this option gives you the ability to be more selective about which attributes are synchronized between the on-premises environment and Azure AD.

- **Password Synchronization**   Synchronizes a hash of the user's on-premises password to Azure AD. When the user authenticates to Azure AD, the submitted password is hashed using the same process, and if the hashes match, the user is authenticated. Each time a user updates their password on-premises, the updated password hash synchronizes to Azure AD.

- **Password Writeback**   Password writeback allows users to change their passwords in the cloud and have the changed password written back to the on-premises Active Directory instance. Enable this option if you want to support Self-Service Password Reset (SSPR).

- **Group Writeback**   Changes made to groups in Azure AD are written back to the on-premises AD instance.

- **Device Writeback**   Information about devices registered by the user in Azure AD is written back to the on-premises AD instance. You need to select this option if you want to allow users on hybrid-joined Windows 10 and Windows 11 devices to sign in using Windows Hello for Business.

- **Directory Extension Attribute Sync**   Allows you to extend Azure AD schema based on extensions made to your organization's on-premises Active Directory instance.

- **Hybrid Azure AD join**   Allows computer accounts in the on-premises AD DS forest to register with Azure AD. Configuring this option allows you to use features including conditional access in Azure.

14. On the **Ready to Configure** page, you can choose to start synchronization or to enable staging mode. When you configure staging mode, Azure AD Connect will prepare the synchronization process, but it will not synchronize any data with Azure AD.

## User principal name (UPN) suffixes

Prior to configuring and performing synchronization between an on-premises Active Directory environment and an Azure Active Directory instance, you must ensure that all user account objects in the on-premises Active Directory environment are configured with a value for the

UPN suffix that can function for both the on-premises environment and any application that you want to use it with in the cloud.

This is not a problem when an organization's internal Active Directory domain suffix is a publicly routable domain. For example, a domain name, such as contoso.com or adatum.com, that is resolvable by public DNS servers will suffice. Things become more complicated when the organization's internal Active Directory domain suffix is not publicly routable.

If a domain is nonroutable, the default Azure AD instance domain, such as adatum2020. onmicrosoft.com, should be used for the UPN suffix. This requires modifying the UPN suffix of accounts stored in the on-premises Active Directory instance. Modification of UPN after initial synchronization has occurred is not supported. So, you need to ensure that on-premises Active Directory UPNs are properly configured before performing initial synchronization using Azure AD Connect.

Follow these steps to add a UPN suffix to the on-premises Active Directory in the event that the Active Directory domain uses a nonroutable namespace:

1. Open the Active Directory Domains and Trust console and select **Active Directory Domains and Trusts**.

2. On the **Action** menu, select **Properties**.

3. On the **UPN Suffixes** tab, enter the UPN suffix to be used with Azure Active Directory. Figure 1-29 shows the UPN suffix of epistemicus.com.

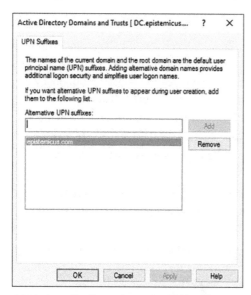

**FIGURE 1-29** Configure alternative UPN suffixes.

4. After the UPN suffix has been added in Active Directory Domains and Trusts, you can assign the UPN suffix to user accounts. You can do this manually, as shown in Figure 1-30, by using the **Account** tab of the user's **Properties** dialog box in Active Directory Users and Computers.

**FIGURE 1-30** Configure UPN.

5. You can also use Microsoft PowerShell scripts to reset the UPNs of multiple user accounts. For example, the following script resets UPN suffixes of all user accounts in the epistemicus.internal domain to epistemicus.onmicrosoft.com:

```
Get-ADUser -Filter {UserPrincipalName -like "*@epistemicus.internal"} -SearchBase
"DC=epistemicus,DC=internal" |
ForEach-Object {
$UPN =
$_.UserPrincipalName.Replace("epistemicus.internal","epistemicus.onmicrosoft.com")
Set-ADUser $_ -UserPrincipalName $UPN
}
```

## Manage Azure AD Connect Synchronization

By default, synchronization occurs between the on-premises directory and Azure every 30 minutes. In some cases, you'll make a change to a user account or create a collection of user accounts and want to get those changes or new accounts up into the Azure Active Directory instance as fast as possible. You can force synchronization by running the Azure AD Connect wizard again, or you can use the Synchronization Service Manager.

To perform a full synchronization using the Synchronization Service Manager, perform the following steps on the computer on which you have installed Azure AD Connect:

1. Open the Synchronization Service Manager, either by selecting **Synchronization Service** from the **Start** menu or by running miisclient.exe located in the C:\Program Files\Microsoft Azure AD Sync\UIShell folder.

2. Select the **Connectors** tab.

3. On the **Connectors** tab, select the name of your Active Directory domain service, as shown in Figure 1-31.

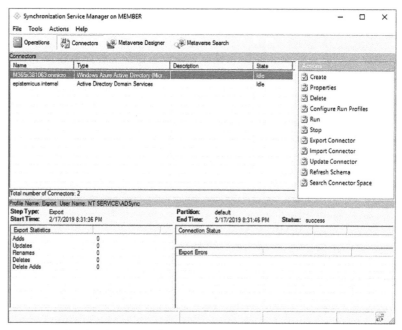

**FIGURE 1-31** Synchronization Service Manager.

4. In the **Actions** pane, select **Run**.

5. In the **Run Connector** dialog box, select **Full Synchronization**, as shown in Figure 1-32, and select **OK**.

**FIGURE 1-32** Full Synchronization.

You can trigger one of the following types of synchronization using the Synchronization Service Manager:

- **Full Import**   A full import and full sync is suitable for initiating the first full synchronization or the first full synchronization after you have changed the filtering parameters.
- **Full Synchronization**   This option performs a full synchronization.
- **Delta Import**   This option imports changed schema and objects.
- **Delta Synchronization**   This option synchronizes only objects changed since the last sync.
- **Export**   This option writes data from the Azure instance to the on-premises instance.

You can also use the Synchronization Service Manager to configure extensive filtering options, though for tasks such as configuring OU-based filtering, Microsoft recommends that you first attempt configuring filtering using the Azure AD Connect setup wizard and rely on a tool such as Synchronization Service Manager only if problems arise.

> **NEED MORE REVIEW?   SYNCHRONIZATION SERVICE MANAGER**
>
> You can learn more about Azure AD Connect Health at *https: https://docs.microsoft.com/ en-us/azure/active-directory/connect/active-directory-aadconnectsync-service-manager-ui*.

## Implement Azure AD Connect cloud sync

Azure AD Connect cloud sync provides an alternative solution for synchronizing identities between an on-premises AD DS instance and Azure AD to Azure AD Connect. Azure AD Connect cloud sync uses a special Azure AD cloud provisioning agent that communicates directly with Azure rather than an on-premises sync agent and database that manages the communication process. Azure AD Connect cloud sync includes the following options:

- Supports synchronization from multi-forest disconnected AD DS forest environments.
- A lightweight provisioning agent with sync configuration managed in Azure.
- Multiple provisioning agent can be deployed, simplifying the process of ensuring high availability.

Because it does not support advanced hash synchronization features, Azure AD Connect cloud sync is not supported to allow an on-premises account to be used to interact with hosts joined to an Azure AD DS domain. Azure AD Connect cloud sync also does not support pass-through authentication, device object synchronization, synchronization filters based on object attribute values, device writeback, group writeback, and groups larger than 50,000 members.

> **NEED MORE REVIEW?   AZURE AD CONNECT CLOUD SYNC**
>
> You can learn more about Azure AD Connect cloud sync at *https://docs.microsoft.com/en-us/ azure/active-directory/cloud-sync/what-is-cloud-sync*.

# Manage Azure AD DS

A simple option for domain-joining an IaaS VM is to deploy an IaaS domain controller VM and to then join other VMs to the domain in the same way that you would in an on-premises environment. The challenge with this is that it means that you have to deploy, maintain, and pay for an IaaS VM configured as a domain controller. Or you can deploy, maintain, and pay for two IaaS VMs if you're following the best practice of having at least two domain controllers for any single domain.

Azure Active Directory Domain Services (Azure AD DS) provides a managed domain service for IaaS VMs running in Azure. This service provides domain join, Group Policy, Lightweight Directory Access Protocol (LDAP), and Kerberos and NTLM authentication, and it is compatible with Windows Server Active Directory Domain Services. Because Azure AD DS is a managed service, Microsoft takes care of the management of the back-end domain controller infrastructure.

Azure AD DS pulls identity data from Azure AD. This includes identities synchronized from an on-premises Windows Active Directory instance through Azure AD Connect. When you deploy Azure AD DS, you select an Azure virtual network on which to make the service available. IaaS VMs placed on that virtual network can then domain-join to Azure AD DS in the same manner as a computer running on a traditional network with a domain controller would.

An Azure AD DS managed domain can also be configured in a trust relationship with an on-premises AD DS domain. This allows you to deploy resources in an Azure AD DS managed domain that functions as a resource forest that is accessible to on-premises accounts stored and managed in an on-premises trusted account forest. You'll learn more about this configuration later in the chapter.

> **NEED MORE REVIEW?**   **AZURE AD DS**
>
> You can learn more about Azure AD DS at *https://docs.microsoft.com/en-us/azure/active-directory-domain-services*.

## Deploying Azure Active Directory Domain Services

Azure AD DS can be enabled within a subscription and can leverage an Azure AD tenancy. Azure AD DS has the following prerequisites:

- To enable Azure AD DS, you'll need Global Administrator privileges within the Azure AD tenancy.
- Creating resources in Azure AD DS requires that you have contributor privileges in the Azure subscription.
- You must have a virtual network with DNS servers that can resolve Azure infrastructure resources, including storage. You can use Azure's DNS servers. If you use custom DNS servers that are unable to resolve internet hosts, you may be unable to create an Azure AD DS domain.

Before creating an Azure AD DS domain, you should decide on the properties of the DNS name that you will assign. Take into account the following:

- The default option will be to use the built-in domain name of the Azure AD directory associated with the managed domain. (This will have an .onmicrosoft.com DNS suffix.) The challenge with this option is that if you wish to enable secure LDAP, you won't be able to create a digital certificate that allows a connection to this default domain because Microsoft owns the domain name associated with the DNS suffix.

- Nonroutable domain names (such as .local and .internal) will cause problems with DNS resolution and should be avoided.

- A custom domain name that you have registered publicly is the best option. Microsoft recommends that you use a domain name separate from any existing or Azure or on-premises DNS namespace. For example, use addstailwindtraders.com for the managed domain, whereas you use tailwindtraders.com for an on-premises domain as well as for some resources in Azure.

The following additional restrictions apply for domain names associated with Azure AD DS managed domains:

- The domain prefix element of the domain name (domainprefix.tailwindtraders.com) cannot be longer than 15 characters. The domain suffix (tailwindtraders.com) is not counted toward this limit.

- The DNS domain name of the managed domain should not already exist in the virtual network. You cannot already have an AD DS domain with the same DNS domain name present, an Azure cloud service with that name, or a VPN connection to an on-premises network with that name.

Deploying an Azure AD Domain Services managed domain involves performing the following steps:

1. In the Azure portal, select **Create a resource** and search for Azure AD Domain Services.

2. On the **Azure AD Domain Services** page, select **Create**.

3. Choose the Azure subscription and resource group that will host the managed domain.

4. Enter the selected DNS name for the Azure AD DS domain.

5. Choose the location in which the domain should be created. If the region supports Azure Availability Zones, the Azure AD DS resources will be distributed across zones for additional redundancy.

6. Choose a SKU (this determines the performance and backup frequency and can be altered after deployment). You can choose between Standard, Enterprise, and Premium.

7. Select between a user forest and a resource forest.

   - User forests synchronize all objects from Azure AD, including any user account synchronized from an on-premises AD DS environment

   - Resource forests only synchronize objects created in Azure AD and will not include any accounts synchronized from an on-premises AD DS environment. A resource forest can be configured in a one-way trust relationship with an on-premises Windows Server AD DS forest. This allows accounts that aren't synchronized to Azure to access resources hosted on Azure IaaS VMs that are domain-joined to an Azure AD DS domain.

8. If you select **Review and Create** and have selected a User forest, the following occurs:

   - A new virtual network named aadds-vnet that uses the IP address range 10.0.0.0/24 is created.

   - A new subnet named aadds-subnet that uses the IP address range 10.0.0.0/24 is deployed within the newly created aadds-vnet.

   - A new network security group is created that contains rules that allow for service communication.

   - You can provide alternate options for virtual network and subnet and should extend the vNet's range at this point if you want to add a VPN gateway.

9. After deployment has completed, you will need to update the DNS server settings for the Azure Virtual Network associated with the Azure AD DS domain so that the DNS server addresses match those associated with the Azure AD DS domain. You can do this automatically by selecting **Configure** on the overview page of the Azure AD DS domain.

## Azure AD DS domain join

You can only perform a domain join to an Azure AD DS instance with an account that is part of the Azure AD tenant. You can't perform a domain join using an account that has been synchronized from an on-premises Windows AD DS instance to perform this task. As is the case when configuring Azure AD Connect, you should consider creating a special account using the default tenancy *onmicrosoft.com* suffix for performing domain-join operations rather than any custom domain name that you have assigned to the tenancy.

You perform the domain-join operation from within the Windows Server VM, either directly by connecting through an RDP or Azure Bastion session or through a remote PowerShell session, either by changing the domain membership on the **Computer Name** tab of the **System Properties** dialog box, or by using the Add-Computer PowerShell cmdlet with the DomainName parameter.

> **NEED MORE REVIEW?  IAAS VM DOMAIN JOIN**
>
> You can learn more about domain-joining a Windows Server IaaS VM at *https://docs.microsoft.com/azure/active-directory-domain-services/join-windows-vm*.

# Integrate Azure AD, AD DS, and Azure AD DS

You can configure Azure AD DS so that an account created on-premises synchronizes using Azure AD Connect to Azure AD and is configured with the appropriate hash synchronization that this account can in turn be used to sign on to an Azure AD DS joined VM.

By default, Azure AD does not automatically generate NTLM or Kerberos password hashes for users. For users to log on to computers that are members of an Azure AD DS domain, they need to have passwords stored in a hash format that can be used by NTLM or Kerberos authentication.

You can configure accounts that are only hosted in Azure AD to support authentication on computers joined to an Azure AD DS domain by changing the account's password once an Azure AD DS instance associated with the Azure AD tenancy is created. Once this is done, generating a new password will create the appropriately stored password hash.

If you are synchronizing accounts and passwords to Azure using Azure AD Connect, you'll need to perform the following steps:

1. Open the Synchronization Service on the computer that hosts Azure AD Connect.

2. On the list of connectors, take note of the connector names.

3. Run the following script, adding the connector names to the location in the script that defines the $azureadConnector and $adConnector variables:

```
# Define the Azure AD Connect connector names and import the required
PowerShell module
$azureadConnector = "<CASE SENSITIVE AZURE AD CONNECTOR NAME>"
$adConnector = "<CASE SENSITIVE AD DS CONNECTOR NAME>"

Import-Module "C:\Program Files\Microsoft Azure AD Sync\Bin\ADSync\ADSync.psd1"
Import-Module "C:\Program Files\Microsoft Azure Active Directory Connect\
AdSyncConfig\AdSyncConfig.psm1"

# Create a new ForceFullPasswordSync configuration parameter object then
# update the existing connector with this new configuration
$c = Get-ADSyncConnector -Name $adConnector
$p = New-Object Microsoft.IdentityManagement.PowerShell.ObjectModel.
ConfigurationParameter "Microsoft.Synchronize.ForceFullPasswordSync", String,
ConnectorGlobal, $null, $null, $null
$p.Value = 1
$c.GlobalParameters.Remove($p.Name)
$c.GlobalParameters.Add($p)
$c = Add-ADSyncConnector -Connector $c

# Disable and re-enable Azure AD Connect to force a full password synchronization
Set-ADSyncAADPasswordSyncConfiguration -SourceConnector $adConnector
-TargetConnector $azureadConnector -Enable $false
Set-ADSyncAADPasswordSyncConfiguration -SourceConnector $adConnector
-TargetConnector $azureadConnector -Enable $true
```

## Manage Azure AD Connect Health

Azure AD Connect Health is a tool available in the Azure Active Directory admin center, shown in Figure 1-33, that allows you to monitor the health of synchronization between your organization's on-premises directory and Azure Active Directory.

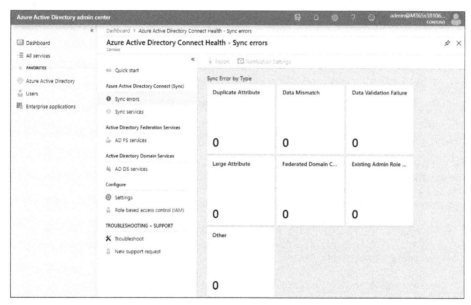

**FIGURE 1-33** Azure AD Connect Health.

You can use Azure AD Connect health to view information about the following:

- **Sync errors**   This option displays errors such as Duplicate Attribute, Data Mismatch, Data Validation Failure, Large Attribute, Federated Domain Change, and Existing Admin Role Conflicts.

- **Sync services**   This option handles information about which services are synchronizing with Azure Active Directory.

- **AD FS services**   This option displays information about AD FS when Azure AD Connect is configured for federation. Includes information about errors and issues.

- **AD DS services**   This option displays information about domains and forests connected to Azure Active Directory.

***NEED MORE REVIEW?*** **AZURE AD CONNECT HEALTH**

You can learn more about Azure AD Connect Health at *https://docs.microsoft.com/en-us/azure/active-directory/hybrid/whatis-azure-ad-connect.*

# Manage authentication in on-premises and hybrid environments

Azure AD Connect supports a variety of user sign-in options, which are related to the method you use to synchronize directory information from Active Directory Domain Services to Azure AD. You configure which sign-in option you will use when setting up Azure AD Connect, as shown in Figure 1-34. The default method, password sync, is appropriate for the majority of organizations that will use Azure AD Connect to synchronize identities to the cloud.

**FIGURE 1-34** User sign-in.

## Password synchronization

Hashes of on-premises Active Directory user passwords synchronize to Azure AD, and changed passwords immediately synchronize to Azure AD. Actual passwords are never sent to Azure AD and are not stored in Azure AD. This allows for single sign-on for users of computers that are joined to an Active Directory domain that synchronizes to Azure AD. Password synchronization also allows you to enable password writeback for self-service password reset functionality through Azure AD.

## Pass-through authentication

When authenticating to Azure AD, the user's password is validated against an on-premises Active Directory domain controller. Passwords and password hashes are not present in Azure AD. Pass-through authentication allows you to apply on-premises password policies. It requires that Azure AD Connect have an agent on a computer joined to the domain that hosts the Active Directory instance that contains the relevant user accounts. Pass-through authentication also allows single sign-on for users of domain-joined machines.

With pass-through authentication, the user's password is validated against the on-premises Active Directory controller. The password doesn't need to be present in Azure AD in any form. This allows for on-premises policies, such as sign-in hour restrictions, to be evaluated during authentication to cloud services.

Pass-through authentication uses a simple agent on a Windows Server 2012 R2, Windows Server 2016, Windows Server 2019, or Windows Server 2022 domain-joined machine in the on-premises environment. This agent listens for password-validation requests. It doesn't require any inbound ports to be open to the internet.

You can also enable single sign-on for users on domain-joined machines that are on the corporate network. With single sign-on, enabled users only need to enter a username to help them securely access cloud resources.

## Active Directory Federation

Active Directory Federation allows users to authenticate to Azure AD resources using on-premises credentials. It also requires the deployment of an Active Directory Federation Services infrastructure. This is the most complex identity synchronization configuration for Azure Active Directory and is only likely to be implemented in environments with complicated identity configurations.

# Configure and manage AD DS passwords

Most of the accounts used in your organization will be domain-based rather than local accounts. Except for the occasional local account, users, services, and computers authenticate against Active Directory Domain Services (AD DS). By using password policies, administrators can specify the rules for allowable passwords. They determine how long and how complicated passwords must be, as well as how often they must be changed, how often they can be changed, and whether previously used passwords can be used again.

Unless you take special steps, the properties of passwords used with domain accounts are determined through domain-based password policies. You configure password policies by editing Group Policy Objects (GPOs) linked at the domain level. This fact is important, and although you can set password policies at GPOs linked at the organizational unit (OU) and site level, these policies have no effect on the properties of user passwords.

Remember that you can have only one set of domain password policies configured through Group Policy. The GPO order at the domain level determines the domain password policy. The exceptions to the rule about one password policy per domain are fine-grained password policies.

Password policies are located in the Computer Configuration\Policies\Windows Settings\ Security Settings\Account Policies node of a GPO. Although most administrators think of password policy and account lockout policy as parts of the same whole, they are actually separate. Windows Server ships with a default password policy, but account lockout policy is not enabled.

## Password policy items

The following list shows five main password policies that you are likely to use when configuring a password policy for your organization, and one that you probably won't use. These password policies are the following:

- **Enforce password history**   This policy means that the configured number of previously used passwords is stored within Active Directory. It stops users from using the same set of small passwords. The default and maximum value is 24 remembered passwords.
- **Maximum password age**   This policy specifies the maximum length of time that can elapse before a password must be changed. The default value is 42 days. You can set it to 999 days. Setting the value to 0 days means that there is no maximum password age.
- **Minimum password age**   You use this policy to restrict users from changing their password instantly. This policy exists because some users spend a couple of minutes repeatedly changing their password until they have exhausted the password history and return to using their original password. Users can change their password after the specified period has elapsed. The default value is 1 day.
- **Minimum password length**   This policy sets the minimum number of characters in a password. Longer passwords are more secure than shorter ones. Windows Server supports passwords up to 128 characters long when changed using GUI tools, and 256 when modified using PowerShell.
- **Password must meet complexity requirements**   This policy ensures that passwords use a mix of numerals, symbols, and uppercase and lowercase alphabet characters. When enabled, it also stops users from using their account name in the password.

The policy that you are unlikely to need is the **Store Passwords Using Reversible Encryption** policy. This policy has been available in most previous versions of the Windows Server operating system. It provides backward compatibility for applications that could not access passwords stored in Active Directory using the native method of encryption. Unless your organization is running some software that was written back when Windows NT 4.0 was the Windows Server operating system, you probably won't need to enable this policy.

## Delegate password settings permissions

People tend to be good at remembering passwords that they have used for a long time. They tend not to be so good at remembering new passwords, especially if those passwords contain a mix of numbers, letters, and symbols. Users who frequently have to change their passwords are more likely to end up forgetting those passwords. If an account lockout policy is enforced, users are more likely to end up calling the service desk to get their password reset. The stricter an organization's password policy is, the more time the service desk has to spend untangling users from forgotten passwords.

Instead of having users call the service desk to have their password reset, you can delegate the ability to reset user passwords to someone in the user's own department, such as an administrative assistant or office manager. Taking this step can increase security because someone in the user's own department can more easily verify the user's identity than a service desk technician can. It also shifts work away from the service desk, which enables service desk technicians to concentrate on other tasks.

The default Active Directory settings give members of the Account Operators, Domain Admins, or Enterprise Admins Active Directory groups the right to change user passwords. You can delegate the ability to manage password settings on a per-OU basis through the delegation of a control wizard. When you do this, you move user accounts into specific OUs that match your administrative requirements. For example, you can move all user accounts of people who work in the research department to the Research OU, and then delegate the right to reset passwords and force password change at the next logon to the research department's departmental manager. You can also delegate the ability to manage password settings at the domain level, though most organizations do this by adding users to the Account Operators, Domain Admins, or Enterprise Admins groups.

To delegate the right to reset passwords and force password changes at the next logon, run the **Delegation of Control Wizard**. You can access this wizard by right-clicking an OU in Active Directory Users and Computers and then selecting **Delegate Control**. You should be careful to select only the **Reset user passwords and force password change at next logon** task and not grant non-IT department users the right to perform other tasks.

Larger organizations should consider providing a self–service password reset portal. Self–service password reset portals enable users to reset their Active Directory user account passwords after performing a series of tasks that verify their identity. This process provides users with a quick method of resetting forgotten passwords and reduces the number of password reset requests for service desk technicians. Connecting your on-premises interest of AD DS to Azure Active Directory provides you with the option of implementing self-service password reset.

## Fine-grained password policies

Fine-grained password policies enable you to have separate password policies within a single domain. For example, with fine-grained password policies you can have a password policy that applies to general users and have a stricter set of policies that apply to users with sensitive accounts, such as members of the IT department. Unlike Group Policy–based password policies, which apply at the domain level, you apply fine-grained password policies to global security groups or individual user accounts. This means that multiple fine-grained password policies might apply to a single account. In this situation, use precedence settings to ensure that the appropriate policy always applies. (Precedence is covered later in this lesson.) Fine-grained password policies can't be applied to domain local or universal security groups, only to global security groups. The Active Directory domain must be at the Windows Server 2008 or later functional level or higher before you can use fine-grained password policies.

### MANAGING FINE-GRAINED PASSWORD POLICIES

You create and manage fine-grained password policies through the Active Directory Administrative Center. To create a new Password Settings Object (PSO), open the Active Directory Administrative Center and navigate to the Password Settings Container (PSC), which is located in the System Container of the domain. From the **Tasks** menu, select **New**, and then select **Password Settings**. The PSC enables you to view the precedence of PSOs. Password settings with lower precedence values override password settings with higher precedence values.

### CONFIGURING PASSWORD SETTINGS OBJECTS

A Password Settings Object (PSO) contains settings for both password policy and account lockout policy. A PSO applies to the groups and users specified in the Directly Applies To area. If a PSO applies to a user account, either directly or indirectly through group membership, that PSO overrides the existing password and account lockout policies configured at the domain level.

PSOs contain the following options:

- **Name**  Enables you to configure a name for the PSO.
- **Precedence**  When multiple PSOs apply to an account, the PSO with the lowest precedence value has priority.
- **Enforce Minimum Password Length**  Minimum password length that can be used by users subject to the policy.
- **Enforce Password History**  The number of passwords remembered by Active Directory. Remembered passwords can't be reused.
- **Password Must Meet Complexity Requirements**  A password must contain a mix of numbers, symbols, and uppercase and lowercase letters.
- **Store Password Using Reversible Encryption**  Provides backward compatibility with older software and is rarely used in Windows Server 2012 environments.
- **Protect From Accidental Deletion**  The user account can't be accidentally deleted. Although this setting is not available in Group Policy password or account lockout settings, you can edit an object directly to configure it.
- **Enforce Minimum Password Age**  The minimum length of time users must have a password before they are eligible to change it.
- **Enforce Maximum Password Age**  The maximum number of days that users can go without changing their password.

- **Enforce Account Lockout Policy**   You can configure the following three policies with this policy enabled:
  - **Number of Failed Logon Attempts Allowed**   The number of incorrect password entries that can be made in succession before a lockout is triggered.
  - **Reset Failed Logon Attempts Count After**   The period of time in which the incorrect password entries must be made.
  - **Account Will Be Locked Out**   Can be set either to a specific number of minutes or to a setting for which the administrator must manually unlock the account.

## Determining password settings

If your organization uses a number of fine-grained password policies, it might be difficult to determine, at a glance, which password policy applies to a particular user because PSOs can be applied to multiple groups and users, and users can be members of multiple groups. Rather than work everything out manually, the Active Directory Administrative Center's Global Search function provides the following criteria to determine which fine-grained password policy applies to a specific user or group:

- **Directly Applied Password Settings For A Specific User**   You can determine which PSOs directly apply to a specific user account. PSOs that apply to security groups of which the user account is a member are not listed.
- **Directly Applied Password Settings For A Specific Global Security Group**   You can determine which PSOs directly apply to a specific security group.
- **Resultant Password Settings For A Specific User**   You can determine which PSO applies to a specific user account based on directly applied PSOs as well as PSOs that apply indirectly through group membership.

## Establishing balanced password policies

Password policies require balance, and a password policy that is too strict can be as detrimental as one that is not strict enough. For example, some organizations that implement strict password policies find that users write complicated passwords down because they can't remember them. By increasing the severity of their password policies, the IT department may prompt users to behave in a way that makes the organization less secure.

When considering password policies, keep the following in mind:

- Users dislike changing their password. Many want to log on and get to work rather than coming up with a new password to remember that also meets the requirements of the password policy.
- Users are more likely to forget a new password than one they have been using for some time. Users who constantly forget passwords tend to do things that decrease security such as writing those passwords on notes taped to their monitors.
- If you increase the minimum password length, forcing users to use pass phrases, you can also increase the maximum time before the password expires. Increasing password

length increases security by making the password less guessable. Although increasing maximum password age reduces password security, this decrease is not as significant as the improvement achieved by increasing password length.

Remember that each call to the service desk costs the organization money and time. You should aim to minimize the number of password reset requests without decreasing password security. An alternative option is to implement Self-Service Password Reset through integration with Azure Active Directory. This strategy is addressed further by the AZ-801 Configuring Windows Server Hybrid Advanced Services exam.

## Account lockout settings

An account lockout policy determines what happens when a person enters an incorrect password a certain number of times. The default Windows Server settings do not have account lockout policy configured, so users can keep entering incorrect passwords until they give up in frustration. Unfortunately, enabling users to keep entering incorrect passwords is a security risk because it allows "dictionary attacks," in which an automated system keeps entering passwords from a list until it locates the correct one.

These policies enable you to do the following:

- **Account Lockout Duration**   Use this policy to specify how long an account is locked out. When enabled, this setting defaults to 30 minutes. If you set this policy to 0, the account is locked out until someone with the appropriate privileges can unlock it.

- **Account Lockout Threshold**   Use this policy to specify the number of invalid logon attempts that trigger an account lockout. When enabled, the default value is 5, but you can set it to 999. The number of invalid logons must occur within the period specified in the Reset Account Lockout Counter After policy. A value of 0 will mean that account lockout will not be triggered.

- **Reset Account Lockout Counter After**   Use this policy to specify the amount of time in which the number of invalid logon attempts must occur. When enabled, this policy defaults to a value of 30 minutes. If the defaults are used and a user enters an incorrect password three times in 30 minutes, the account is locked out for 30 minutes. If a user enters an incorrect password three times in 31 minutes, however, the account is not locked out.

You have to consider balance when configuring lockout policies. How many failed attempts suggest that users won't remember their password? For the average user, a lockout of 30 minutes is functionally equivalent to a lockout that never expires. Even if you explain to users a thousand times that they have to wait 30 minutes and try again, they will still ring the help desk within moments of being locked out. Consider a 1-minute lockout and mention it using the logon disclaimer Group Policy item. It enables you to protect against dictionary attacks and probably minimize calls to the service desk.

## Account management tasks

Having a set of account policies in place is only the first step in a comprehensive account management strategy. Administrators must regularly check the status of user accounts to determine how well account policies are functioning, as well as locate any accounts in which there is suspicious activity.

### ACCOUNTS WITH NONEXPIRING PASSWORDS

You can configure an account so that the password never expires. When you do this, the user associated with the account never has to change the password. Password policies don't override accounts that have been explicitly configured so that their passwords do not expire. Selecting the **Password never expires** setting, as shown in Figure 1-35, exempts an account from any password-expiration policies.

**FIGURE 1-35** Password never expires setting.

To configure an account so that password policies apply, you need to deselect the **Password never expires** option. You should also force the user to change the password at the next logon as if the password was configured not to expire because it is reasonable to assume that the user hasn't changed it recently. You can figure out which accounts have been configured not to expire by using the Active Directory Administrative Center and performing a query to find all accounts that have been configured with no expiration date, as shown in Figure 1-36.

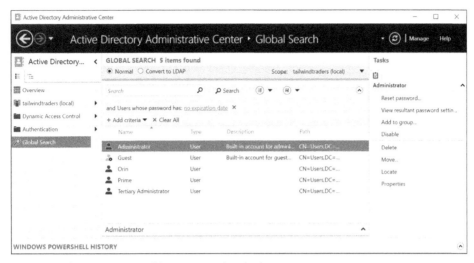

**FIGURE 1-36** Locate accounts with no password expiration.

You can then modify the properties of these accounts by selecting them all and selecting the **Password never expires** option in the **Multiple User Account properties** dialog box, which is available when you select and view the properties of multiple accounts in the Active Directory Administrative Center console. When performing this task, you should also force users to change their passwords on their next logon, which ensures that password policies apply in the future.

Many systems administrators have the bad habit of configuring their passwords not to expire simply because they realize how annoying it is to have to change passwords constantly. Given that systems administrator accounts are usually the most powerful in the organization, it is a bad idea to enable them to exempt themselves from an organizational password policy. If anything, systems administrators should be subject to more stringent password policies than ordinary users. You can configure stricter password policies for a specific subset of users using fine-grained password policies.

### LOCKED-OUT ACCOUNTS

As you learned earlier, the length of time an account is locked out depends on account lockout policies. Many organizations that permanently lock out accounts when a user enters incorrect passwords in succession wait for the locked-out user to call the service desk to request a password reset. Although most users contact the service desk quickly when their user account is locked out, there are situations in which this does not occur, such as when someone attempts to gain access to a coworker's account while that coworker is on leave. You can use the Active Directory Administrative Center Global Search option to locate users with enabled but locked-out accounts. You do this by selecting the **Users with enabled but locked accounts** search criteria. You should further investigate locked accounts when the user associated with the account has not contacted the service desk.

### INACTIVE ACCOUNTS

Although the IT department is often notified when a person new to the organization needs a new user account, the IT department is not always notified when people leave the organization. As a result, most organizations have a number of inactive user accounts that are associated with people no longer directly associated with the organization. There can be good reasons for the inactivity; for example, a person may be on maternity or long service leave. As an administrator, you should frequently search for accounts in which the user has not signed on for a good length of time. You can disable user accounts associated with users who have temporarily departed the organization. This gives you the option of reenabling the account when the user returns. You can later remove user accounts associated with users who have left the organization.

Disabling an account allows you to reactivate the account if it is necessary to access resources to which the departed user had access. Some organizations have a special "Disabled User Accounts" OU to store these accounts. Deleting an account is a more permanent option. Although it is possible to recover deleted items if backups are available, it gets increasingly difficult once the tombstone lifetime expires.

You can locate inactive accounts by using the Global Search function in the Active Directory Administrative Center to search for users with enabled accounts who have not signed on for more than a given number of days. The value you choose here will depend on the nature of your environment, but you should definitely investigate any active enabled accounts in which a logon has not occurred for more than 50 days.

## Azure AD Password Protection

Azure AD Password Protection allows you to detect and block known weak passwords. You can also use Azure AD Password Protection to block specific terms from being used in passwords, such as those associated with your organization, popular anime characters, or the local football team.

Checks for weak passwords occur on the domain controller, and password hash synchronization is not required for the implementation of Azure AD Password Protection. Communication with Azure occurs through a domain-joined computer that has the Azure AD Password Protection Proxy service deployed. This service is responsible for ensuring that password hygiene policies configured in Azure are distributed to domain controllers. Azure AD Password Protection does not require domain controllers to be able to directly communicate with Azure.

Password policies are only enforced on domain controllers where the Azure AD Password Protection agent is installed. To ensure that password protection enforcement occurs consistently, you will need to deploy the password protection agent on all domain controllers in a domain.

***EXAM TIP***

**Remember the difference between password synchronization, pass-through authentication, and Active Directory Federation Services when configuring Azure AD Connect.**

# Skill 1.5: Manage Windows Server by using domain-based Group Policies

Group Policy is the primary method by which you configure settings for users and computers in an Active Directory Domain Services environment. Even though other technologies exist through which configuration of servers and client computers can be accomplished, an understanding of how Group Policies function is critical to the practice of Windows Server administration.

**This skill covers how to:**

- Implement Group Policy in AD DS
- Implement Group Policy Preferences in AD DS
- Implement Group Policy in Azure AD DS

## Implement Group Policy in AD DS

Group Policy provides a central way of managing user and computer configuration. You can use Group Policy to configure everything from password and auditing policies to software deployment, desktop background settings, and mappings between file extensions and default applications.

### Managing Group Policy Objects

As an experienced systems administrator, you are aware that GPOs enable you to configure settings for multiple users and computers. After you get beyond editing GPOs to configure settings, you need to start thinking about issues such as GPO maintenance. For example, if an important document is lost, you need to know how to recover it from backup. Do you know what to do if someone accidentally deletes a GPO that has hundreds of settings configured over a long period of time?

The main tool you'll use for managing GPOs is the Group Policy Management Console (GPMC), shown in Figure 1-37. You can use this console to back up, restore, import, copy, and migrate. You can also use this console to delegate GPO management tasks.

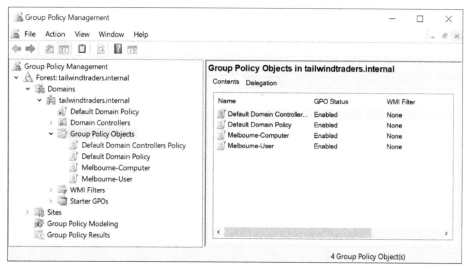

**FIGURE 1-37** Group Policy Management Console.

There are also a substantial number of cmdlets available in the PowerShell Group Policy module, including the following:

- **Get-GPO**   Enables you to view GPOs
- **Backup-GPO**   Enables you to back up GPOs
- **Import-GPO**   Enables you to import a backed-up GPO into a specified GPO
- **New-GPO**   Enables you to create a new GPO
- **Copy-GPO**   Enables you to copy a GPO
- **Rename-GPO**   Enables you to change a GPO's name
- **Restore-GPO**   Enables you to restore a backed-up GPO to its original location
- **Remove-GPO**   Enables you to remove a GPO

## Backup GPOs

Backing up a GPO enables you to create a copy of a GPO as it exists at a specific point in time. A user must have read permission on a GPO to back it up. When you back up a GPO, the backup version of the GPO is incremented. It is good practice to back up GPOs prior to editing them so that if something goes wrong, you can revert to the unmodified GPO.

If your organization doesn't have access to the Microsoft Desktop Optimization Pack (MDOP), you should back up GPOs before you or other people modify them. If a problem occurs, it's quicker to restore a backup than it is to reconfigure the modified GPO with the existing settings. MDOP provides the ability to use GPO versioning as well as other advanced functionality. You'll learn about Advanced Group Policy Management later in this chapter.

To back up a GPO, perform the following steps:

1.  Open the GPMC.

2. Right-click the GPO that you want to back up, and select **Back Up**. In the **Back Up Group Policy Object** dialog box enter the location of the backup and a description for the backup and then select **Back Up**.

You can restore a GPO using the `Restore-GPO` cmdlet. Restoring a GPO overwrites the current version of the GPO if one exists or re-creates the GPO if the GPO has been deleted. To restore a GPO, right-click the Group Policy Objects node in the GPMC and select **Manage Backups**. In the **Manage Backups** dialog box select the GPO you want to restore and select **Restore**. If multiple backups of the same GPO exist, you can select which version of a GPO to restore.

### IMPORT AND COPY GPOS

Importing a GPO enables you to take the settings in a backed-up GPO and import them into an existing GPO. To import a GPO, perform the following steps:

1. Right-click an existing GPO in the GPMC and select **Import Settings**.

2. In the **Import Settings Wizard**, you are given the option of backing up the destination GPO's settings. This enables you to roll back the import.

3. Specify the folder that hosts the backed-up GPO.

4. On the **Source GPO** page of the Import Settings Wizard. select the source GPO. You can view the settings that have been configured in the source GPO prior to importing it. Complete the wizard to finish importing the settings.

Remember that when you import settings from a backed-up GPO, the settings in the backed-up GPO overwrite the settings in the destination GPO.

Copying a GPO creates a new GPO and copies all configuration settings from the original to the new. You can copy GPOs from one domain to another. You can also use a migration table when copying a GPO to map security principals referenced in the source domain to security principals referenced in the destination domain.

To copy a GPO, perform the following steps:

1. Right-click the GPO that you want to copy and select **Copy**.

2. Right-click the location that you want to copy the GPO to and select **Paste**.

3. In the **Copy GPO** dialog box, choose between using the default permissions and preserving the existing permissions assigned to the GPO.

### FIXING GPO PROBLEMS

Windows Server includes command-line utilities that allow you to repair a GPO after you perform a domain rename or re-create default GPOs. If you need to re-create the default GPOs for a domain, use the `DCGPOFix` command. If you perform a domain rename, you can use the `GPFixup` command to repair name dependencies in GPOs and Group Policy links.

## Migrate Group Policy Objects

When moving GPOs between domains or forests, you need to ensure that any domain-specific information is accounted for, so locations and security principals in the source domain aren't used in the destination domain. You can account for these locations and security principals using migration tables. You use *migration tables* when copying or importing GPOs.

Migration tables enable you to alter references when moving a GPO from one domain to another, or from one forest to another. An example is when you are using GPOs for software deployment and need to replace the address of a shared folder that hosts a software installation file so that it is relevant to the target domain. You can open the Migration Table Editor (MTE) by right-clicking **Domains** in the GPMC and selecting **Open Migration Table Editor**.

When you use the MTE, you can choose to populate from a GPO that is in the current domain or to populate the MTE from a backed-up GPO. When you perform this action, the MTE will be populated with settings that reference local objects. If when you perform this action there are no results, then no local locations are referenced in the GPO that you are going to migrate.

## GPO management

In larger environments, there is more than one person in the IT department. In very large organizations, one person's entire job responsibility might be creating and editing GPOs. Delegation enables you to grant the permission to perform specific tasks to a specific user or group of users. You can delegate some or all of the following Group Policy management tasks:

- GPO creation
- GPO modification
- GPO linking to specific sites, organizational units (OUs), or domains
- Permission to perform Group Policy Modeling analysis at the OU or domain level
- Permission to view Group Policy Results information at the OU or domain level
- Windows Management Instrumentation (WMI) filter creation

Users in the Domain Admins and Enterprise Admins groups can perform all Group Policy management tasks. Users that are members of the Group Policy Creator Owners domain group can create GPOs. They also have the right to edit and delete any GPOs that they have created. You can delegate permissions to GPOs directly using the GPMC.

### CREATING GPOS

Creating a GPO is simply creating a new Group Policy Object. Newly created GPOs have no settings applied. To create a new GPO:

1. Open the Group Policy Management Console.
2. Under Forest\Domains\Domain Name, right-click **Group Policy Objects** and select **New**.
3. Provide a name for the new GPO and select **OK**.

If you want to delegate the ability for users to create GPOs, you can add them to the Group Policy Creator Owners group. You can also explicitly grant them permission to create GPOs using the GPMC. To do this, perform the following steps:

1. Open the GPMC from the Tools menu of Server Manager.

2. Expand the domain in which you want to delegate the ability to create GPOs, select **Group Policy Objects**, and select the **Delegation** tab.

3. Select **Add** and select the group or user that you want to give the ability to create GPOs in that domain.

### EDITING GPOS

To edit a GPO, users must be either a member of the Domain Admins or Enterprise Admins group. Users can edit a GPO if they:

- Created it
- Have been given Read/Write permissions on the GPO through the GPMC

To grant a user permission to edit a GPO, perform the following steps:

1. Select the GPO in the GPMC.

2. Select the **Delegation** tab.

3. Select **Add**, specify the user or group that should have permission to edit the GPO, and then specify the permissions that you want to give this user or group. You can choose from one of the following permissions:

  - Read
  - Edit Settings
  - Edit Settings, Delete, Modify Security

### LINKING GPOS

Linking a GPO to an object such as a domain or OU involves navigating to the location in the Group Policy Management Console, right-clicking on that location, and selecting **Link Existing GPO**. You then select which of the existing GPOs you want to link to the domain or OU. You also have the ability to create and link a GPO using this method.

To enable a user to link a GPO to a specific object, you need to edit the permission on that object. You can perform this task in the GPMC. For example, to grant a user or group permission to link a GPO to an OU, select the OU in the GPMC, select the **Delegation** tab, select **Add**, and then select the user or group to which you want to grant this permission.

### MODELING, RESULTS, AND WMI FILTERS

The Group Policy Modeling Wizard allows you to simulate a policy deployment for planning and testing purposes without actually assigning a policy to the production environment. You can determine what the resultant set of policy will be using this wizard without it actually impacting existing users or computers.

Group Policy Results allows you to calculate which policies apply given the existing configuration to a specific user or computer. This wizard differs from the Group Policy Modeling Wizard in that it will tell you what policies apply at the current moment rather than modeling a hypothetical policy deployment configuration.

Delegating permissions to perform tasks related to Group Policy Modeling and Group Policy Results is performed at the domain level. You can delegate the ability to create WMI filters by selecting the WMI Filters node in the GPMC and granting the permission on the Delegation tab.

## Advanced Group Policy Management

Advanced Group Policy Management (AGPM) is available to Software Assurance customers through the Microsoft Desktop Optimization Pack. AGPM integrates with the existing Group Policy Management Console, extending its functionality. AGPM has several benefits over the standard Group Policy Management Console.

The biggest advantage of AGPM is that it enables you to apply a workflow to the management of GPOs, allowing you to use versioning and offline editing. This is an advantage over the standard Group Policy Management Console, where any changes made to an active Group Policy are automatically propagated to clients that are influenced by that policy. Having offline functionality for editing GPOs allows GPOs that are already active to be more extensively tested during the revision process than might be the case in a traditional GPO deployment.

AGPM offers a more advanced model for editing GPOs because it allows administrators to track precisely which person in an organization made a specific change to a GPO. In a traditional Windows Server deployment, even though it is possible to control who has the permissions required to edit and apply a GPO, if multiple people have these permissions, it can be almost impossible to determine who made a specific change to an existing GPO. Being able to track the changes made to a GPO is very important in a high-security environment.

AGPM uses the following roles in its delegation architecture:

- **AGPM Administrator**   Users assigned this role are able to perform all tasks in AGPM. This includes configuring domain-wide options as well as delegating permissions.

- **Approver**   Users assigned this role are able to deploy GPOs into the domain. Approvers are also able to approve or reject requests from users assigned the Editor role. Users assigned this role are also able to create and delete GPOs, but they cannot edit GPOs unless assigned the Editor role.

- **Reviewer**   Users assigned the Reviewer role are able to view and compare the contents of GPOs, but they do not have the ability to modify or deploy GPOs. The Reviewer role is designed to review and audit GPO management.

- **Editor**   Users assigned this role are able to view and compare GPOs as Reviewers can. They are also able to check GPOs out of the archive, edit them offline, and then check those GPOs back into the archive. They are unable to deploy GPOs but can request GPO deployment.

# Group Policy processing

In organizations with large Group Policy deployments, multiple GPOs might apply to a single user account or computer account, or when a user is signed on to a specific computer, or both. Group Policy processing precedence is the set of rules that determines which Group Policy items apply when multiple GPOs are configured.

Group Policies are processed in the following manner:

- **Local**  Settings configured at the local level apply first. If multiple local policies apply, settings in machine policies apply first, settings in admin and nonadmin local policies override them, and settings in per-user policies override any configured at the machine and admin/nonadmin level.

- **Site**  Policies based on location apply next. Any settings configured at the site level override settings configured at the local level. You can link multiple GPOs at the site level. When you do this, policies with a lower numerical link order override policies with a higher numerical link order.

- **Domain**  Settings applied at the domain level override settings applied at the site and local levels. You can link multiple GPOs at the domain level. The Default Domain Policy is linked at this level.

- **Organizational unit (OU)**  Settings applied at the organizational unit level override settings applied at the domain, site, and local levels. When an account is a member of a child OU, policies applied at the child OU level override policies applied at the parent OU level. You can apply multiple GPOs at the OU level. Policies with a lower numerical link order override policies with a higher numerical link order.

Group Policy processing precedence is relevant only when there are conflicts in policies. If policy A applies at the domain level and policy B applies at the OU level, both policy A and policy B apply.

### POLICY ENFORCEMENT AND BLOCKING

When configuring a Group Policy, you can choose to enforce that policy. To enforce a Group Policy, right-click that policy at the location in which you link the policy and then select Enforced. When you choose to enforce a policy, that policy will apply and override settings configured at other levels. For example, normally a policy linked at the OU level would override a policy linked at the domain level. If you configure the policy at the domain level as Enforced, it instead overrides the policy linked at the OU level.

The Block Inheritance function enables you to block policies applied at earlier levels. For example, you can use Block Inheritance at the OU level to block policies applied at the domain and site level. Block Inheritance does not stop the application of policies configured as Enforced.

### GROUP POLICY SECURITY FILTERING

Security filtering enables you to configure permissions on GPOs. By default, Group Policies apply to the Authenticated Users group. By changing the default permissions, you can make the Group Policy apply only to a specific group. For example, if you remove the Authenticated Users group and add another security group such as the Melbourne-Users group, the Group Policy applies to only that configured security group.

When considering whether to use security filtering, keep the following in mind:

- A security filter applies to the GPO, so it applies wherever the GPO is linked. You can't have one security filter apply to the GPO when linked at the domain level and another security filter apply to the GPO when linked at the OU level.

- Filtered policies still need to be checked during the Group Policy processing process, which can increase the amount of time spent on Group Policy processing. Startup and logon times may increase.

- Apply Group Policy and Read permissions are the minimum required for user settings to take effect. If you have removed the Authenticated Users group, you will need to assign the Read only permission to a security principal associated with the computer account so that the computer account can process that user settings element of the GPO.

It is also possible to apply a Deny permission on the basis of security account or group. Deny permissions override Allow permissions. You block a particular security group from receiving a Group Policy by setting the Apply Group Policy (Deny) advanced permission. You can do this on the Delegation tab of a GPO's properties instead of the Scope tab.

### GROUP POLICY WMI FILTERING

WMI filtering enables you to filter the application of policy based on the results of a WMI query. For example, you might write a WMI query to determine whether a computer has an x86 or x64 processor, or whether there is more than a certain amount of disk space available. WMI queries are often used with policies related to software deployment to determine whether the target computer has the appropriate system resources to support the installation of the application.

The drawback of WMI queries is that they are complicated for systems administrators who are unfamiliar with programming beyond simple scripting. WMI queries also cause significant delays in Group Policy processing. In environments in which sophisticated logic needs to be applied to targeted application distribution, products such as Configuration Manager are more appropriate. Configuration Manager enables administrators performing software deployment to configure ways of checking hardware configuration before software deployment that do not require writing queries in WMI Query Language (WQL).

### LOOPBACK PROCESSING

Each GPO has two distinct sections: Computer Configuration and User Configuration. The resultant policies for a user are based on the cumulative user configuration settings in GPOs that apply to the user's accounts at the site, domain, and OU setting. The resultant computer policies are applied based on the cumulative computer configuration settings in GPOs that apply to the computer's account at the site, domain, and OU level.

In some situations, you'll want only the GPOs that apply to the computer account to apply. You might want to do this with conference room computers, for which you want people to be able to sign on with domain accounts but to have a very controlled configuration. When you enable loopback processing, user settings are determined based on the settings in the User Configuration settings area of **GPOs** that apply to the computer account.

There are two types of loopback processing that you can configure by setting the Group Policy loopback processing mode policy. This policy is located under Computer Configuration\Administrative Templates\System\Group Policy node and can be configured with the following settings:

- **Replace** When you configure Replace, only the GPOs that apply to the computer account will apply. Settings in the User Configuration area of the GPOs that apply to the computer account will apply.

- **Merge** The settings in the User Configuration area of GPOs that apply to the user account will still apply but will be overridden by settings in the User Configuration area of GPOs that apply to the computer account.

Slow-link processing enables you to configure Group Policy application to be performed in a different manner, depending on the speed of the connection from the client to the domain controller. It enables you to block activities such as software deployment when the connection between Active Directory and the client is detected as falling below a particular threshold. You configure slow-link detection by configuring the Group Policy slow-link detection policy located under Computer Configuration\Administrative Templates\System\Group Policy. When a slow link is detected, Registry settings from administrative templates, security policies, Encrypting File System (EFS) recovery policy, and firewall policies are applied. Policies related to application deployment, scripts, folder redirection, and disk quotas will not be applied.

### GROUP POLICY CACHING

Group Policy caching reduces the amount of time taken to process Group Policy during computer startup and user sign-on. Rather than retrieve the Group Policies that apply to the computer from a domain controller when a computer starts up or a user signs on, the client will use a cached copy of the last Group Policies downloaded from the domain controller. After this initial application of the cached policies during startup and user sign-on, policies will be retrieved and applied normally from a domain controller. You enable Group Policy caching by configuring the Configure Group Policy Caching policy. This policy is located under Computer Configuration\Policies\Administrative Templates\System\Group Policy.

### FORCE GROUP POLICY UPDATE

Remote Group Policy update allows you to force a remote computer to perform a Group Policy update without having to sign on to the computer and run the GPUpdate command or the Invoke-GPUpdate PowerShell cmdlet. Remote Group Policy requires that the following firewall rules be enabled on clients:

- Remote Scheduled Tasks Management (RPC)
- Remote Scheduled Tasks Management (RPC-EPMAP)
- Windows Management Instrumentation (WMI-In)

You can run remote Group Policy update from the Group Policy Management Console by right-clicking on a container or OU. An update will run on all computers within the container or OU as well as on any computer accounts stored within child OUs. You can also use the Invoke-GPUpdate PowerShell cmdlet to trigger a remote Group Policy update. The advantage of the PowerShell cmdlet is that you can target a specific computer rather than all computer accounts in an OU.

## Resultant Set of Policy tool

The Resultant Set of Policy tool allows you to generate a model of Group Policy application, allowing you to figure out which policies apply to particular objects within the domain. Resultant Set of Policy allows you to figure out why Group Policy application isn't behaving in the way that you expect and allows you to resolve Group Policy conflicts.

There are two ways you can calculate Resultant Set of Policy. The first is to use Group Policy Modeling. The second is to use Group Policy Results. The difference between these is as follows:

- Group Policy Modeling allows you to view the impact of altering site membership, security group membership, filtering, slow links, loopback processing, and the movement of accounts to new OUs on the application of policy.

- Group Policy Results allows you to troubleshoot the application of policy by telling you which settings apply to a specific user or computer account.

By default, members of the Domain Admins and Enterprise Admins groups can generate Group Policy Modeling or Group Policy Results information. You can delegate permissions so that users can perform these tasks at the OU or domain level.

Policies linked at the site level in multi-domain forests are stored in the root domain. This can cause challenges with Group Policy application in scenarios in which a site-linked policy applies but where no DC with a root domain membership is present in the local site.

If Group Policy processing takes too long because of site-linked GPOs, the simplest solution is to not link polices at the site level; instead, you apply the links at the domain level and use Group Policy filtering through a WMI query to ensure that location-specific GPOs are applied. An alternative is to place domain controllers that have root domain membership at each site, although this is likely to be more expensive than the policy filtering option.

## Administrative templates

Group Policy Administrative Templates allow you to extend Group Policy beyond the settings available in GPOs. Common software packages, such as Microsoft Office, often include Administrative Templates that you can import to manage software-specific settings. In early versions of Windows Server, Administrative Templates were available as files in ADM format. Since the release of Windows Server 2008, Administrative Templates are available in a standards-based XML file format called ADMX.

To be able to use an Administrative Template, you can import it directly into a GPO using the Add/Remove Templates option when you right-click the Administrative Templates node. A second option is to copy the Administrative Template files to the Central Store, located in the c:\Windows\Sysvol\sysvol\<domainname>\Policies\PolicyDefinitions folder on any domain controller. You might need to create this folder if it does not already exist. After the folder is present, the template is then replicated to all domain controllers, and you can access the newly imported Administrative Templates through the Administrative Templates node of a GPO.

## Implement Group Policy preferences in AD DS

Group Policy preferences work around the idea of eliminating (or at least substantially reducing) the need for traditional start-up and log-in scripts. Log-in scripts have a way of becoming convoluted over time. Group Policy preferences allow simplification of common log-in and start-up script tasks such as drive mappings and setting of environment variables.

By reducing or eliminating some of the complexity of log-in scripts, you can use Group Policy preferences to reduce configuration errors. You can use Group Policy preferences to configure the following:

- Applications
- Drive mappings
- Environment variables
- File updates
- Folders
- INI files
- Registry settings
- Shortcuts
- Data sources
- Devices
- Folder options
- Internet settings
- Local users and groups
- Network options
- Network shares
- Power options
- Printer settings
- Regional options
- Scheduled tasks
- Start Menu settings

Some of these items can also be configured using a traditional Group Policy. In the event that an item is configured in the same GPO using both policy and preferences, the traditional setting takes precedence. The difference between a Group Policy preference and a normal

Group Policy setting is that users can change a Group Policy preference if they have the appropriate permissions. For example, users can unmap a mapped network drive. The drive would remain unmapped until the user logged in again, at which point it would be remapped. Generally, if you want to enforce a setting, use a standard Group Policy. If you want to apply the setting and allow users to change it, use a Group Policy preference. The closest you can come to enforcing a Group Policy preference is to disable the **Apply Once and Do Not Reapply** setting in the policy item's configuration. This way, the preference is applied each time Group Policy refreshes.

You can target Group Policy preferences so that different preferences can apply to the same item types within a single GPO. Use the following items to restrict how a Group Policy preference applies:

- The computer has a battery.
- The computer has a specific name.
- The computer has a specific CPU speed.
- Apply by or after a specific date.
- The computer has a certain amount of disk space.
- The computer is a member of a domain.
- The computer has a particular environment variable set.
- A certain file is present on the computer.
- The computer is within a particular IP address range.
- The computer uses specific language settings.
- The computer meets the requirements of an LDAP query.
- The computer has a MAC address within a specific range.
- The computer meets the requirements of a WMI query.
- The computer uses a specific type of network connection.
- The computer is running a specific operating system.
- The computer is a member of a specific OU.
- The computer has PCMCIA present.
- The computer is portable.
- The computer uses a specific processing mode.
- The computer has a certain amount of RAM.
- The computer has a certain Registry entry.
- User or computer is a member of a specific security group.
- The computer is in a specific Active Directory site.
- The computer has a Remote Desktop Setting.
- A specific time range is present.
- The user has a specific name.

## Implement Group Policy in Azure AD DS

Azure AD DS includes two built-in GPOs, AADDC Users and AADDC Computers. You configure all Group Policy settings that you need to have applied in your Azure AD DS domain through these policies. Members of the AAD DC administrators group have Group Policy administration privileges in an Azure AD DS domain. You can manage these built-in GPOs by installing the Group Policy Management Tools on a computer that is a member server of the Azure AD DS domain. Although Azure AD DS does not allow you to create GPOs and link them at the domain level, you can create custom GPOs and link them to a custom OU that you create separately in Azure AD DS.

> **NEED MORE REVIEW?** **GROUP POLICY IN AZURE AD DS**
>
> You can learn more about Group Policy in Azure AD DS at *https://docs.microsoft.com/en-us/ azure/active-directory-domain-services/manage-group-policy.*

**EXAM TIP**

Remember the order in which group policies apply and how the Enforced and Block Override settings influence policy application.

## Chapter summary

- On-premises domain controllers should be deployed using the Server Core configuration. You should minimize who has access and manage them remotely using Windows Admin Center, Microsoft Management Consoles, or PowerShell.
- You can deploy domain controllers in Azure as IaaS VMs. When connected via VPN or ExpressRoute, they can be configured as a separate AD DS site, child domain, or trusted forest of the on-premises environment.
- Read-only domain controllers allow many AD DS functions but limit which objects are replicated and stored.
- When a computer hosting an FSMO role is not available, certain functions such as domain join or password change do not work.
- Trusts allow security principals in one domain or forest to be assigned permissions to resources in another domain or forest.
- Active Directory sites are used to manage replication, with computers located in a site assumed to be in high bandwidth proximity with each other. Site links allow you to define which sites have network connectivity to each other.
- Replication occurs over site links and can be managed with site link bridges.

- Active Directory security principals include user, computer, service, and group accounts. Domain Local, Global, and Universal groups all have different properties and visibility within a forest.

- Group Managed Service Accounts are a special type of account used by services on domain-joined computers that have their passwords automatically managed.

- Azure AD Connect allows you to synchronize on-premises identities to Azure AD.

- Azure AD DS allows IaaS VMs to perform a domain-join and leverage Active Directory Domain Services like Group Policy without requiring the deployment of domain controllers.

- Group Policy allows you to apply configuration settings to users and computers.

# Thought experiment

In this thought experiment, demonstrate your skills and knowledge of the topics covered in this chapter. You can find answers to this thought experiment in the next section.

Tailwind Traders has begun to extend their on-premises infrastructure into Azure. As a part of this move they need to ensure that an appropriate hybrid identity solution exists and that they are able to address the following challenges:

1. Remediate existing on-premises service accounts that were configured as privileged user accounts with nonexpiring passwords.

2. Deploy several VMs that rely on an application that requires those VMs to be a part of an AD DS domain to Azure, but minimize the administrative overhead related to directly managing and maintaining domain controllers in Azure.

3. Ensure that administrative users in the single on-premises AD DS domain have a more rigorous set of password policies than standard users.

With this information in mind, answer the following questions:

1. What type of account should you create for a service on a set of on-premises Windows Server computers if you want the password for that account automatically managed by Active Directory?

2. Which service should you deploy in an Azure virtual network if you want to have a set of domain-joined Windows Server 2022 IaaS virtual machines that host an application but do not wish to manage domain controllers directly?

3. You want to have a separate set of password policies for administrative users compared to standard users in a single domain forest. Which technology should you implement to achieve this goal?

# Thought experiment answers

This section contains the solution to the thought experiment. Each answer explains why the answer choice is correct.

1. You should create a Group Managed Service Account if you want a service account used by multiple computers managed by Active Directory Domain Services.

2. You should deploy Azure AD DS if you want to have domain-joined IaaS virtual machines in Azure but do not want to manage a domain controller.

3. You should implement fine-grained password policies.

# CHAPTER 2

# Manage Windows Servers and workloads in a hybrid environment

A critical element in any complex hybrid cloud deployment is the set of tools used to manage, maintain, and monitor workloads. Windows Server hybrid administrators have several options when it comes to choosing which tools they will use to manage the Windows Server instances that they are responsible for. Some tools allow you to manage up to the cloud from an on-premises administrative workstation; other tools allow you to manage down from the cloud from the Azure portal or Azure CLI.

## Skills covered in this chapter:

- Skill 2.1: Manage Windows Servers in a hybrid environment
- Skill 2.2: Manage Windows Servers and workloads by using Azure Services

## Skill 2.1: Manage Windows Servers in a hybrid environment

This objective deals with the technologies and techniques that you can use to manage Windows Server instances in on-premises and cloud environments. You'll learn about choosing and configuring administration tools as well as constrained delegation and Just Enough Administration.

> **This skill covers how to:**
> - Choose administration tools
> - Deploy a WAC gateway server
> - Configure a target machine for WAC
> - Manage Azure hybrid services with WAC
> - Configure PowerShell remoting
> - Configure CredSSP or Kerberos Delegation for second hop remoting
> - Configure Just Enough Administration for PowerShell remoting

# Choose administration tools

You can use a variety of tools to manage Windows Server 2019. Some, such as PowerShell, the Microsoft Management Console, and Server Manager, are built into the operating systems. You'll need to download others, such as Windows Admin Center, for free from the Microsoft website.

The company's general systems administration philosophy is that while you can do almost everything with a graphical console such as Windows Admin Center, Active Directory Administrative Center, or the Server Manager console, any task that you do repeatedly should be automated using PowerShell. Microsoft best practice is that almost all administration tasks should be performed remotely rather than by signing in directly to the server and performing them locally.

## Remote not local

Windows Server is designed to be administered remotely rather than locally. This "remote first" philosophy shouldn't come as a surprise to experienced administrators. The vast majority of Windows Server instances are running as virtual machines, either in datacenters or in the cloud, and we are long past the days where your primary method of switching between different servers that you were working on was by selecting different options on a KVM switch.

You need to be familiar with how to use your tools remotely. You should avoid signing in to each server individually using Remote Desktop and firing up the console that is relevant to the role or feature that you want to manage. You should also avoid using Remote Desktop to connect to a server just to run a PowerShell script because this is a task more appropriately performed using PowerShell remoting.

## Privileged Access Workstations

Servers are only as secure as the computers that you use to manage them. An increasing number of security incidents have occurred because a privileged user's computer was infected with malware and that computer was then used to perform server administration tasks. Privileged Access Workstations (PAWs) are specially configured computers that you use to perform remote administration tasks. The idea of a PAW is that you have a computer with a locked-down configuration that you only use to perform server administration tasks. You don't use this computer to read your email or browse the internet; you just use it to perform server administration tasks.

Consider configuring a PAW in the following way:

- Configure Windows Defender Application Control to allow only specifically authorized and digitally signed software to run on the computer.
- Configure Credential Guard to protect credentials stored on the computer.
- Use BitLocker to encrypt the computer's storage and protect the boot environment.
- The computer should not be used to browse the internet or to check email. Server administrators should have completely separate computers to perform their other

daily job tasks. Block internet browsing on the PAW both locally and on the perimeter network firewall.

- Block the PAW from accessing the internet. Software updates should be obtained from a dedicated secure update server on the local network. External tools should be obtained from another computer and transferred to the PAW.
- Server administrators should not sign in to the PAW using an account that has administrative privileges on the PAW.
- Only specific user accounts used by server administrators should be able to sign on to the PAW. Consider additional restrictions such as sign-in hours. Block privileged accounts from signing in to computers that are not PAWs or servers to be managed, such as the IT staff's everyday work computers.
- Configure servers to only accept administrator connections from PAWs. This can be done through Windows Defender Firewall with Advanced Security.
- Use configuration-management tools to monitor the configuration of the PAW. Some organizations rebuild PAWs entirely every 24 hours to ensure that configurations are not altered. Use these tools to restrict local group membership and ensure that the PAW has all appropriate recent software updates applied.
- Ensure that audit logs from PAWs are forwarded to a separate secure location.
- Disable the use of unauthorized storage devices. For example, you can configure policies so that only USB storage devices that have a specific BitLocker organizational ID can be used with the computer.
- Block unsolicited inbound network traffic to the PAW using Windows Defender Firewall.

## Jump servers

Jump servers are another security procedure that can be used in conjunction with privileged-access workstations. Jump servers allow servers to accept administrative connections only from specific hosts. For example, you only allow domain controllers to be administered from computers that have a specific IP address and a computer certificate issued by a specific certification authority. You can configure jump servers to only accept connections from PAWs and servers to be administered to only accept connections from jump servers. As mentioned earlier, some organizations that use jump servers have them rebuilt and redeployed every 24 hours to ensure that their configuration does not drift from the approved configuration. Azure provides a service, Azure Bastion, that functions as a managed jump server. You'll learn more about using Azure Bastion to access Windows Server IaaS VMs in Chapter 3.

## Remote Desktop

Remote Desktop is the way that many administrators are likely to remotely perform one-off tasks on servers running the GUI version of Windows Server. While best practice is to use PowerShell or Windows Admin Center for remote administration, sometimes it's quicker to just establish a Remote Desktop session. This is because using Remote Desktop allows you to perform tasks on the remote server in a manner that appears similar to being directly signed in at the console.

By default, Remote Desktop is disabled on newly deployed computers running Windows Server (though this is not the case for new Azure IaaS instances of Windows Server). You enable Remote Desktop either through the Remote tab of the System Properties dialog box or by running the following PowerShell command:

```
Set-ItemProperty -Path "HKLM:\System\CurrentControlSet\Control\Terminal Server" -Name
"fDenyTSConnections" -Value 0
```

You can make Remote Desktop connections to computers running the Server Core installation option if Remote Desktop is enabled.

By default, Remote Desktop Connection connects to Remote Desktop services on port 3389. When you enable Remote Desktop using the GUI, a remote desktop related firewall is automatically enabled. If you enable Remote Desktop using PowerShell, you also need to manually enable a firewall rule to allow connections. You can do this using the following PowerShell command:

```
Enable-NetFirewallRule -DisplayGroup "Remote Desktop"
```

By default, the **Allow connections only from computers running Remote Desktop with Network Level Authentication** option is selected. Network Level Authentication requires that a user be authenticated prior to the Remote Desktop session being established. Network Level Authentication is supported by the Remote Desktop Connection client, which is available on all Windows operating systems, but it might not be supported by third-party Remote Desktop clients.

Only users who are members of the local Administrators group and members of the local Remote Desktop Users group can make connections via Remote Desktop. If you want to grant a user account permission to access the server without the account full administrative privileges, add the account to the local Remote Desktop Users group.

You can map local volumes to a remote host in an active Remote Desktop Connection session by configuring the **Local Resources and Devices** setting on the **Local Resources** tab of the **Remote Desktop Connection** dialog box. While it is less effective over low-bandwidth connections, it can provide a simple way to transfer files from your client computer to a remote server instead of setting up FTP or another file transfer method.

## Deploy a WAC gateway server

Windows Admin Center (WAC) is a web-based console that allows you to remotely manage Windows Server through a web browser. You can connect to and use Windows Admin Center using Edge, Chrome, or any standards-compliant browser. You can use WAC to manage computers running Windows Server 2012 and later and Windows 10 or later client computers.

You can install WAC on computers running Windows 10 and later and Windows Server 2016 and later. You can install WAC on a Windows Server instance deployed using the Server Core installation option.

When you deploy WAC on a Windows Server instance, it functions as a *gateway server*. Gateway servers allow any client on the network to connect to the Windows Admin Center instance using their standards-compliant web browser without requiring Windows Admin Center be installed locally. A WAC gateway server can function as an administration connection point for multiple administrative sessions from different administrative users. Some organizations only deploy a single highly available gateway server and have all WAC administration tasks performed using that single WAC gateway instance. You should not deploy Windows Admin Center on a Windows Server instance that hosts the AD DS role.

## Installing WAC

Windows Admin Center isn't included in Windows Server. You have to download the installation files from the Microsoft website. There are four Windows Admin Center deployment options:

- **Local client**   When you choose this installation option, you install Windows Admin Center on your workstation. You connect to the WAC instance locally, which is similar to installing the Remote Server Administration Tools (RSAT) on a local workstation. When you install WAC locally, a shortcut to the WAC console is placed on your desktop.

- **Gateway server**   When you install WAC in the gateway server configuration, you install it on a computer running Windows Server 2016 or later and then make remote connections to the WAC instance hosted on that computer through your preferred browser. Once connected to the WAC instance, you can add servers that you want to manage to the web-based console. When you perform an administrative task, the instructions to perform that task are issued from the gateway server and are run against the target server.

- **Managed server**   The managed server deployment is a version of WAC in a gateway server configuration deployed on a cluster node to manage the cluster.

- **Failover cluster**   The gateway server is deployed as a highly available service. This requires the configuration of a Cluster Shared Volume to store persistent data used by WAC. A script is available from the Microsoft website that simplifies the process of performing a high availability deployment.

When you install WAC on a Windows Server instance, you get the option of configuring which port will be used. You can choose between using a self-signed SSL (TLS) certificate or an SSL (TLS) certificate that is already installed on the computer. If you're deploying a gateway server, things will be a lot simpler if you deploy a TLS certificate from a trusted CA because it won't be necessary to go through the hassle of responding to dialog boxes about whether to trust the self-signed certificate when connecting to the gateway server from a variety of different administrative systems.

You can install Windows Admin Center on a Server Core instance of Windows Server using `msiexec` and by specifying the management port and SSL certificate option. (It should be the TLS certificate since the SSL protocol has been phased out, but most of the world still uses the legacy terminology.) The syntax of the command-line installation where a trusted certificate is used is as follows:

```
msiexec /i <WACInstallerName>.msi /qn /L*v log.txt SME_PORT=<port> SME_
THUMBPRINT=<thumbprint> SSL_CERTIFICATE_OPTION=installed
```

SME_PORT is the port you want to use, and SME_THUMBPRINT is the thumbprint of the installed SSL (TLS) certificate. By default, installing WAC updates the computer's trusted host files. When you deploy WAC, you can configure it to update automatically or manually. When you configure WAC to update automatically, new versions will be installed as they become available through Microsoft Update. If you don't configure this option, you'll need to manually install newer versions of WAC as they become available.

To update an expired certificate on a WAC gateway server, you need to obtain and install the new certificate, obtain the certificate's thumbprint, and then rerun Setup and change the certificate used by WAC by specifying the new thumbprint.

> **NEED MORE REVIEW?** **DEPLOY WAC GATEWAY**
>
> You can learn more about deploying a WAC gateway at *https://docs.microsoft.com/en-us/windows-server/manage/windows-admin-center/deploy/install*.

## Windows Admin Center extensions

Windows Admin Center extensions allow for the extension of WAC functionality. Windows Admin Center includes extensions for roles built into Windows Server such as Storage Migration Services and third-party extensions. Microsoft encourages third-party partners to add extensions to Windows Admin Center as an alternative to requiring systems administrators to use product-specific consoles.

By default, Windows Admin Center will display extensions published to the Microsoft official NuGet feed. This feed includes extensions published and updated by Microsoft as well as those published by trusted third-party vendors. Also, you can configure Windows Admin Center to display extensions or installations from any NuGet feed that supports the NuGet V2 APIs or a specially configured file share accessible to the computer hosting Windows Admin Center.

Extensions are available in Windows Admin Center by selecting the **Settings** icon and then selecting **Extensions**. The **Available Extension** pane displays all extensions that are available but not installed from the currently configured feed. You can update currently installed extensions if new versions of those extensions are available through the **Installed Extensions** pane. You can also configure Windows Admin Center to automatically update extensions.

## Show script

When you perform a task in Windows Admin Center, you can select the PowerShell icon in the Windows Admin Center title bar to view PowerShell source code relevant to the tasks.

This allows you to copy and save useful PowerShell code for reuse later rather than having to perform all tasks through WAC.

## Configure a target machine for WAC

Just like you need to configure a Windows Server instance so that you can connect to it using Remote Desktop, a Microsoft Management Console, or a remote PowerShell session, you will also have to configure a Windows Server instance so that it can be managed from a remote WAC instance.

To allow administration from a WAC instance, Remote Management must be enabled on a Windows Server instance you intend to manage. WAC traffic from the WAC instance to target servers uses PowerShell and WMI over WinRM. WinRM connections over HTTP use port 5985 and WinRM connections over HTTPS uses port 5986. If WinRM over HTTPS is not configured, you can configure a WinRM HTTPS listener using the following command:

```
winrm quickconfig -transport:https
```

In addition to the WinRM ports, WAC uses the SMB file sharing protocol for some file copying tasks. To configure a target machine for remote management by WAC, you will need to ensure any firewalls between the WAC instance and the target computer allow inbound connections on ports 445, 5985, and 4986.

To use Windows Admin Center from the Azure portal to manage Windows Server instances in Azure, it's necessary to deploy Windows Admin Center to each Windows Server Azure IaaS instance.

> **NEED MORE REVIEW?** **CONFIGURE TARGET MACHINE**
>
> You can learn more about configuring a target machine at *https://docs.microsoft.com/windows-server/manage/windows-admin-center/azure/manage-vm*.

## Manage Azure hybrid services with WAC

Windows Admin Center can also be used to manage Azure hybrid services, such as Azure Backup, Azure Software Update, Azure Site Recovery, Azure Network Adapter, and Azure Monitor. Before you can integrate Azure hybrid services with WAC, you need to register the Windows Admin Center gateway with your Azure subscription. This process requires that you have access to an Azure AD account with the necessary permissions to configure an Azure AD application that has access to the Azure AD tenancy associated with your Azure subscription.

## Configure PowerShell remoting

PowerShell is the primary scripting, automation, and management tool from Microsoft. In almost all cases, you can access greater functionality and settings through PowerShell than you can through WAC or the Azure console.

PowerShell includes a substantial amount of documentation explaining what each cmdlet can do and how you can do it. Once you know the name of the command you want to use to perform a task, you can use the PowerShell built-in help to learn the precise details of how to use that cmdlet to perform that task. You can get help for each cmdlet by typing **help cmdletname**. For example, to get help with the get-service cmdlet, type **help get-service** into a PowerShell session.

## Modules

Modules are collections of PowerShell cmdlets. In older versions of PowerShell, you needed to manually load a module each time you wanted to use one of its associated cmdlets. In Windows Server 2016 and later, any module that is installed will load automatically when you try to run an associated cmdlet. Viewing cmdlets by module using the Get-Command-Module <modulename> cmdlet allows you to view just those cmdlets associated with a specific role or feature.

## PowerShell Gallery

The PowerShell Gallery is a collection of modules published by the community that extend the functionality of PowerShell beyond what is available with a default installation of Windows Server. Table 2-1 lists the commands that you can use to get started with the PowerShell Gallery.

**TABLE 2-1** PowerShell Gallery basics

| Command | Functionality |
|---|---|
| Find-Module -Repository PSGallery \| out-host -paging | This will list the available modules in the PowerShell Gallery in a paged format. You'll be prompted to install the NuGetProvider to interact with the PowerShell Gallery. |
| Find-Module -Repository PSGallery -Name <ModuleName> | This will list the modules with a specific name. You can use wild-cards. For example, to view all modules that start with the name AzureRM, run the command Find-Module -Repository PSGallery -Name AzureRM*. |
| Install-Module -Repository PSGallery -Name <ModuleName> | This will install the Modulename module. For example, to install the AzureRM module, run the command Install-Module -Repository PSGallery -Name AzureRM. |
| Update-Module | This will update any module that you've installed using Install-Module. |
| Get-InstalledModule | Use this command to view all modules installed from the Power-Shell Gallery. |

## PowerShell remoting

PowerShell remoting allows you to establish a remote interactive PowerShell session from a local PowerShell session on an administrative workstation or Cloud Shell. By default, Power-Shell remoting is enabled on Windows Server instances but also requires a connection from a private network and an account that is a member of the local Administrators group. PowerShell uses WMI over WinRM. WinRM connections over HTTP use port 5985, and WinRM connections over HTTPS uses port 5986. If PowerShell remoting has been disabled, you can enable it using the `Enable-PSRemoting` cmdlet. If WinRM over HTTPS is not configured, you can configure a WinRM HTTPS listener using the following command:

```
winrm quickconfig -transport:https
```

You initiate a remote PowerShell session using the `enter-pssession` command. If you do not specify alternate credentials, the credentials of the currently signed-on user will be used. If you want to use alternate credentials, one method to do so securely is by using the `get-credential` command and assigning it to a PowerShell variable, and then using the variable with the `enter-pssession` command. When you use `get-credential`, you will be prompted to enter a set of credentials. For example, to enter a set of credentials and then to use those credentials to establish a remote PowerShell session to a host named dc1.tailwindtraders.com, use the following commands:

```
$creds = get-credential
Enter-pssession -Computername dc1.tailwindtraders.com -credential $creds
```

To enable PowerShell remoting to computers that are not domain-joined, you must configure the trusted hosts list on the client computer from which you want to establish the remote session. You do this on the client computer using the `set-item` cmdlet. For example, to trust the computer at IP address 192.168.3.200, run this command:

```
Set-Item wsman:\localhost\Client\TrustedHosts -Value 192.168.3.200 -Concatenate
```

Once you've run the command to configure the client, you'll be able to establish a PowerShell remote session using the `Enter-PSSession` cmdlet. If you want more information about remoting, run the following command to bring up help text on the subject:

```
Help about_Remote_faq -ShowWindow
```

PowerShell allows you to run one command against many machines, which is known as *one-to-many remoting* or *fan-out administration*. You can use one-to-many remoting to run the same command against any number of computers. Rather than signing in to each computer to check whether a particular service is running, you can use PowerShell remoting to run the same command that checks the status of the service against each computer within the scope of the command.

For example, you could use the following command to read a list of computers from a text file named computers.txt:

```
$Computers = Get-Content c:\Computers.txt
```

You could then use the following command to get the properties of the Windows Update service:

```
Invoke-Command -ScriptBlock { get-service wuauserv } -computername $Computers
```

You can also use the `Invoke-Command` cmdlet to run a script from the local computer against a number of remote computers. For example, to run the script FixStuff.ps1 against the computers in the file computers.txt, run this command:

```
$Computers = Get-Content c:\Computers.txt
Invoke-Command -FilePath c:\FixStuff.ps1
```

> **NEED MORE REVIEW?** **POWERSHELL REMOTING**
>
> You can learn more about PowerShell remoting at *https://docs.microsoft.com/powershell/ scripting/learn/remoting/powershell-remoting-faq*.

## Configure CredSSP or Kerberos Delegation for second hop remoting

Second hop remoting is when you are signed in to one host, make a remote PowerShell connection to a second host, and perform a task that requires resource access to a third host that requires your account credentials. Unless the second host has a way of forwarding your credentials to the third host, the task may not complete because your credentials can't be used for that task. The process of a server acting on behalf of a signed-on user is termed *delegation*.

Kerberos delegation allows a computer to interact with the Kerberos Key Distribution Center to obtain a service ticket derived from the user's permissions that is used to access resources on the network.

For example, say you need to allow users with accounts in the tailwindtraders.com domain to use a WAC to manage a server named app1.adatum.com in the adatum.com domain. The following conditions exist:

- You have deployed a WAC gateway server on host wac.tailwindtraders.com.
- There is a two-way forest trust between the adatum.com and the tailwindtraders.com single-domain forests.

You can configure constrained delegation in this scenario by running the following PowerShell command:

```
Set-ADComputer -Identity (Get-ADComputer wac.tailwindtraders.com) -PrincipalsAllowed
ToDelegateToAccount (Get-ADComputer app1.adatum.com)
```

Kerberos constrained delegation allows you to limit which of a computer's services can interact with the KDC to obtain the appropriate ticket on the user's behalf. You can configure constrained delegation on the **Delegation** tab of a computer account's properties in Active Directory Users and Computers. When you do this, you specify the service type, the user or computer account that can leverage delegated credentials, the port, and the service principal name of the service that can perform the action.

**NEED MORE REVIEW?** **SECOND HOP REMOTING**

You can learn more about second hop remoting at *https://docs.microsoft.com/powershell/scripting/learn/remoting/ps-remoting-second-hop*.

# Configure Just Enough Administration for PowerShell remoting

Just Enough Administration (JEA) allows you to implement role-based access control (RBAC) functionality through Windows PowerShell remoting. JEA allows you to specify which PowerShell cmdlets and functions can be used when connected to a specific endpoint. You can go further and specify which parameters within those cmdlets and functions are authorized and even specify which values can be used with those parameters.

For example, you could create a JEA endpoint where a user is able to run the Restart-Service command, but only where the Name parameter is set to DHCPServer. This would allow the user to restart the DHCPServer on the computer they connected to, but it would not restart any other service on the computer.

You can also configure a JEA endpoint to allow other command-line commands such as whoami to be run, though the drawback of this is that you don't have the same level of control when restricting how that command can be run.

JEA endpoints can leverage virtual accounts. This means that activities performed on the computer through the endpoint use a special temporary virtual account rather than the user's account. This temporary virtual account has local administrator privileges but is constrained to only using the cmdlets, functions, parameters, and values defined by JEA. The benefits of this include:

- The user's credentials are not stored on the remote system. If the remote system is compromised, the user's credentials are not subject to credential theft and cannot be used to traverse the network to gain access to other hosts.

- The user account used to connect to the endpoint does not need to be privileged. The endpoint simply needs to be configured to allow connections from specified user accounts.

- The virtual account is limited to the system on which it is hosted. The virtual account cannot be used to connect to remote systems. Attackers cannot use a compromised virtual account to access other protected servers.

- The virtual account has local administrator privileges but is limited to performing only the activities defined by JEA. You have the option of configuring the virtual account with the membership of a group other than the local administrators group, to further reduce privileges.

# Role-capability files

A role-capability file is a special file that allows you to specify what tasks can be performed when connected to a JEA endpoint. Only tasks that are explicitly allowed in the role-capability file can be performed.

You can create a new blank role-capability file by using the `New-PSRoleCapabilityFile` cmdlet. Role-capability files use the .psrc extension. For example, run this command to create a new role-capability file for a role that allows someone to manage a DNS server:

```
New-PSRoleCapabilityFile -Path .\DNSOps.psrc
```

Once the PSRC file is created, you edit the role-capability file and add the cmdlets, functions, and external commands that are available when a user is connected to the endpoint. You can allow entire Windows PowerShell cmdlets or functions or list which parameters and parameter values can be used.

You can edit a role-capability file in PowerShell ISE, Visual Studio Code (though only the first is available on Windows Server), or any capable text editor. Editing the file involves commenting out the appropriate sections and filling them in with the configuration items that you want to set.

Authoring role-capability files is one of those few times when you need to know whether something in PowerShell is a cmdlet or a function. Mostly, people refer to commands in PowerShell as cmdlets, but some are actually functions and others are aliases. You need to know the appropriate type when configuring a role-capability file because if you put a function in as an allowed cmdlet, you won't get the expected result. You can figure out which designation is appropriate by using the `Get-Command` cmdlet.

Table 2-2 describes the different options that you can configure in a role-capability file.

**TABLE 2-2** Role-capability files

| Capability | Description |
| --- | --- |
| *ModulesToImport* | JEA auto-loads standard modules, so you probably don't need to use this unless you need to import custom modules. |
| *VisibleAliases* | Specifies which aliases to make available in the JEA session. Even if an aliased cmdlet is available, the alias won't be available unless it's here. |
| *VisibleCmdlets* | Lists which Windows PowerShell cmdlets are available in the session. You can extend this by allowing all parameters and parameter values to be used or you can limit cmdlets to particular parameters and parameter values. For example, use the following syntax, if you wanted to allow the `Restart-Service` cmdlet to only be used to restart the DNS service:<br>`VisibleCmdlets = @{ Name = 'Restart-Service'; Parameters = @{`<br>`Name='Name'; ValidateSet = 'DNS'}}` |

| Capability | Description |
|---|---|
| *VisibleFunctions* | This field lists which Windows PowerShell functions are available in the session. You can choose to list functions, allowing all parameters and parameter values to be used, or you can limit functions to particular parameters and parameter values. For example, if you wanted to allow the Add-DNSServerResourceRecord, Get-DNSServer ResourceRecord, and Remove-DNSServerResource functions to be used, you would use the following syntax:<br>`VisibleFunctions = 'Add-DNSServerResourceRecord',`<br>`'Get-DNSServerResourceRecord','Remove-DNSServerResourceRecord'` |
| *VisibleExternal Commands* | This field allows users who are connected to the session to run external commands. For example, you can use this field to allow access to *c:\windows\system32\whoami.exe* so that users connected to the JEA session can identify their security context by using the following syntax:<br>`VisibleExternalCommands = 'C:\Windows\System32\whoami.exe'` |
| *VisibleProviders* | This field lists Windows PowerShell providers that are visible to the session. |
| *ScriptsToProcess* | This field allows you to configure Windows PowerShell scripts to run automatically when the session is started. |
| *AliasDefinitions* | This field allows you to define Windows PowerShell aliases for the JEA session. |
| *FunctionDefinitions* | This field allows you to define Windows PowerShell functions for the JEA session. |
| *VariableDefinitions* | This field allows you to define Windows PowerShell variables for the JEA session. |
| *EnvironmentVariables* | This field allows you to specify environment variables for the JEA session. |
| *TypesToProcess* | This field allows you to configure Windows PowerShell type files to load for the JEA session. |
| *FormatsToProcess* | This field allows you to configure Windows PowerShell formats to load for the JEA session. |
| *AssembliesToLoad* | This field allows you to specify which assemblies to load for the JEA session. |

## Session-configuration files

Session-configuration files determine which role capabilities are mapped to specific security groups. For example, if you wanted to allow only members of the CONTOS\DNSOps security group to connect to the JEA endpoint that is defined by the DNSOps role-capability file, you would configure this security group in the session-configuration file.

You use the `New-PSSessionConfigurationFile` cmdlet to create a session-configuration file. These files use the .pssc extension. For example, to create a new session-configuration file for the DNSOps role, run the following command:

`New-PSSessionConfigurationFile -Path .\DNSOps.pssc -Full`

Session-configuration files have elements described in Table 2-3.

**TABLE 2-3** Session-configuration files

| Field | Explanation |
|---|---|
| SessionType | This field allows you to configure the session's default settings. If you set this to *RestrictedRemoteServer*, you can use the `Get-Command`, `Get-FormatData`, `Select-Object`, `Get-Help`, `Measure-Object`, `Exit-PSSession`, `Clear-Host`, and `Out-Default` cmdlets. The session execution policy is set to *RemoteSigned*. Example: `SessionType = 'RestrictedRemoteServer'` |
| RoleDefinitions | You use the *RoleDefinitions* entry to assign role capabilities to specific security groups. These groups do not need to have any privileges and can be standard security groups. Example: `RoleDefinitions =@{'CONTOSO\DNSOps' = @{RoleCapabilities='DNSOps'}}` |
| RunAsVirtualAccount | When enabled, this field allows JEA to use a privileged virtual account created just for the JEA session. This virtual account has local administrator privileges on member servers and is a member of the Domain Admins group on a domain controller. Use this option to ensure that credentials are not cached on the server that hosts the endpoint. Remember that you can configure the virtual account to be a member of groups other than the local administrators group. |
| TranscriptDirectory | This field allows you to specify the location where JEA activity transcripts are stored. |
| RunAsVirtual AccountGroups | If you do not want the virtual account to be a member of the local administrators group (or Domain Admins on a domain controller), you can instead use this field to specify the groups in which the virtual account is a member. |

## JEA endpoints

A JEA endpoint is a Windows PowerShell endpoint that you configure so that only specific authenticated users can connect to it. When those users do connect, they only have access to the Windows PowerShell cmdlets, parameters, and values defined by the appropriate session-configuration file that links security groups and role capabilities. When you use endpoints with virtual accounts, the actual activity that a user performs on the server that hosts the endpoint occurs using the virtual account. This means that no domain-based administrative credentials are stored on the server that hosts the endpoint.

A server can have multiple JEA endpoints, and each JEA endpoint can be used for a different administrative task. For example, you could have a DNSOps endpoint to perform DNS administrative tasks and an IISOps endpoint to perform Internet Information Server–related administrative tasks. Users are not required to have privileged accounts that are members of groups, such as the local administrators group, to connect to an endpoint. Once connected, users have the privileges assigned to the virtual account configured in the session-configuration file.

You create JEA endpoints by using the `Register-PSSessionConfiguration` cmdlet. When using this cmdlet, you specify an endpoint name and a session-configuration file hosted on the local machine.

For example, to create the endpoint DNSOps using the DNSOps.pssc session-configuration file, issue the following command and then restart the WinRM service:

```
Register-PSSessionConfiguration -Name DNSOps -Path .\DNSOps.pssc
```

You can use the `Get-PSSessionConfigurationFile` cmdlet to determine which endpoints are present on a computer. A user wanting to connect to a JEA session endpoint uses the `Enter-PSSession` cmdlet with the ConfigurationName parameter. For example, to connect to the DNSOps JEA endpoint on server MEL-DNS1, you would use this command:

```
Enter-PSSession -ComputerName MEL-DNS1 -ConfigurationName DNSOps
```

Once you've verified that JEA works, you'll need to lock down the default PowerShell endpoint. By default, only members of the local administrators group can connect to this default endpoint, and if you've implemented JEA properly, this group shouldn't need to have very many members anyway.

> **NEED MORE REVIEW?** **JUST ENOUGH ADMINISTRATION**
>
> You can learn more about Just Enough Administration at *https://docs.microsoft.com/powershell/scripting/learn/remoting/jea/overview*.

**EXAM TIP**
Remember which PowerShell cmdlets are relevant to specific JEA tasks.

# Skill 2.2: Manage Windows Servers and workloads by using Azure Services

This objective deals with managing Windows Server instances in hybrid environments using Azure services, including Azure Arc, Microsoft Defender for Cloud, Microsoft Update, and Desired State Configuration.

**This skill covers how to:**

- Manage Windows Servers by using Azure Arc
- Assign Azure Policy guest configuration
- Deploy Azure services using the Azure VM extensions on non-Azure machines
- Manage updates for Windows machines
- Integrate Windows Servers with Log Analytics
- Integrate Windows Servers with Microsoft Defender for Cloud
- Manage IaaS VMs in Azure that run Windows Server
- Create runbooks to automate tasks on target VMs
- Implement Azure Automation for hybrid workloads
- Implement Desired State Configuration to prevent configuration drift in IaaS machines

# Manage Windows Servers by using Azure Arc

Azure Arc allows you to manage Windows Server instances in hybrid and multicloud environments. A Windows Server instance enrolled through Azure Arc has an Azure resource ID, which allows you to include those instances in an Azure resource group.

Connecting a Windows Server instance to Azure Arc involves deploying and configuring the Azure Connected Machine Agent on each instance. The Azure Connected Machine Agent is separate from the Log Analytics Agent. You will need both agents installed to perform tasks requiring the Log Analytics Agent. These tasks include OS and workload monitoring as well as management of Azure Automation runbooks, updates, and services such as Microsoft Defender for Cloud.

## Azure Arc functionality

Much of the functionality that Azure Arc provides can be achieved by deploying individual elements that are covered in more detail in the rest of this chapter. An advantage of Azure Arc is that rather than deploying this functionality on a per-service basis, Azure Arc allows everything to be configured and maintained from the moment you enroll the connected Windows Server instance. Azure Arc can leverage the following services:

- **Assign Azure Policy guest configuration**   Allows you to audit settings inside the Windows Server instance to determine compliance against baselines.
- **Manage security**   Allows you to manage Microsoft Defender for Endpoint, which is included with Microsoft Defender for Cloud. Microsoft Defender for Endpoint also provides threat detection, vulnerability management, security threat monitoring, and remediation suggestions.

- **Configuration management** Allows you to deploy Azure Automation runbooks based on PowerShell and Python to connected instances to set instance configuration. VM extensions allow further automation and management tasks to be performed.
- **Monitoring** Azure Arc configures change tracking and inventory and allows you to monitor processes and dependencies through VM insights. Performance data and events are siphoned to a Log Analytics workspace.
- **Update Management** Onboards connected Windows Server instances to Update Management.

Azure Arc also supports Azure Automanage, an umbrella services that automatically onboards and configures a connected Windows Server instance according to Microsoft best practices.

## Deploy Azure Arc

You can use a variety of methods to obtain the agent software, deploy that software on a Windows Server instance, and configure the software to communicate with Azure Arc. The method that you use depends on the technologies you have available and the number of Windows Server instances you wish to connect to Azure Arc. Connecting a Windows Server instance to Azure Arc requires access to an account that holds the Azure Connected Machine Onboarding role.

You can use the following techniques to connect Windows Server instances to Azure Arc interactively:

- Create an installation script through the Azure portal that automates agent download and installation and the Azure Arc connection.

- Use Windows Admin Center to connect a Windows Server instance to Azure Arc by specifying appropriate subscription properties, including resource group, Azure region, and any proxy configuration. The agent will be retrieved, installed, and configured.

- Use PowerShell to connect a Windows Server instance to Azure Arc. The script uses the `Connect-AzConnectedMachine` PowerShell cmdlet to obtain the Connected Machine agent, install that agent, and register the Windows Server instance with Azure Arc. This technique requires Azure PowerShell to be available on an administrative computer, but the process can be performed remotely so it is not necessary to install Azure PowerShell on each Windows Server instance that you wish to configure with Azure Arc.

- Use PowerShell Desired State Configuration to connect the Windows Server instance to Azure Arc. Requires the AzureConnectedMachineDsc desired state configuration module. Also requires that an Azure Active Directory service principal be created to connect Windows Server instances to Azure Arc noninteractively.

Creating and configuring an Azure Active Directory service principal allows you to automate the deployment and configuration of Azure Arc because this allows you to bypass the need to log into Azure with an Azure AD account that has been delegated appropriate permissions. This Azure AD service principal must be assigned the Azure Connected Machine Onboarding role to be used for this task. You can use the `New-AzADServicePrincipal` Azure PowerShell cmdlet to create this principal by specifying the role as **Azure Connected Machine Onboarding**. For example, to create an Azure AD service principal named WinServArc to be used in the process of automating the onboarding of a large number of on-premises Windows Server instances to Azure Arc, use the following Azure PowerShell command:

```
New-AzADServicePrincipal -DisplayName WinServArc -Role 'Azure Connected Machine
Onboarding'
```

After you have created and configured the Azure AD service principal, you can use the following techniques to deploy and connect the Connected Machine Agent to Azure Arc:

- Use the Azure AD service principal with an installation script generated through the Azure portal. Once the script has installed the agent, the azcmagent command included with the agent is used to connect to Azure Arc.

- Use a Configuration Manager script or task sequence to deploy the agent and then connect the Windows Server instance to Azure Arc.

- Use Azure Automation Update Management to launch a runbook that downloads, installs, and configures the Connected Machine Agent using Azure PowerShell.

> **NEED MORE REVIEW**   **ONBOARDING WINDOWS SERVERS TO AZURE ARC**
>
> You can learn more about onboarding Windows Servers to Azure Arc at *https://docs.microsoft. com/azure/azure-arc/servers/onboard-windows-admin-center.*

## Assign Azure Policy guest configuration

Azure Policy guest configuration allows you to audit or configure Windows Server operating system settings. You can deploy Azure Policy guest configuration on a per-instance basis or apply it to a large number of systems using Azure Policy. Azure Policy guest configuration can be deployed to Windows Server IaaS instances or to Azure Arc–enabled Windows Server instances. To be able to use the Azure Policy guest configuration feature with an Azure virtual machine, the virtual machine must have a system-managed identity.

When using Azure Policy guest configuration for configuration management, you specify which properties the Windows Server should have—for example, to ensure that the server has specific roles installed or services configured in a specific manner. When using Azure Policy guest configuration for compliance auditing, you are checking the configuration of settings on a server and determining which settings are not configured in the manner defined in the configuration baseline. Sometimes it is necessary to audit and then resolve misconfigurations manually since there might be no way to automate remediation actions.

Guest configuration checks for new or altered guest assignments every 300 seconds. Once a guest assignment is obtained, settings related to that configuration will be checked every 15 minutes. When multiple configurations are assigned to a Windows Server instance, each configuration will be checked in sequence. A new configuration will not be checked until the previous configuration has completed validation.

Azure Policy guest configuration uses PowerShell Desired State Configuration v3. This instance is side-loaded to a separate folder and will only be used by Azure Policy. If the server already uses Windows PowerShell DSC, no conflict will occur since the DSC instances are partitioned from each other.

---

*NEED MORE REVIEW*   **AZURE POLICY GUEST CONFIGURATION**

**You can learn more about Azure Policy guest configuration at** *https://docs.microsoft.com/azure/azure-arc/servers/learn/tutorial-assign-policy-portal.*

---

# Deploy Azure services using the Azure VM extensions on non-Azure machines

VM extensions are special software that performs configuration and automation tasks on hybrid Windows Server instances. When a hybrid Windows Server instance is Arc-enabled, you can deploy, remove, and update Azure VM extensions through the Azure portal or the Azure CLI. You can also add and remove extensions using Azure PowerShell and ARM templates, but you can't use these management technologies to update existing extensions in a Windows Server instance.

You can use Azure Arc–enabled VM extensions to configure the following functionality on hybrid Windows Server instances:

- Enable and manage the Log Analytics Agent to collect log and performance data and to transmit that data to a Log Analytics Workspace for later analysis.
- Enable and manage VM insights to analyze the performance of Windows Server instances as well as workload processes and dependencies.
- Download and run scripts using the Custom Script Extension.
- Update and refresh certificates stored in Azure Key Vault.

The specific extensions you can deploy and manage with Azure Arc–enabled Windows Server instances include the following:

- Microsoft Defender for Cloud Integrated vulnerability scanner
- Microsoft Antimalware extension
- Custom Script extension
- Log Analytics Agent
- Azure Monitor for VMs (insights)
- Azure Key Vault Certificate Sync
- Azure Monitor Agent
- Azure Automation Hybrid Runbook Worker extension

# Manage updates for Windows machines

Azure Update Management allows you to automate the deployment of updates to computers running both the Windows and the Linux operating systems. You can configure on-premises Windows Servers to use Azure Update Management using Windows Admin Center. You can also manage the deployment of updates to those servers using Windows Admin Center. Update Management also enables you to view update compliance across the Windows Server instances that you are managing with the service, allowing you to quickly determine which instances aren't patched, something that can be challenging with existing tools such as Windows Server Update Services (WSUS).

Update Management is integrated with Azure Monitor Logs, allowing you to record update assessments and update deployment results as log data. The automation account used for Update Management and the Log Analytics workspaces are linked together. It's also necessary for the Log Analytics Agent to be configured to communicate with the Log Analytics workspaces.

You can configure a Windows Server instance to use Update Management through Windows Admin Center or by automatically enrolling the instance using Azure Arc or PowerShell.

## Update Deployment

To deploy updates, select Schedule Update Deployment in the Update Management blade of the Azure console. When configuring a scheduled update, you need to provide the following information:

- **Name of the update deployment** This is especially useful if you configure a recurring schedule.
- **Operating system** Azure Update Management allows you to deploy updates to computers running either Windows or Linux in a single update deployment, but not to both operating systems in the one deployment.
- **Groups** You can configure query-based groups so that the update deployment targets computers that meet the criteria specified in the query.
- **Machines to update** Allows you to select specific computers to which the update deployment applies.
- **Update classifications** Rather than select specific updates, you configure an update deployment so that all updates that meet a specific update classification will be deployed (though you do have the option of excluding specific updates by Update

ID). For Windows computers, the update classifications are Critical Updates, Security Updates, Update Rollups, Feature Packs, Service Packs, Definition Updates, Tools, and Updates.

- **Include/Exclude Updates** Allows you to choose specific updates based on KB identifiers (KBIDs). You can find relevant KBIDS in the list of missing updates in the Azure Update Management console.

- **Schedule Settings** Allows you to specify when updates will be deployed. You can configure a schedule to recur. When you do this, all updates that meet the classification characteristics specified in the update deployment will be deployed.

- **Maintenance window** The amount of time that can be taken to install updates, with the final 20 minutes of the assigned maintenance window reserved for restart operations. For example, if you set a maintenance window of 120 minutes, update installation will be halted after 100 minutes have elapsed so that restart operations can occur.

- **Reboot options** Allow you to specify whether the server can restart automatically after update deployment or whether this step must be performed manually.

## Assess update compliance

You can view an update assessment for a Windows Server instance by selecting the instance in the Update Management dashboard. The update assessment will provide information about the Windows Server instance, missing updates, scheduled update deployments, and a list of completed update deployments.

## Update Management permissions

The permissions listed in Table 2-4 are required to manage update deployments.

**TABLE 2-4** Update Management permissions

| Resource | Role | Scope |
|---|---|---|
| Automation account | Virtual Machine Contributor | Resource Group |
| Log Analytics workspace | Log Analytics Contributor | Log Analytics workspace |
| Log Analytics workspace | Log Analytics Reader | Subscription |
| Solution | Log Analytics Contributor | Solution |
| Virtual Machine | Virtual Machine Contributor | Virtual Machine |
| Update schedule execution history | Reader | Automation account |
| Create update schedule | Microsoft.Compute/virtualMachines/write | Virtual machine or resource group |
| Create update schedule | Microsoft.OperationalInsights/workspaces/analytics/query/action | Workspace resource ID |

## Integrate Windows Servers with Log Analytics

Azure Monitor is the umbrella solution for collecting, analyzing, and responding to telemetry from workloads in a hybrid environment. You can use Azure Monitor to perform the following tasks:

- Detect and diagnose problems with workloads and workload dependencies with application insights.
- Correlate infrastructure problems with VM insights and container insights.
- Explore monitoring data with Log Analytics.
- Perform automated operations tasks with smart alerts and automated actions.
- Create visualizations derived from collected data using dashboards and workbooks.
- Ingest data from monitored resources using Azure Monitor Metrics.

Azure Monitor data collection fits into one of two distinct categories, metrics and logs. A metric is a point-in-time numerical value that describes a property of the system, such as the amount of disk space used at 10.30 p.m. on November 3. Logs are records, each of which has its own properties. It includes everything recorded by the Windows Server event logs as well as any other application running on a Windows Server instance that generates event log data in an ingestible format. Specifically, Azure Monitor collects the following data:

- **Application monitoring data**   Data related to performance and functionality of workloads
- **Guest OS monitoring data**   Data about the Windows Server instance on which the application is hosted
- **Azure resource monitoring data**   Data generated by Azure resources such as storage, networks, database instances, or any other Azure service that can generate log data (which is almost all of them)
- **Azure subscription monitoring data**   Data generated about the operation and management of an Azure subscription
- **Azure tenant monitoring data**   Data generated about the operation and management of tenant-level Azure services (Azure Active Directory)

To prepare an Azure subscription for Azure Monitor, you need to deploy at least one Log Analytics workspace. A single Log Analytics workspace can support multiple Azure services, including Microsoft Sentinel and Microsoft Defender for Cloud, though there might be governance reasons why you need different teams to have different levels of access to log data and it may be simpler to store different log information in a separate Log Analytics workspace.

To install Azure Monitor on a Windows Server instance, connect to the server using Windows Admin Center and perform the following steps:

1. In Windows Admin Center, select Azure Hybrid Services and then select Discover Azure Services. If you haven't connected the Windows Admin Center instance to an Azure subscription, you'll be prompted to do so.

2. On the list of Azure Resources, select Set Up in the section on Azure Monitor.

3. If an appropriate resource group and Log Analytics workspace already exists within the subscription, the Azure Monitor setup process will detect them automatically. If these workspaces are not present, you will be prompted to create them.

4. Once the connection is configured, you can review analytics information in the appropriate Log Analytics workspace in the Azure portal.

An alternative to using Windows Admin Center is to download the Azure Monitor Agent (also called the Log Analytics Agent) from your Log Analytics workspace. When installing the agent, you will need to provide the Log Analytics workspace ID and the workspace's primary key.

> ***NEED MORE REVIEW?*** **AZURE MONITOR LOGS**
>
> You can learn more about Azure Monitor Logs at *https://docs.microsoft.com/en-us/azure/azure-monitor/logs/data-platform-logs*.

## Integrate Windows Servers with Microsoft Defender for Cloud

Microsoft Defender for Cloud is the current name for what was Azure Security Center. Microsoft Defender for Servers is an element of Microsoft Defender for Cloud that allows you to add threat detection and defense functionality to Windows Server instances located in Azure or hybrid environments. You have to enable Microsoft Defender for Cloud on a subscription before you can connect Windows Server instances.

You can connect hybrid Windows Server instances to Microsoft Defender for Cloud using the following methods:

- Configure the Windows Server as an Arc-enabled instance.
- Use Defender for Cloud's Getting Started and Inventory page.

Deployment of Azure Arc was covered earlier in this chapter. To connect a hybrid Windows Server instance to Microsoft Defender for Cloud to enable Microsoft Defender for Servers, you first need to install and configure the Microsoft Monitoring agent (also called the Log Analytics Agent) on the instance. If the agent is installed, you are able to configure the instance for Microsoft Defender for Cloud by selecting the Windows Server instance on the Asset Inventory page of Microsoft Defender for Cloud.

## Manage IaaS VMs in Azure that run Windows Server

Windows Server IaaS VMs are only visible to users in the Azure portal if they have a role that grants them that right. The default Azure IaaS VM role-based access control (RBAC) roles are as follows:

- **Virtual Machine Contributor**   Users who hold this role can manage virtual machines through the Azure console and perform operations such as starting, stopping, restarting, and deleting the virtual machine. Membership in this role does not provide the user with access to the VM itself. It also does not provide access to the virtual network or storage account to which the VM is connected.

- **Virtual Machine Administrator Login**   If the VM is configured to allow login using Azure AD accounts, assigning this role grants the user local administrator privileges in the virtual machine. Users who hold this role can view the details of a VM in the portal but not change its properties.

- **Virtual Machine User Login**   Users who hold this role are able to view the details of a virtual machine in the Azure portal and can log in using their Azure AD account with user permissions. Users who hold this role cannot change the properties of the VM.

As long as a local account with the appropriate permissions is present on a Windows Server IaaS VM instance, you can use that account to make a connection to perform administrative tasks. For example, if you want to allow someone to connect to a Windows Server IaaS VM instance using Remote Desktop, they need to be a member of the Remote Desktop Users group or have local administrative privileges.

You can use the following tools to make connections to a properly configured Windows Server IaaS VM instance to perform management tasks on that VM:

- **Cloud Shell**   Cloud Shell is a web app command-line environment that you can use to manage your Azure subscription. You can also initiate a remote PowerShell session from Cloud Shell to a properly configured Windows Server IaaS VM instance.

- **Remote PowerShell**   You can establish a remote PowerShell session to a properly configured Windows Server IaaS VM instance.

- **Azure Bastion**   Creates a managed temporary jump server through which you can make connections.

- **Just in Time VM Access**   Configures temporary firewall rules to allow authorized users to establish remote access connections.

- **Windows Admin Center in the Azure portal**   Allows you to make Windows Admin Center connections to specially configured IaaS VMs without deploying a separate Windows Admin Center gateway server.

- **Azure Serial Console**  Connect to an IaaS VM through virtual serial console instead of a network connection.

As with any tool that allows you to perform management of a remote computer, you should use the appropriate firewall and network security group tools to allow connections only from approved hosts. You will learn more about these tools and managing Windows Server IaaS VMs in Chapter 3, "Manage virtual machines and containers."

## Create runbooks to automate tasks on target VMs

Process Automation in Azure Automation allows you to create and deploy runbooks. A runbook is a set of executable tasks that run on the target Windows Server instance. Process Automation supports the following types of runbooks:

- **Graphical**  A graphical runbook is a set of automation steps that you create and edit in a graphical editor that is then translated into PowerShell code that executes on the target instance.

- **Graphical PowerShell workflow**  A graphical PowerShell workflow is a special type of PowerShell script that uses Windows Workflow Foundation. Windows Workflow Foundation is suited to scripts that need to run against multiple instances simultaneously while also being able to automatically recover from failures. Without using Windows Workflow Foundation, this resiliency would need to be built into the script.

- **PowerShell**  A text-edited PowerShell script that executes on the target instance.

- **PowerShell Workflow**  A PowerShell script that leverages Windows Workflow Foundation to scale to many instances and to be more resilient to failures.

- **Python**  A Python script for environments where automation occurs using Python rather than PowerShell.

Automation executes runbooks as jobs. A special process called a worker runs each job during runbook execution. Azure Automation runbooks run either in an Azure sandbox or as a Hybrid Runbook Worker. The Azure sandbox is appropriate for workloads that exist entirely within Azure. Hybrid Runbook Worker is appropriate for automation tasks that will enact on an instance that needs to access local resources in the environment that may not be connected to Azure.

> **NEED MORE REVIEW?**  **AUTOMATION RUNBOOKS**
>
> You can learn more about Automation runbooks at *https://docs.microsoft.com/azure/automation/automation-runbook-execution*.

## Implement Azure Automation for hybrid workloads

Azure Automation's Hybrid Runbook Worker feature allows you to enact runbooks on Windows Server instances running as IaaS VMs or registered as an Azure Arc–enabled server. The Hybrid Runbook Worker role is integrated into a connected instance through the Azure virtual machine extension framework. Hybrid Runbook Workers can be deployed in the following manner:

- **Extension based (V2)**   This is installed as a VM extension and has no dependency on the Azure Monitor Agent (also known as Log Analytics Agent).
- **Agent based (V1)**   This agent is deployed after the Azure Monitor Agent and reports to a Log Analytics workspace.

The two different types of Hybrid Runbook Workers are as follows:

- **System**   Used by the Update Management feature and designed to install software updates on Windows Server instances. It's not a member of a Runbook Worker group and cannot enact runbooks targeted to Runbook Worker groups.
- **User**   Used with user-defined runbooks that enact directly on a Windows Server instance that are members of one or more Runbook Worker groups.

Installing the Hybrid Runbook Worker requires enrollment through Azure Arc or that you enable Azure Automation in a Log Analytics workspace and then deploy the Azure Monitor Agent.

> **NEED MORE REVIEW?   HYBRID AUTOMATION**
>
> You can learn more about hybrid automation at *https://docs.microsoft.com/azure/ architecture/hybrid/azure-automation-hybrid*.

## Implement Desired State Configuration to prevent configuration drift in IaaS machines

State Configuration in Azure Automation is the current version of the functionality provided by Desired State Configuration (DSC). State Configuration uses DSC version 3 with PowerShell version 7. DSC version 3 can coexist with older versions of DSC since implementations are separate. It is important to note that no conflict detection exists if you are running DSC version 3 with prior implementations.

State Configuration allows you to write, manage, and compile DSC configuration for Windows Server instances running as IaaS VMs or hybrid instances connected to Azure. State Configuration hosts a DSC pull server that functions in a manner similar to the Windows Feature DSC-Service. State Configuration target nodes receive configurations, converge with the desired state, and report on compliance status to the State Configuration service. Data returned to State Configuration is forwarded to a Log Analytics workspace.

> **NEED MORE REVIEW?   STATE CONFIGURATION**
>
> You can learn more about State Configuration at *https://docs.microsoft.com/en-us/azure/ automation/automation-dsc-overview*.

## Chapter summary

- WAC servers are accessible to administrators over HTTPS. WAC traffic from the WAC instance to target servers uses PowerShell and WMI over WinRM. WinRM connections over HTTP use port 5985, and WinRM connections over HTTPS use port 5986.

- To update an expired certificate on a WAC gateway server, you'll need to obtain and install the new certificate, obtain the certificate's thumbprint, and then rerun Setup and change the certificate used by WAC by specifying the new thumbprint.

- Constrained delegation can be configured in Active Directory Users and Computers on the Delegation tab of a computer account's properties or by using the `Set-ADComputer` cmdlet with the `PrincipalsAllowedToDelegate` parameter.

- Onboarding a Windows Server instance requires an Azure AD account that has the Azure Connected Machine Onboarding role. If you are onboarding a large number of Windows Server instances, you can use an Azure AD Service principal that has been assigned this role.

- Azure Monitor requires that a Log Analytics workspace be present in Azure.

- To leverage Update Management in Azure Automation, hybrid instances require an Azure Automation account and that the Azure Monitor agent be installed.

- A Windows Server IaaS instance requires a system-managed identity to use Azure Policy guest configuration.

- Microsoft Defender for Servers is an element of Microsoft Defender for Cloud that allows you to add threat detection and defense functionality to Windows Server instances located in Azure or hybrid environments.

- To connect a hybrid Windows Server instance to Microsoft Defender for Cloud to enable Microsoft Defender for Servers, you first need to install and configure the Microsoft Monitoring Agent (also called the Log Analytics Agent) on the instance.

- State Configuration in Azure Automation allows you to write, manage, and compile DSC configuration for Windows Server instances running as IaaS VMs or hybrid instances connected to Azure.

## Thought experiment

In this thought experiment, demonstrate your skills and knowledge of the topics covered in this chapter. You can find answers to this thought experiment in the next section.

You are one of the hybrid administrators at Tailwind Traders. You have a variety of challenges you need to resolve related to Windows Server management. Specifically:

- You want to enroll 500 servers across several remote datacenters into Azure Arc using an onboarding script.

- You want to allow Sonia to manage the DNS server service on the domain controllers in the root domain from PowerShell without providing her with the ability to perform any other tasks using PowerShell on those systems.

- You want to allow Rick to connect using PowerShell to an administrative jump server and then to be able to use his credentials to run PowerShell scripts hosted on the jump server against a set of 10 remote servers.

With these requirements in mind, answer the following questions:

1. What type of Azure AD account should you create and what role should you delegate this account to onboard the 500 servers?

2. How can you provide Sonia with the appropriate restricted PowerShell access to the domain controllers in the root domain?

3. How can you ensure that Rick is able to run scripts against remote servers from the jump servers?

# Thought experiment answers

This section contains the solution to the thought experiment. Each answer explains why the answer choice is correct.

1. Use an Azure AD Service principal delegated the Azure Connected Machine Onboarding role. An Azure AD Service principal is required to perform onboarding in this manner.

2. Configure a JEA endpoint that allows Sonia to perform a restricted set of tasks related to DNS management. This will ensure that she is able to perform tasks without unnecessary permissions.

3. Configure Kerberos delegation that allows Rick's credentials to be used by the jump server. Kerberos delegation allows the jump server to use Rick's credentials to run the PowerShell scripts.

# CHAPTER 3

# Manage virtual machines and containers

Windows Server functions as a host platform for virtual machines (VMs) and containers. Many hybrid administrators who deploy and manage Windows Server in Azure also run Windows Server as infrastructure as a service (IaaS) virtual machines. In this chapter you learn about managing Windows Server and guest virtual machines, configuring and managing Windows Server as a container host, and managing and maintaining Windows Server VMs in Azure.

## Skills covered in this chapter:

- Skill 3.1: Manage Hyper-V and guest virtual machines
- Skill 3.2: Create and manage containers
- Skill 3.3: Manage Azure Virtual Machines that run Windows Server

## Skill 3.1: Manage Hyper-V and guest virtual machines

Hyper-V is a virtualization platform that is built into Windows Server. Not only can you use Hyper-V to host virtual machines and a special type of containers, but Hyper-V is integrated into the very fabric of the Microsoft Azure cloud. Hyper-V is also available on some editions of Windows 10 and Windows 11, meaning that it's possible to transfer a virtual machine from a Windows client to a Windows server to Azure and back without needing to alter the virtual machine's format.

> **This skill covers how to:**
> - Understand virtual machine types
> - Manage VM using PowerShell Remoting, PowerShell Direct, and HVC.exe
> - Enable VM Enhanced Session Mode
> - Configure nested virtualization
> - Configure VM Memory
> - Configure Integration Services

- Configure Discrete Device Assignment
- Configure VM resource groups
- Configure VM CPU groups
- Configure hypervisor scheduling types
- Manage VM checkpoints
- Implement high availability for virtual machines
- Manage VHD and VHDX files
- Configure Hyper-V network adapter
- Configure NIC teaming
- Configure Hyper-V switch

## Virtual machine types

Hyper-V on Windows Server supports two different types of VM virtual hardware configurations. Generation 2 VMs are a special type of VM that differs in configuration from the VMs that are now termed "Generation 1 VMs," which could be created on Hyper-V virtualization hosts running the Windows Server 2008, Windows Server 2008 R2, and Windows Server 2012 operating systems. Generation 2 VMs are supported on Windows Server 2012 R2 and later operating systems and are supported in Azure.

Generation 2 VMs provide the following functionality:

- Can boot from a SCSI virtual hard disk
- Can boot from a SCSI virtual DVD
- Supports UEFI firmware on the VM
- Supports VM Secure Boot
- Can PXE boot using standard network adapter
- Supports Virtual TPM

Generation 2 VMs don't attempt to replicate the hardware configuration of existing physical systems in the way that Generation 1 VMs did. There are no legacy network adapters with Generation 2 VMs, and the majority of legacy devices, such as COM ports and the diskette drive, are no longer present. Generation 2 VMs are "virtual first" and are not designed to simulate hardware for computers that have undergone physical-to-virtual (P2V) conversion. To deploy a VM that requires an emulated component such as a COM port, you have to deploy a Generation 1 VM. You configure the generation of a VM during the VM creation. After a VM is created, Hyper-V doesn't allow you to modify the VM's generation.

Generation 2 VMs boot more quickly and allow the installation of operating systems more quickly than generation 1 VMs. Generation 2 VMs have the following limitations:

- You can only use Generation 2 VMs if the guest operating system is running an x64 version of Windows Server 2012 or later server or the Windows 8 or later client operating systems.
- Generation 2 VMs only support virtual hard disks in VHDX format.

## Manage VM using PowerShell remoting, PowerShell Direct, and HVC.exe

You can use a variety of methods to connect remotely to a virtual machine from a command prompt. The method you choose depends on whether you are trying to access the VM from the Hyper-V host, what operating system the VM is running, and whether the VM has network connectivity.

### PowerShell remoting

PowerShell remoting is the primary method you use to run PowerShell sessions on Windows Server VMs that have network connectivity. PowerShell remoting allows you to have an inter-active PowerShell session where you are signed on locally to a remote Windows Server VM. The account used to make a connection to this remote VM needs to have local Administrator privileges on the target VM. PowerShell remoting is enabled by default on Windows Server, but also by default, it requires a connection from a private network.

You can enter a remote session to a Windows Server VM that is a member of the same Active Directory forest by using the following commands, which will prompt you for the cre-dentials that you'll use to connect to the remote computer:

```
$cred = Get-Credential
Enter-PSSession -computername <computername> -Credential $cred
```

You can enable PowerShell remoting using the `Enable-PSRemoting` cmdlet if it has been disabled. PowerShell remoting relies on WSMan (Web Server Management). WSMan uses port 5985 and can be configured to support TLS over port 5986.

To enable PowerShell remoting to VMs that are not domain-joined, you must configure the trusted hosts list on the client computer from which you want to establish the remote session. You do this on the client computer using the `set-item` cmdlet. For example, to trust the com-puter at IP address 192.168.3.200, run this command:

```
Set-Item wsman:\localhost\Client\TrustedHosts -Value 192.168.3.200 -Concatenate
```

After you've run the command to configure the client, you'll be able to establish a Pow-erShell remote session by using the `Enter-PSSession` cmdlet. If you want more information about remoting, you can run the following command to bring up help text on the subject:

```
Help about_Remote_faq -ShowWindow
```

## PowerShell Direct

PowerShell Direct allows you to create a remote PowerShell session directly from a Hyper-V host to a virtual machine hosted on that Hyper-V host without requiring the VM to be configured with a network connection. PowerShell Direct requires that both the Hyper-V host and the VM be running Windows Server 2016 or later server or Windows 10 or later client operating systems.

To use PowerShell Direct, you must be signed in locally to the Hyper-V host with Hyper-V Administrator privileges. You also must have access to valid credentials for the virtual machine. If you don't, you won't be able to establish a PowerShell Direct connection.

To establish a PowerShell Direct connection, use this command:

```
Enter-PSSession -vmname NameOfVM
```

You exit the PowerShell Direct session by using the `Exit-PSSession` cmdlet.

## HVC for Linux

HVC.exe, which is included with Windows Server 2019 and later and Windows 10 and later, allows you to make a remote SSH connection from a Hyper-V host to a Linux virtual machine guest without requiring the Linux VM to have a functioning network connection. It provides similar functionality to PowerShell Direct. For HVC.exe to work, you must ensure that the Linux VM has an updated kernel and that the Linux integration services are installed. You also need the SSH server on the Linux VM to be installed and configured before you'll be able to use HVC. exe to initiate an SSH connection.

# Enable VM Enhanced Session Mode

Enhanced Session Mode allows you to perform actions such as cutting and pasting, audio redirection, and volume and device mapping when using Virtual Machine Connection (VMConnect) windows. For example, you can use Enhanced Session Mode to sign in to a VM with a smart card and view your local storage as a volume accessible to the VM. You enable Enhanced Session Mode on the Hyper-V server by selecting **Allow Enhanced Session Mode** in the Enhanced Session Mode Policy section of the Hyper-V server's Properties dialog box.

You can only use Enhanced Session Mode with guest VMs running Windows Server 2012 R2 or later server operating systems or Windows 8.1 and later client operating systems. To use Enhanced Session Mode, you must have permission to connect to the VM using Remote Desktop through the account you use to sign in to the guest VM. You can grant permission to the VM by adding the user to the Remote Desktop Users group. A user who is a member of the local Administrators group also has this permission. The Remote Desktop Services service must be running on the guest VM.

# Configure nested virtualization

Hyper-V on Windows Server 2016 and later servers and Windows 10 and later client OSs support nested virtualization. *Nested virtualization* allows you to enable Hyper-V and host virtual machines on a VM running under Hyper-V as long as that VM is running Windows Server 2016 and later servers or Windows 10 and later client operating systems. Nested virtualization can be enabled on a per-VM basis through Windows Admin Center or by running the following PowerShell command:

```
Set-VMProcessor -VMName NameOfVM -ExposeVirtualiationExtensions $true
```

### Nested virtualization dynamic memory

You won't be able to adjust the memory of a virtual machine that is enabled for nested virtualization while that VM is running. Although it is possible to enable dynamic memory, the amount of memory allocated to a VM configured for nested virtualization will not fluctuate while the VM is running.

### Nested virtualization networking

To route network packets through the multiple virtual switches required during nested virtualization, you can either enable MAC address spoofing or configure network address translation (NAT).

To enable MAC address spoofing on the virtual machine that you have configured for nested virtualization, run the following PowerShell command:

```
Get-VMNetworkAdapter -VMName NameOfVM | Set-VMNEtworkAdapter -MacAddressSpoofing On
```

To enable NAT, create a virtual NAT switch in the VM that has been enabled for nested virtualization by using the following PowerShell commands:

```
New-VMSwitch -name VMNAT -SwitchTypeInternal
New-NetNAT -Name LocalNAT -InternalIPInterfaceAddressPrefix "192.168.15.0/24"
Get-NetAdapter "vEthernet (VmNat)" | New-NetIPAddress -IPAddress 192.168.15.1
-AddressFamily IPv4 -PrefixLength 24
```

After you've done this, you need to manually assign IP addresses to VMs running under the VM enabled for nested virtualization, using the default gateway of 192.168.15.1. You can use a separate internal addressing scheme other than 192.168.15.0/24 by altering the appropriate PowerShell commands in the previous code.

> **NEED MORE REVIEW?** **ENABLE NESTED VIRTUALIZATION**
>
> You can learn more about enabling nested virtualization at *https://docs.microsoft.com/virtualization/hyper-v-on-windows/user-guide/nested-virtualization*.

## Configure VM memory

You have two options when assigning memory to VMs. You can assign a static amount of memory, or you can configure dynamic memory. When you assign a static amount of memory, the amount of memory assigned to the VM remains the same, whether the VM is starting up, currently running, or in the process of shutting down.

When you configure dynamic memory, you can configure the following values in Windows Admin Center:

- **Startup Memory** This is the amount of memory allocated to the VM during startup. The value can be the same as the minimum amount of memory, or it can be as large as the maximum amount of allocated memory. Once the VM has started, it will instead use the amount of memory configured as the Minimum Memory.

- **Minimum Memory** This is the minimum amount of memory that the VM will be assigned by the virtualization host when dynamic memory is enabled. When multiple VMs are demanding memory, Hyper-V may reallocate memory away from the VM until the Minimum Memory value is met. You can reduce the Minimum Memory setting while the VM is running, but you cannot increase it while the VM is running.

- **Maximum Memory** This is the maximum amount of memory that the VM will be allocated by the virtualization host when dynamic memory is enabled. You can increase the Maximum Memory setting while the VM is running, but you cannot decrease it while the VM is running.

- **Memory Buffer** This is the percentage of memory that Hyper-V should allocate to the VM as a buffer.

- **Memory Weight** This setting allows you to configure how memory should be allocated to this particular VM as compared to other VMs running on the same virtualization host.

Generally, when you configure dynamic memory the amount of memory used by a VM will fluctuate between the Minimum Memory and Maximum Memory values. You should monitor VM memory utilization and tune these values so that they accurately represent the VM's actual requirements. If you allocate a Minimum Memory value below what the VM would actually need to run, this shortage might cause the virtualization host to reduce the amount of memory allocated to this Minimum Memory value, which will cause the VM to stop running.

## Smart paging

Smart paging is a special technology in Hyper-V that functions in certain conditions when a VM is restarting. *Smart paging* uses a file on the disk to simulate memory to meet Startup Memory requirements when the Startup Memory setting exceeds the Minimum Memory setting. Startup Memory is the amount of memory allocated to the VM when it starts, but not when it is in a running state. For example, you could set Startup Memory to 2,048 MB and the Minimum Memory to 512 MB for a specific virtual machine. In a scenario where 1,024 MB of free memory was available on the virtualization host, smart paging would allow the VM to access the required 2,048 MB of memory.

Because smart paging uses disk to simulate memory, it's only active if the following three conditions occur at the same time:

- The VM is being restarted.

- There is not enough memory on the virtualization host to meet the Startup Memory setting.
- Memory cannot be reclaimed from other VMs running on the same host.

Smart paging doesn't allow a VM to perform a "cold start" if the required amount of Startup Memory is not available but the Minimum Memory amount is. Smart paging is used only when a VM that was already running restarts and those three conditions have been met.

You can configure the location of the smart paging file on a per-VM basis. By default, smart paging files are written to the C:\ProgramData\Microsoft\Windows\Hyper-V folder. The smart paging file is created only when needed and is deleted within 10 minutes of the VM restarting.

## Configure integration services

Integration services allow the virtualization host to extract information and perform operations on a hosted VM. By default, Windows Server 2012 R2 and later include Hyper-V integration services. If you are running a supported Linux guest VM on your Hyper-V server, you can download the Linux Integration Services for Hyper-V and Azure from the Microsoft website. Integration service installation files are available for all operating systems that are supported on Hyper-V. You can enable the following integration services:

- **Operating System Shutdown**   This integration service allows you to shut down the VM from the virtualization host, rather than from within the VM's OS.
- **Time Synchronization**   This service synchronizes the virtualization host's clock with the VM's clock; it ensures that the VM clock doesn't drift when the VM is started, stopped, or reverted to a checkpoint.
- **Data Exchange**   This service allows the virtualization host to read and modify specific VM registry values.
- **Heartbeat**   This service allows the virtualization host to verify that the VM OS is still functioning and responding to requests.
- **Backup (Volume Shadow Copy)**   For VMs that support Volume Shadow Copy, this service synchronizes with the virtualization host, allowing backups of the VM while the VM is in operation.
- **Guest Services**   Guest services allow you to copy files from the virtualization host to the VM using the Copy-VMFile Windows PowerShell cmdlet.

## Configure Discrete Device Assignment

Discrete Device Assignment (DDA) allows you to directly assign a physical GPU or an NVMe storage device to a specific virtual machine. Each physical GPU or NVMe storage device can be associated with only one VM. DDA involves installing the device's native driver in the VM associated with that GPU. This process works for both Windows and Linux VMs as long as the drivers are available for the VM's operating system. DDA is supported for Generation 1 or 2 VMs running Windows Server 2012 R2 or later, Windows 10 or later, and some Linux guest operating systems.

Before assigning the physical GPU or storage device to a specific VM, you must dismount the device from the Hyper-V host. Some device vendors provide partitioning drivers for the Hyper-V host. Partitioning drivers are different from the standard device drivers and improve the security of the DDA configuration. If a partitioning driver is available, you should install this driver before dismounting the device from the Hyper-V host. If no driver is available, you'll have to use the `-Force` option with the `Dismount-VMHostAssignableDevice` cmdlet.

After you've dismounted the physical device from the Hyper-V host, you can assign it to a specific guest VM using the `Add-VMAssignableDevice` cmdlet. If you want to remove a physical device from its assignment to a VM, you'll need to stop the VM it is assigned to, then dismount it using the `Remove-VMAssignableDevice` cmdlet. Then, you'll be able to assign it to another VM or make it available to the host computer by enabling it in Device Manager.

Enabling DDA requires that you disable the VM's automatic stop action. You can do so using this command:

```
Set-VM -Name VMName -AutomaticStopAction TurnOff
```

The following functionality is also not available to VMs configured with DDA:

- VM Save and Restore
- VM live migration
- Use of dynamic memory
- Deployment of VM to a high availability cluster

RemoteFX is a technology available in Windows Server 2016 that performs a similar function to DDA in Windows Server 2019 and Windows Server 2022. RemoteFX provides a 3D virtual adapter and USB redirection support for VMs. You can only use RemoteFX if the virtualization host has a compatible GPU. RemoteFX allows one or more compatible graphics adapters to perform graphics processing tasks for multiple VMs. As with DDA, you can use RemoteFX to provide support for graphic-intensive applications, such as CAD, in virtual desktop infrastructure (VDI) scenarios. RemoteFX is deprecated from version 1803 of Windows Server on.

> **NEED MORE REVIEW?**   **DISCRETE DEVICE ASSIGNMENT**
>
> You can learn more about DDA at *https://docs.microsoft.com/en-us/windows-server/ virtualization/hyper-v/plan/plan-for-deploying-devices-using-discrete-device-assignment.*

## Configure VM resource groups

Instead of instituting resource constraints on a per-virtual machine basis, virtual machine resource controls allow you to create groups of virtual machines where each group is allocated a different proportion of the Hyper-V host's total CPU resources. For example, you can have a group of six virtual machines used by a specific department that are limited to a specific proportion of the Hyper-V host's CPU capacity that they cannot exceed. VM resource groups also allow you to limit what resources the Hyper-V host can use; for example, ensuring that the

Hyper-V host has a limit on processor and memory use that can't be exceeded, which would limit the processor and memory available to VMs.

> **NEED MORE REVIEW?** **VIRTUAL MACHINE RESOURCE CONTROLS**
>
> You can learn more about virtual machine resource controls at *https://docs.microsoft.com/ windows-server/virtualization/hyper-v/manage/manage-hyper-v-cpugroups*.

## Configure VM CPU groups

VM CPU groups allow you to isolate VM groups to specific host processors; for example, on a multi-processor Hyper-V host, you might choose to allow a group of VMs exclusive access to specific processor cores. This can be useful in scenarios where you must ensure that different VMs are partitioned from one another, with Hyper-V network virtualization providing completely separate tenant networks and VM CPU groups ensuring that separate VM groups never share the same physical CPUs.

CPU groups are managed through the Hyper-V Host Compute Service (HCS). You cannot directly manage CPU groups through PowerShell or the Hyper-V console and instead need to download the cpugroups.exe command-line utility from the Microsoft Download Center.

> **NEED MORE REVIEW?** **HYPER-V CPU GROUPS**
>
> You can learn more about Hyper-V CPU groups at *https://docs.microsoft.com/windows-server/ virtualization/hyper-v/manage/manage-hyper-v-cpugroups*.

## Configure hypervisor scheduling types

Hyper-V supports a "classic" scheduler and a new hypervisor core scheduler. The differences between these are as follows:

- **Classic scheduler**    Uses fair-share round-robin method of scheduling processor tasks across the Hyper-V host, including processors used by the host and those used by guest VMs. The classic scheduler is the default type used on all versions of Hyper-V until Windows Server 2019. When used on a host with Symmetric Multi-Threading (SMT) enabled, the classic scheduler will schedule guest virtual processors from any VM running on the host so that one VM runs on one SMT thread of a processor core while another VM runs on another SMT thread of the same processor core.
- **Core scheduler**    The core scheduler uses SMT to ensure isolation of guest workloads. This means that a CPU core is never shared between VMs, which is not the case if SMT is enabled and the classic scheduler is used. The core scheduler ensures a strong security boundary for guest workload isolation. It also allows the use of SMT within guest VMs, allowing programming interfaces to control and distribute tasks across SMT threads.

Windows Server 2019 and Windows Server 2022 use the core scheduler by default. New virtual machines created using VM version 9.0 or later will inherit the SMT properties of the physical host. VMs that may have been migrated to Windows Server 2019 or Windows Server 2022 and have been updated to VM version 9.0 or later will need to have their setting updated to enable SMT using the Set-VMProcessor cmdlet with the HWThreadCountPerCore parameter.

**NEED MORE REVIEW?**   **HYPER-V SCHEDULING TYPES**

You can learn more about Hyper-V scheduling types at *https://docs.microsoft.com/windows-server/virtualization/hyper-v/manage/about-hyper-v-scheduler-type-selection*.

## Manage VM checkpoints

Checkpoints represent the state of a VM at a particular point in time. You can create checkpoints when the VM is running or when the VM is shut down. When you create a checkpoint of a running VM, the running VM's memory state is also stored in the checkpoint. Restoring a checkpoint taken of a running VM returns the running VM to a restored state. Creating a checkpoint creates either an AVHD or an AVHDX file (depending on whether the VM is using virtual hard disks in the VHD or VHDx format).

Windows Server 2016 and later support two types of checkpoints:

- **Standard checkpoints**   These function just as checkpoints have functioned in previous versions of Hyper-V. They capture the state, date, and hardware configuration of a virtual machine. They are designed for development and test scenarios.

- **Production checkpoints**   Available only in Windows Server 2016 and later, production checkpoints use backup technology inside the guest as opposed to the saved-state technology used in standard checkpoints. Production checkpoints are fully supported by Microsoft and can be used with production workloads, which is something that was not supported with the standard version of checkpoints available in previous versions of Hyper-V.

You can switch between standard and production checkpoints on a per-virtual machine basis by editing the properties of the virtual machine; in the Management section of the Properties dialog box, choose between Production and Standard checkpoints.

You can create checkpoints from Windows PowerShell with the Checkpoint-VM cmdlet. The other checkpoint-related Windows PowerShell cmdlets in Windows Server actually use the VMSnapshot noun, though on Windows 10, they confusingly have aliases for the VMCheckPoint noun.

The Windows Server checkpoint-related cmdlets are as follows:

- **Restore-VMSnapshot**   Restores an existing VM checkpoint.

- **Export-VMSnapshot** Allows you to export the state of a VM as it exists when a particular checkpoint was taken. For example, if you took checkpoints at 2 p.m. and 3 p.m., you could choose to export the checkpoint taken at 2 p.m. and then import the VM in the state that it was in at 2 p.m. on another Hyper-V host.
- **Get-VMSnapshot** Lists the current checkpoints.
- **Rename-VMSnapshot** Allows you to rename an existing VM checkpoint.
- **Remove-VMSnapshot** Deletes a VM checkpoint. If the VM checkpoint is part of the chain but not the final link, changes are merged with the successive checkpoint so that the checkpoint remains a representation of the VM at the point in time when the snapshot was taken. For example, if checkpoints were taken at 1 p.m., 2 p.m., and 3 p.m., and you delete the 2 p.m. checkpoint, the AVHD/AVHDX files associated with the 2 p.m. snapshot would be merged with the AVHD/AVHDX files associated with the 3 p.m. snapshot so that the 3 p.m. snapshot retains its integrity.

Checkpoints do not replace backups. Checkpoints are almost always stored on the same volume as the original VM hard disks, so a failure of that volume will result in all VM storage files—both original disks and checkpoint disks—being lost. If a disk in a checkpoint chain becomes corrupted, then that checkpoint and all subsequent checkpoints will be lost. Disks earlier in the checkpoint chain will remain unaffected. Hyper-V supports a maximum of 50 checkpoints per VM.

# Implement high availability for virtual machines

There are several methods that you can use to make virtual machines fault tolerant and resilient. These include configuring VM replication as well as running VMs on more traditional failover clusters as well as combinations of these technologies.

## Hyper-V Replica

Hyper-V Replica provides a replica of a VM running on one Hyper-V host that can be stored and updated on another Hyper-V host. For example, you could configure a VM hosted on a Hyper-V failover cluster in Melbourne to be replicated through Hyper-V Replica to a Hyper-V failover cluster in Sydney. Hyper-V Replica allows for replication across site boundaries and does not require access to shared storage in the way that failover clustering does.

Hyper-V Replica is asynchronous. While the replica copy is consistent, it is a lagged copy with changes sent only as frequently as once every 30 seconds. Hyper-V Replica supports multiple recovery points, with a recovery snapshot taken every hour. (This incurs a resource penalty, so the setting is off by default.) This means that when activating the replica, you can choose to activate the most up-to-date copy or a lagged copy. You would choose to activate a lagged copy in the event that some form of corruption or change made the up-to-date copy problematic.

When you perform a planned failover from the primary host to the replica, you need to switch off the primary host. This ensures that the replica is in an up-to-date and consistent state. This is a drawback compared to failover or live migration, where the VM will remain available during the process. A series of checks are completed before performing planned failover to ensure that the VM is off, that reverse replication is allowed back to the original primary Hyper-V host, and that the state of the VM on the current replica is consistent with the state of the VM on the current primary. Performing a planned failover will start the replicated VM on the original replica, which will now become the new primary server.

Hyper-V Replica also supports unplanned failover. You perform an unplanned failover in the event that the original Hyper-V host has failed or the site that hosts the primary replica has become unavailable. When performing an unplanned failover, you can choose either the most recent recovery point or a previous recovery point. Performing unplanned failover will start the VM on the original replica, which will now become the new primary server.

Hyper-V extended replication allows you to create a second replica of the existing replica server. For example, you could configure Hyper-V replication between a Hyper-V virtualization host in Melbourne and Sydney, with Sydney hosting the replica. You could then configure an extended replica in Brisbane using the Sydney replica.

### CONFIGURING HYPER-V REPLICA SERVERS

To configure Hyper-V Replica, you must configure the Replication Configuration settings. The first step is to select **Enable This Computer As A Replica Server**. Next, select the authentication method you are going to use. If the computers are parts of the same Active Directory environment, you can use Kerberos. When you use Kerberos, Hyper-V replication data isn't encrypted when transmitted across the network. If you are concerned about encrypting network data, you could configure IPsec. If you are concerned about encrypting replication traffic, another option is to use certificate-based authentication. This is useful if you are transmitting data across the public internet without using an encrypted VPN tunnel. When using certificate-based authentication, you'll need to import and select a public certificate issued to the partner server.

The final step when configuring Hyper-V Replica is to select the servers from which the Hyper-V virtualization host will accept incoming replicated VM data. One option is to have the Hyper-V virtualization host accept replicated VMs from any authenticated Hyper-V virtualization host, using a single default location to store replica data. The other option is to configure VM replica storage on a per-server basis. For example, if you wanted to store VM replicas from one server on one volume and VM replicas from another server on a different volume, you'd configure VM replica storage on a per-server basis.

Once replication is configured on the source and destination servers, you'll also need to enable the predefined firewall rules to allow the incoming replication traffic. There are two rules: one for replication using Kerberos (HTTP) on port 80 and the other for using certificate-based authentication on port 443.

### CONFIGURING VM REPLICAS

After you have configured the source and destination replica servers, you have to configure replication on a per-VM basis. You do so by running the Enable Replication Wizard, which you can trigger by selecting **Enable Replication** when the VM is selected in Hyper-V Manager. To configure VM replicas, you must perform the following steps:

- **Select Replica Server** Select the replica server name. If you are replicating to a Hyper-V failover cluster, you'll need to specify the name of the Hyper-V Replica Broker. You'll learn more about Hyper-V Replica Broker later in this chapter.

- **Choose Connection Parameters** Specify the connection parameters. The options will depend on the configuration of the replica servers. On this page, depending on the existing configuration, you can choose the authentication type and whether replication data will be compressed when transmitted over the network.

- **Select Replication VHDs** When configuring replication, you have the option of not replicating some of a VM's virtual hard disks. In most scenarios, you should replicate all of a VM's hard disk drives. One reason not to replicate a VM's virtual hard disk would be if the virtual hard disk only stores frequently changing temporary data that wouldn't be required when recovering the VM.

- **Replication Frequency** Use this page to specify the frequency with which changes are sent to the replica server. You can choose between intervals of 30 seconds, 5 minutes, and 15 minutes.

- **Additional Recovery Points** You can choose to create additional hourly recovery points. Doing so gives you the option of starting the replica from a previous point in time rather than the most recent. The advantage is that this allows you to roll back to a previous version of the VM in the event that data corruption occurs and the VM has replicated to the most recent recovery point. The replica server can store a maximum of 24 recovery points.

- **Initial Replication** The last step in configuring Hyper-V Replica is choosing how to seed the initial replica. Replication works by sending changed blocks of data, so the initial replica, which sends the entire VM, will be the largest transfer. You can perform an offline transfer with external media, use an existing VM on the replica server as the initial copy (the VM for which you are configuring a replica must have been exported and then imported on the replica server), or transfer all VM data across the network. You can perform replication immediately or at a specific time in the future, such as 2 a.m. when network utilization is likely to be lower.

### REPLICA FAILOVER

You perform a planned replica failover when you want to run the VM on the replica server rather than on the primary host. Planned failover involves shutting down the VM, which ensures that the replica will be up to date. Contrast this with Hyper-V live migration, which you perform while the VM is running. When performing a planned failover, you can configure the VM on the replica server to automatically start once the process completes; you can also configure reverse replication so that the current replica server becomes the new primary server and the current primary becomes the new replica server.

In the event that the primary server becomes unavailable, you can trigger an unplanned failover. You would then perform the unplanned failover on the replica server (as the primary is not available). When performing an unplanned failover, you can select any of the up to 24 previously stored recovery points.

### HYPER-V REPLICA BROKER

You need to configure and deploy Hyper-V Replica Broker if your Hyper-V replica configuration includes a Hyper-V failover cluster as a source or destination. You don't need to configure and deploy Hyper-V Replica Broker if both the source and destination servers are not participating in a Hyper-V failover cluster. You install the Hyper-V Replica Broker role using Failover Cluster Manager after you've enabled the Hyper-V role on cluster nodes.

## Hyper-V failover clusters

One of the most common uses for failover clustering is to host Hyper-V virtual machines. Hyper-V failover clusters allow VMs to move to another virtualization host in the event that the original experiences a disruption or when you need to rebalance the way that VMs across the cluster use Hyper-V host resources.

### HYPER-V HOST CLUSTER STORAGE

When deployed on Hyper-V host clusters, the configuration and virtual hard disk files for highly available VMs are hosted on shared storage. This shared storage can be one of the following:

- **Serial Attached SCSI (SAS)**   Suitable for two-node failover clusters where the cluster nodes are in close proximity to each other.
- **iSCSI storage**   Suitable for failover clusters with two or more nodes. Windows Server includes iSCSI Target Software, allowing it to host iSCSI targets that can be used as shared storage by Windows failover clusters.
- **Fibre Channel**   Fibre Channel/Fibre Channel over Ethernet storage requires special network hardware. While generally providing better performance than iSCSI, Fibre Channel components tend to be more expensive.
- **SMB 3.0 file shares configured as continuously available storage**   This special type of file share is highly available, with multiple cluster nodes able to maintain access to the file share. This configuration requires multiple clusters. One cluster hosts the highly available storage used by the VMs, and the other cluster hosts the highly available VMs.
- **Cluster Shared Volumes (CSVs)**   CSVs can also be used for VM storage in Hyper-V failover clusters. As with continuously available file shares, multiple nodes in the cluster have access to the files stored on CSVs, ensuring that failover occurs with minimal disruption. As with SMB 3.0 file shares, multiple clusters are required, with one cluster hosting the CSVs and the other cluster hosting the VMs.

When considering storage for a Hyper-V failover cluster, remember the following:

- Ensure volumes used for disk witnesses are formatted as either NTFS or ReFS.
- Avoid allowing nodes from separate failover clusters to access the same shared storage by using LUN masking or zoning.
- Where possible, use storage spaces to host volumes presented as shared storage.

## CLUSTER QUORUM

Hyper-V failover clusters remain functional until they do not have enough active votes to retain quorum. Votes can consist of nodes that participate in the cluster as well as disk or file share witnesses. The calculation on whether the cluster maintains quorum is dependent on the cluster quorum mode. When you deploy a Windows Server failover cluster, one of the following modes will automatically be selected, depending on the current cluster configuration:

- Node Majority
- Node and Disk Majority
- Node and File Share Majority
- No Majority: Disk Only

You can change the cluster mode manually, or with Dynamic Quorum in Windows Server, the cluster mode will change automatically when you add or remove nodes, a witness disk, or a witness share. The following quorum modes are available:

- **Node Majority** This cluster quorum mode is chosen automatically during setup if a cluster has an odd number of nodes. When this cluster quorum mode is used, a file share or disk witness is not used. A failover cluster will retain quorum as long as the number of available nodes is more than the number of failed nodes that retain cluster membership. For example, if you deploy a nine-node failover cluster, the cluster will retain quorum as long as five cluster nodes are able to communicate with each other.

- **Node and Disk Majority** This model is chosen automatically during setup if the cluster has an even number of nodes and shared storage is available to function as a disk witness. In this configuration, cluster nodes and the disk witness each have a vote when calculating quorum. As with the Node Majority model, the cluster will retain quorum as long as the number of votes that remain in communication exceeds the number of votes that cannot be contacted. For example, if you deployed a six-node cluster and a witness disk, there would be a total of seven votes. As long as four of those votes remained in communication with each other, the failover cluster would retain quorum.

- **Node and File Share Majority** This model is used when a file share is configured as a witness. Each node and the file share have a vote when it comes to determining if quorum is retained. As with other models, a majority of the votes must be present for the cluster to retain quorum. Node and File Share Majority is suitable for organizations that are deploying multisite clusters; for example, placing half the cluster nodes in one site, half the cluster nodes in another site, and the file share witness in a third site. If one site fails, the other site is able to retain communication with the site that hosts the file share witness, in which case quorum is retained.

- **No Majority: Disk Only** This model must be configured manually and must only be used in testing environments because the only vote that counts toward quorum is that of the disk witness on shared storage. The cluster will retain quorum as long as the witness is available, even if every node but one fails. Similarly, the cluster will be in a failed state if all the nodes are available but the shared storage hosting the disk witness goes offline.

### CLUSTER NODE WEIGHT

Rather than every node in the cluster having an equal vote when determining quorum, you can configure which cluster nodes can vote to determine quorum by running the Configure Cluster Quorum Wizard. Configuring node weight is useful if you are deploying a multisite cluster and you want to control which site retains quorum in the event that communication between the sites is lost. You can determine which nodes in a cluster are currently assigned votes by selecting **Nodes** in the **Failover Cluster Manager**.

### DYNAMIC QUORUM

Dynamic quorum allows cluster quorum to be recalculated automatically each time a node is removed from or added to a cluster. By default, dynamic quorum is enabled on Windows Server clusters. Dynamic quorum works in the following manner:

- The vote of the witness is automatically adjusted based on the number of voting nodes in the cluster. If the cluster has an even number of nodes, the witness has a vote. If a cluster has an even number of nodes and a node is added or removed, the witness loses its vote.

- In the event of a 50 percent node split, dynamic quorum can adjust the vote of a node. This is useful in avoiding "split brain" syndrome during site splits with multisite failover clusters.

An advantage of dynamic quorum is that as long as nodes are evicted in a graceful manner, the cluster will reconfigure quorum appropriately. This means that you could change a nine-node cluster to a five-node cluster by evicting nodes, and the new quorum model would automatically be recalculated assuming that the cluster only had five nodes. With dynamic quorum, it is a good idea to specify a witness even if the initial cluster configuration has an odd number of nodes; doing so means a witness vote will automatically be included in the event that an administrator adds or removes a node from the cluster.

### CLUSTER NETWORKING

In lab and development environments, it's reasonable to have failover cluster nodes that are configured with a single network adapter. In production environments with mission-critical workloads, you should configure cluster nodes with multiple network adapters, institute adapter teaming, and leverage separate networks. Separate networks should include:

- A network dedicated for connecting cluster nodes to shared storage
- A network dedicated for internal cluster communication
- The network that clients use to access services deployed on the cluster

When configuring IPv4 or IPv6 addressing for failover cluster nodes, ensure that addresses are assigned either statically or dynamically to cluster node network adapters. Avoid using a mixture of statically and dynamically assigned addresses, as this will cause an error with the Cluster Validation Wizard. Also ensure that cluster network adapters are configured with a default gateway. While the Cluster Validation Wizard will not provide an error if a default gateway is not present for the network adapters of each potential cluster node, you will be unable to create a failover cluster unless a default gateway is present.

You can use the Validate-DCB tool to validate cluster networking configuration. This tool is useful in situations where you need to check networking configuration to support RDMA and Switch Embedded Teaming (SET).

### FORCE QUORUM RESILIENCY

Imagine you have a five-node, multisite cluster in Melbourne and Sydney, with three nodes in Sydney. Also, imagine that internet connectivity to the Sydney site is lost. Within the Sydney site itself, the cluster will remain running because with three nodes, it has retained quorum. But if external connectivity to the Sydney site is not available, you may instead need to forcibly start the cluster in the Melbourne site (which will be in a failed state because only two nodes are present) using the /fq (forced quorum) switch to provide services to clients.

In the past, when connectivity was restored, this would have led to a "split brain" or partitioned cluster, as both sides of the cluster would be configured to be authoritative. To resolve this with failover clusters running Windows Server 2012 or earlier, you would need to manually restart the nodes that were not part of the forced quorum set using the /pq (prevent quorum) switch. Windows Server 2019 and later provide a feature known as Force Quorum Resiliency that automatically restarts the nodes that were not part of the forced quorum set so that the cluster does not remain in a partitioned state.

### CLUSTER SHARED VOLUMES

Cluster Shared Volumes (CSVs) are a high-availability storage technology that allows multiple cluster nodes in a failover cluster to have read-write access to the same LUN. This has the following advantages for Hyper-V failover clusters:

- VMs stored on the same LUN can be run on different cluster nodes. This reduces the number of LUNs required to host VMs because the VMs stored on a CSV aren't tied to one specific Hyper-V failover cluster node; instead, the VMs can be spread across multiple Hyper-V failover cluster nodes.
- Switch-over between nodes is almost instantaneous in the event of failover because the new host node doesn't have to go through the process of seizing the LUN from the failed node.

CSVs are hosted from servers running the Windows Server 2012 or later operating systems and allow multiple nodes in a cluster to access the same NTFS- or ReFS-formatted file system. CSVs support BitLocker, with each node performing decryption of encrypted content using a cluster computer account. CSVs also integrate with SMB (Server Message Block) Multichannel and SMB Direct, allowing traffic to be sent through multiple networks and to leverage network cards that include Remote Direct Memory Access (RDMA) technology. CSVs can also automatically scan and repair volumes without requiring storage to be taken offline. You can convert cluster storage to a CSV using the Disks node of the Failover Cluster Manager.

### ACTIVE DIRECTORY DETACHED CLUSTERS

Active Directory detached clusters, also called "clusters without network names," are a feature of Windows Server 2012 R2 and later operating systems. Detached clusters have their names stored in DNS but do not require the creation of a computer account within Active Directory. The benefit of detached clusters is that it is possible to create them without requiring that a computer object be created in Active Directory to represent the cluster; also, the account used to create the cluster need not have permissions to create computer objects in Active Directory. Although the account used to create a detached cluster does not need permission to create computer objects in Active Directory, the nodes that will participate in the detached cluster must still be domain-joined.

### PREFERRED OWNER AND FAILOVER SETTINGS

Cluster role preferences settings allow you to configure a preferred owner for a cluster role. When you do this, the role will be hosted on the node listed as the preferred owner. You can specify multiple preferred owners and configure the order in which a role will attempt to return to a specific cluster node.

Failover settings allow you to configure how many times a service will attempt to restart or fail over in a specific period. By default, a cluster service can fail over twice in a six-hour period before the failover cluster will leave the cluster role in a failed state. The failback setting allows you to configure the amount of time a clustered role that has failed over to a node that is not its preferred owner will wait before falling back to the preferred owner.

### VM NETWORK HEALTH DETECTION

VM Network Health Detection is a feature for VMs that are deployed on Hyper-V host clusters. With VM Network Health Detection, you configure a VM's network adapter settings and mark certain networks as being protected. You do this in the Advanced Features section of the Network Adapter properties dialog box.

In the event that a VM is running on a cluster node where the network marked as protected becomes unavailable, the cluster will automatically live migrate the VM to a node where the protected network is available. For example, say you have a four-node Hyper-V failover cluster. Each node has multiple network adapters, and a virtual switch named Alpha maps as an external virtual switch to a physical network adapter on each node. A VM, configured as highly available and hosted on the first cluster node, is connected to a virtual switch, Alpha. The network adapter on this VM is configured with the protected network option. After the VM has been switched on and has been running for some time, a fault occurs, causing the physical network adapter mapped to the virtual switch Alpha on the first cluster node to fail. When this happens, the VM will automatically be live migrated to another cluster node where the virtual switch Alpha is working.

### VM DRAIN ON SHUTDOWN

*VM drain on shutdown* is a feature that will automatically live migrate all running VMs off a node if you shut down that node without putting it into maintenance mode. If you are following best practice, you'll be putting nodes into maintenance mode and live migrating running workloads away from nodes that you will restart or intend to shut down anyway. The main benefit of VM drain on shutdown is that, in the event that you are having a bad day and forget to put a cluster node into maintenance mode before shutting it down or restarting it, any running VMs will be live migrated without requiring your direct intervention.

## Hyper-V guest clusters

A guest cluster is a failover cluster that consists of two or more VMs as cluster nodes. You can run a guest cluster on a Hyper-V failover cluster, or you can run guest clusters with nodes on separate Hyper-V failover clusters. While deploying a guest cluster on Hyper-V failover clusters may seem as though it is taking redundancy to an extreme, there are good reasons to deploy guest clusters and Hyper-V failover clusters together:

■ Failover clusters monitor the health of clustered roles to ensure that they are functioning. This means that a guest failover cluster can detect when the failure of a clustered role occurs and can take steps to recover the role. For example, say you deploy an SQL Server failover cluster as a guest cluster on a Hyper-V failover cluster. One of the SQL Server instances that participates in the guest cluster suffers a failure. In this scenario, failover occurs within the guest cluster, and another instance of SQL Server hosted on the other guest cluster node continues to service client requests.

■ Deploying guest and Hyper-V failover clusters together allows you to move applications to other guest cluster nodes while you are performing servicing tasks. For example, you may need to apply software updates that require a restart to the operating system that hosts an SQL Server instance. If this SQL Server instance is participating in a Hyper-V guest cluster, you could move the clustered role to another node, apply software updates to the original node, perform the restart, and then move the clustered SQL Server role back to the original node.

■ Deploying guest and Hyper-V failover clusters together allows you to live migrate guest cluster VMs from one host cluster to another host cluster while ensuring clients retain connectivity to clustered applications. For example, suppose a two-node guest cluster hosting SQL Server is hosted on one Hyper-V failover cluster in your organization's datacenter. You want to move the guest cluster from its current host Hyper-V failover cluster to a new Hyper-V failover cluster. By migrating one guest cluster node at a time from the original Hyper-V failover cluster to the new Hyper-V failover cluster, you'll be able to continue to service client requests without interruption, failing over SQL Server to the guest node on the new Hyper-V failover cluster after the first node completes its migration and before migrating the second node across.

### HYPER-V GUEST CLUSTER STORAGE

Just as you can configure a Hyper-V failover cluster where multiple Hyper-V hosts function as failover cluster nodes, you can configure failover clusters within VMs, where each failover cluster node is a VM. Even though failover cluster nodes must be members of the same Active Directory domain, there is no requirement that they be hosted on the same cluster. For example, you could configure a multisite failover cluster where the cluster nodes are hosted as highly available VMs, each hosted on its own Hyper-V failover clusters in each site.

When considering how to deploy a VM guest cluster, you'll need to choose how you will provision the shared storage that is accessible to each cluster node. The options for configuring shared storage for VM guest clusters include:

- iSCSI
- Virtual Fibre Channel
- Cluster Shared Volumes
- Continuously Available File Shares
- Shared virtual hard disks

The conditions for using iSCSI, Virtual Fibre Channel, Cluster Shared Volumes, and Continuously Available File Shares with VM guest clusters are essentially the same for VMs as they are when configuring traditional physically hosted failover cluster nodes.

### SHARED VIRTUAL HARD DISK

Shared virtual hard disks are a special type of shared storage only available to VM guest clusters. With shared virtual hard disks, each guest cluster node can be configured to access the same shared virtual hard disk. Each VM cluster node's operating system will recognize the shared virtual hard disk as shared storage when building the VM guest failover cluster.

Shared virtual hard disks have the following requirements:

- Can be used with Generation 1 and Generation 2 VMs.
- Can only be used with guest operating systems running Windows Server 2012 or later. If the guest operating systems are running Windows Server 2012, they must be updated to use the Windows Server 2012 R2 integration services components.
- Can only be used if virtualization hosts are running the Windows Server 2012 R2 or later version of Hyper-V.
- Must be configured to use the VHDX virtual hard disk format.
- Must be connected to a virtual SCSI controller.
- When deployed on a failover cluster, the shared virtual hard disk itself should be located on shared storage, such as a Continuously Available File Share or Cluster Shared Volume. This is not necessary when configuring a guest failover cluster on a single Hyper-V server that is not part of a Hyper-V failover cluster.
- VMs can only use shared virtual hard disks to store data. You can't boot a VM from a shared virtual hard disk.

The configuration of shared virtual hard disks differs from the traditional configuration of VM guest failover clusters because you configure the connection to shared storage by editing the VM properties rather than connecting to the shared storage from within the VM. Windows Server 2016 and later support shared virtual hard disks being resized and used with Hyper-V Replica.

### HYPER-V VHD SETS

VHD Sets are a newer version of shared virtual hard disks. Hyper-V VHD Sets use a new virtual hard disk format that uses the .vhds extension. VHD Sets support online resizing of shared virtual disks, Hyper-V Replica, and application-consistent Hyper-V checkpoints.

You can create a VHD Set file from Hyper-V Manager or by using the New-VHD cmdlet with the file type set to VHDS when specifying the virtual hard disk name. You can use the Convert-VHD cmdlet to convert an existing shared virtual hard disk file to a VHD Set file as long as you have taken the VMs that use the shared virtual hard disk file offline and removed the shared virtual hard disk from the VM using the Remove-VHHardDiskDrive cmdlet.

## Hyper-V live migration

*Live migration* is the process of moving an operational VM from one physical virtualization host to another with no interruption to VM clients or users. Live migration is supported between cluster nodes that share storage between separate Hyper-V virtualization hosts that are not participating in a failover cluster using an SMB 3.0 file share as storage; live migration is even supported between separate Hyper-V hosts that are not participating in a failover cluster using a process called "shared nothing live migration."

Live migration has the following prerequisites:

- There must be two or more servers running Hyper-V that use processors from the same manufacturer (for example, all Hyper-V virtualization hosts configured with Intel processors or all Hyper-V virtualization hosts configured with AMD processors).
- Hyper-V virtualization hosts need to be members of the same domain, or they must be members of domains that have a trust relationship with each other.
- VMs must be configured to use virtual hard disks or virtual Fibre Channel disks; pass-through disks are not allowed.

It is possible to perform live migration with VMs configured with pass-through disks under the following conditions:

- VMs are hosted on a Windows Server Hyper-V failover cluster.
- Live migration will be within nodes that participate in the same Hyper-V failover cluster.
- VM configuration files are stored on a Cluster Shared Volume.
- The physical disk that is used as a pass-through disk is configured as a storage disk resource that is controlled by the failover cluster. This disk must be configured as a dependent resource for the highly available VM.

If performing a live migration using shared storage, the following conditions must be met:

- The SMB 3.0 share needs to be configured so that the source and the destination virtualization host's computer accounts have read and write permissions.
- All VM files (virtual hard disks, configuration files, and snapshot files) must be located on the SMB 3.0 share. You can use storage migration to move VM files to an SMB 3.0 share while the VM is running before performing a live migration using this method.

You must configure the source and destination Hyper-V virtualization hosts to support live migrations by enabling live migrations in the Hyper-V settings. When you do this, you specify the maximum number of simultaneous live migrations and the networks that you will use for live migration. Microsoft recommends using an isolated network for live migration traffic, though this is not a requirement.

The next step in configuring live migration is choosing which authentication protocol and live migration performance options to use. You select these in the Advanced Features area of the Live Migrations settings. The default authentication protocol is CredSSP (Credential Security Support Provider). CredSSP requires local sign-in to both the source and the destination Hyper-V virtualization host to perform live migration. Kerberos allows you to trigger live migration remotely. To use Kerberos, you must configure the computer accounts for each Hyper-V virtualization host with constrained delegation for the CIFS (Common internet File System) and Microsoft Virtual System Migration Service services, granting permissions to the virtualization hosts that will participate in the live migration partnership. The performance options allow you to speed up live migration. Compression increases processor utilization. SMB will use SMB Direct if both the network adapters used for the live migration process support remote direct memory access (RDMA) and RDMA capabilities are enabled.

## Manage VHD and VHDX files

Hyper-V supports two separate virtual hard disk formats. Virtual hard disk files in VHD format are limited to 2,040 GB. Virtual hard disks in this format can be used on all supported versions of Hyper-V. Other than the size limitation, the important thing to remember is that you cannot use virtual hard disk files in VHD format with Generation 2 VMs.

Virtual hard disk files in VHDX format are an improvement over virtual hard disks in VHD format. The main limitation of virtual hard disks in VHDX format is that they cannot be used with Hyper-V on Windows Server 2008 or Windows Server 2008 R2, which shouldn't be as much of a problem now since these operating systems no longer have mainstream support. Virtual hard disks in VHDX format have the following benefits:

- Can be up to 64 TB in size
- Have larger block size for dynamic and differential disks
- Provide 4 KB logical sector virtual disks
- Have an internal log that reduces chance of corruption
- Support TRIM to reclaim unused space

You can convert hard disks between VHD and VHDX format. You can create virtual hard disks at the time you create the VM, by using the New Virtual Hard Disk Wizard, or by using the New-VHD PowerShell cmdlet. You can convert virtual hard disks using the Convert-VHD PowerShell cmdlet.

## Fixed-sized disks

Virtual hard disks can be dynamic, differencing, or fixed. When you create a fixed-size disk, all space used by the disk is allocated on the hosting volume at the time of creation. Fixed disks increase performance if the physical storage medium does not support Windows Offloaded Data Transfer (ODX). Improvements in Windows Server reduce the performance benefit of fixed-size disks when the storage medium supports ODX. The space to be allocated to the disk must be present on the host volume when you create the disk. For example, you can't create a 3 TB fixed disk on a volume that has only 2 TB of space.

## Dynamically expanding disks

A dynamically expanding disk uses a small file initially and then grows as the VM allocates data to the virtual hard disk. This means you can create a 3 TB dynamic virtual hard disk on a 2 TB volume because the entire 3 TB will not be allocated at disk creation. However, in this scenario, you would need to ensure that you extend the size of the 2 TB volume before the dynamic virtual disk outgrows the available storage space.

## Differencing disks

Differencing disks are a special type of virtual hard disk that has a child relationship with a parent hard disk. Parent disks can be fixed size or dynamic virtual hard disks, but the differencing disk must be the same type as the parent disk. For example, you can create a differencing disk in VHDX format for a parent disk that uses VHDX format, but you cannot create a differencing disk in VHD format for a parent disk in VHDX format.

Differencing disks record the changes that would otherwise be made to the parent hard disk by the VM. For example, differencing disks are used to record Hyper-V VM checkpoints. One parent virtual hard disk can have multiple differencing disks associated with it.

For example, you can create a specially prepared parent virtual hard disk by installing Windows Server on a VM by running the sysprep utility within the VM and then shutting the VM down. You can use the virtual hard disk created by this process as a parent virtual hard disk. In this scenario, when you create new Windows Server VMs, you would configure the VMs to use a new differencing disk that uses the sysprepped virtual hard disk as a parent. When you run the new VM, it will write any changes that it would normally make to the full virtual hard disk to the differencing disk. In this scenario, deploying new Windows Server VMs becomes a simple matter of creating new VMs that use a differencing disk that uses the sysprepped Windows Server virtual hard disk as a parent.

You can create differencing hard disks using the New Virtual Hard Disk Wizard or the New–VHD Windows PowerShell cmdlet. You must specify the parent disk during the creation process.

The key to using differencing disks is to ensure that you don't make changes to the parent disk; doing so will invalidate the relationship with any child disks. Generally, differencing disks can provide storage efficiencies because the only changes are recorded on child disks. For example, rather than storing 10 different instances of Windows Server 2022 in its entirety, you could create one parent disk and have 10 much smaller differencing disks to accomplish the same objective. If you store VM virtual hard disks on a volume that has been deduplicated, these efficiencies are reduced.

## Modifying virtual hard disks

You can perform the following tasks to modify existing virtual hard disks:

- Convert a virtual hard disk in VHD format to VHDX format.
- Convert a virtual hard disk in VHDX format to VHD format.
- Change the disk from fixed size to dynamically expanding or from dynamically expanding to fixed size.
- Shrink or enlarge the virtual hard disk.

You convert virtual hard disk type (VHD to VHDX, VHDX to VHD, dynamic to fixed, or fixed to dynamic) by using the Edit Virtual Hard Disk Wizard or by using the Convert-VHD PowerShell cmdlet. When converting from VHDX to VHD, remember that virtual hard disks in VHD format cannot exceed 2,040 GB in size. So, while it is possible to convert virtual hard disks in VHDX format that are smaller than 2,040 GB to VHD format, you will not be able to convert virtual hard disks that are larger than 2,040 GB.

You can only perform conversions from one format to another and from one type to another while the VM is powered off. You must shrink the virtual hard disk using the disk manager in the VM operating system before shrinking the virtual hard disk using the Edit Virtual Hard Disk Wizard or the Resize-VHD cmdlet. You can resize a virtual hard disk while the VM is running under the following conditions:

- The virtualization host is running Windows Server 2012 R2 or later.
- The virtual hard disk is in VHDX format.
- The virtual hard disk is attached to a virtual SCSI controller.
- The virtual hard disk must have been shrunk. You must shrink the virtual hard disk using the disk manager in the host operating system before shrinking the virtual hard disk using the Edit Virtual Hard Disk Wizard or the Resize-VHD cmdlet.

## Pass-through disks

Pass-through disks, also known as directly attached disks, allow a VM to directly access the underlying storage rather than accessing a virtual hard disk that resides on that storage. For example, with Hyper-V you normally connect a VM to a virtual hard disk file hosted on a volume formatted with NTFS or ReFS. With pass-through disks, the VM instead accesses the disk directly, and there is no virtual hard disk file.

Pass-through disks allow VMs to access larger volumes than are possible when using virtual hard disks in VHD format. In earlier versions of Hyper-V—such as the version available with Windows Server 2008—pass-through disks provide performance advantages over virtual hard disks. The need for pass-through disks has diminished with the availability of virtual hard disks in VHDX format because that format allows you to create much larger volumes.

Pass-through disks can be directly attached to the virtualization host, or they can be attached to Fibre Channel or iSCSI disks. When adding a pass-through disk, you will need to ensure that the disk is offline. You can use the Disk Management console or the diskpart.exe utility on the virtualization host to set a disk to be offline.

To add a pass-through disk using PowerShell, use the `Get-Disk` cmdlet to get the properties of the disk that you want to add as a pass-through disk. Next, pipe the result to the Add-VMHardDiskDrive cmdlet. For example, to add physical disk 3 to the VM named Alpha-Test, execute the following command:

```
Get-Disk 3 | Add-VMHardDiskDrive -VMName Alpha-Test
```

A VM that uses pass-through disks will not support VM checkpoints. Pass-through disks also cannot be backed up with backup programs that use the Hyper-V VSS writer.

## Virtual Fibre Channel adapters

Virtual Fibre Channel allows you to make direct connections from VMs running on Hyper-V to Fibre Channel storage. If the following requirements are met, Virtual Fibre Channel is supported on Windows Server 2016 and later:

- The computer functioning as the Hyper-V virtualization host must have a Fibre Channel host bus adapter (HBA) that has a driver that supports Virtual Fibre Channel.
- SAN must be NPIV (N_Port ID) enabled.
- The VM must be running a supported version of the guest operating system.
- Virtual Fibre Channel LUNs cannot be used to boot Hyper-V VMs.

VMs running on Hyper-V support up to four virtual Fibre Channel adapters, each of which can be associated with a separate storage area network (SAN). Before you can use a Virtual Fibre Channel adapter, you will need to create at least one virtual SAN on the Hyper-V virtualization host. A virtual SAN is a group of physical Fibre Channel ports that connect to the same SAN. VM live migration and VM failover clusters are supported; however, virtual Fibre Channel does not support VM checkpoints, host-based backup, or live migration of SAN data.

## Storage QoS

Storage Quality of Service (QoS) allows you to limit the maximum number of IOPS (input/output operations per second) for virtual hard disks. IOPS are measured in 8 KB increments. If you specify a maximum IOPS value, the virtual hard disk will be unable to exceed this value. You use Storage QoS to ensure that no single workload on a Hyper-V virtualization host consumes a disproportionate amount of storage resources.

It's also possible to specify a minimum IOPS value for each virtual hard disk. You would do this if you wanted to be notified that a specific virtual hard disk's IOPS has fallen below a threshold value. When the number of IOPS falls below the specified minimum, an event is written to the event log. You configure Storage QoS on a per-virtual hard disk basis.

## Hyper-V storage optimization

Several technologies built into Windows Server allow you to optimize the performance and data storage requirements for files associated with VMs.

### DEDUPLICATION

In Windows Server 2019 and later, both ReFS and NTFS volumes support deduplication. *Deduplication* is a process by which duplicate instances of data are removed from a volume and replaced with pointers to the original instance. Deduplication is especially effective when used with volumes that host virtual hard disk files because many of these files contain duplicate copies of data, such as the VM's operating system and program files.

Once deduplication is installed, you can enable it through the Volumes node of the **File and Storage Services** section of the Server Manager console. When enabling deduplication, you specify whether you want to use a general file server data deduplication scheme or a virtual desktop infrastructure (VDI) scheme. For volumes that host VM files, the VDI scheme is appropriate. You can't enable deduplication on the operating system volume; deduplication may only be enabled on data volumes. For this reason, remember to store VM configuration files and hard disks on a volume that is separate from the operating system volume.

### STORAGE TIERING

Storage tiering is a technology that allows you to mix fast storage, such as solid-state disk (SSD), with traditional spinning magnetic disks to optimize both storage performance and capacity. Storage tiering works on the premise that a minority of the data stored on a volume is responsible for the majority of read and write operations. Storage tiering can be enabled through the storage spaces functionality, and rather than creating a large volume that consists entirely of SSDs, you create a volume consisting of both solid-state and spinning magnetic disks. In this configuration, frequently accessed data is moved to the parts of the volume hosted on the SSDs, and less frequently accessed data is moved to the parts of the volume hosted on the slower spinning magnetic disks. This configuration allows many of the performance benefits of an SSD-only volume to be realized without the cost of using SSD-only storage.

When used in conjunction with deduplication, frequently accessed deduplicated data is moved to the faster storage, providing reduced storage requirements, while improving performance over what would be possible if the volume hosting VM files were solely composed of spinning magnetic disks. You also have the option of pinning specific files to the faster storage, which overrides the algorithms that move data according to accumulated utilization statistics. You configure storage tiering using PowerShell.

## Storage migration

With storage migration, you can move a VM's virtual hard disk files, checkpoint files, smart paging files, and configuration files from one location to another. You can perform storage migration while the VM is either running or powered off. You can move data to any location that is accessible to the Hyper-V host. This allows you to move data from one volume to another, from one folder to another, or even to an SMB 3.0 file share on another computer. When performing storage migration, choose the **Move the VM's Storage** option.

For example, you could use storage migration to move VM files from one Cluster Share Volume to another on a Hyper-V failover cluster without interrupting the VM's operation. You have the option of moving all data to a single location, moving VM data to separate locations, or moving only the VM's virtual hard disk. To move the VM's data to different locations, select the items you want to move and the destination locations.

### Exporting, importing, and copying VMs

A VM export creates a duplicate of a VM that you can import on the same or a different Hyper-V virtualization host. When performing an export, you can choose to export the VM, which includes all its VM checkpoints, or you can choose to export just a single VM checkpoint. Windows Server 2012 R2 and later support exporting a running VM. With Hyper-V in Windows Server 2012, Windows Server 2008 R2, and Windows Server 2008, it is necessary to shut down the VM before performing an export.

Exporting a VM with all of its checkpoints will create multiple differencing disks. When you import a VM that was exported with checkpoints, these checkpoints will also be imported. If you import a VM that was running at the time of export, the VM is placed in a saved state. You can resume from this saved state, rather than having to restart the VM.

When importing a VM, you can choose from the following options:

- **Register The Virtual Machine In Place (Use The Existing ID)**  Use this option when you want to import the VM while keeping the VM files in their current locations. Because this method uses the existing VM ID, you can only use it if the original VM on which the export was created is not present on the host to which you wish to import the VM.

- **Restore The Virtual Machine (Use The Existing Unique ID)**  Use this option when you want to import the VM while moving the files to a new location; for example, you would choose this option if you are importing a VM that was exported to a network share. Because this method also uses the existing VM ID, you can only use it if the original VM on which the export was created is not present on the host to which you wish to import the VM.

- **Copy The Virtual Machine (Create A New Unique ID)**  Use this method if you want to create a separate clone of the exported VM. The exported files will be copied to a new location, leaving the original exported files unaltered. A new VM ID is created, meaning that the cloned VM can run concurrently on the same virtualization host as the original progenitor VM. When importing a cloned VM onto the same virtualization host as the original progenitor VM, ensure that you rename the newly imported VM; otherwise you may confuse the VMs.

## Configure Hyper-V network adapter

Generation 1 VMs support two types of network adapters: synthetic network adapters and legacy network adapters. A *synthetic network adapter* uses drivers that are provided when you install integration services in the VM operating system. If a VM operating system doesn't have these drivers or if integration services are not available for this operating system, then the network adapter will not function. Synthetic network adapters are unavailable until a VM operating system that supports them is running. This means that you can't perform a PXE boot from a synthetic network adapter if you have configured a Generation 1 VM.

*Legacy network adapters* emulate a physical network adapter, similar to a multiport DEC/Intel 21140 10/100TX 100 MB card. Many operating systems, including those that do not support virtual machine integration services, support this network adapter. This means that if you want to run an operating system in a VM that doesn't have virtual machine integration services support—such as a version of Linux or BSD that isn't officially supported for Hyper-V—you'll need to use a legacy network adapter because it is likely to be recognized by the guest VM operating system.

Legacy network adapters on Generation 1 VMs also function before the VM guest operating system is loaded. You could use a legacy network adapter to PXE boot a Generation 1 VM to deploy an operating system through WDS..

Generation 2 VMs don't separate synthetic and legacy network adapters and only have a single network adapter type. Generation 2 VMs support PXE booting from this single network adapter type. Generation 2 VMs also support "hot add" network adapters, allowing you to add or remove network adapters to or from a virtual machine while it is running. It is important to remember that only recent Windows client and server operating systems and only certain Linux operating systems are supported as Generation 2 VMs.

## Virtual machine MAC addresses

By default, VMs running on Hyper-V hosts use dynamic MAC addresses. Each time a VM is powered on, it will be assigned a MAC address from a MAC address pool. You can configure the properties of the MAC address pool through the **MAC Address Range** settings available through Virtual Switch Manager.

When you deploy operating systems on physical hardware, you can use two methods to ensure that the computer is always assigned the same IP address configuration. The first method is to assign a static IP address from within the virtualized operating system. The second is to configure a DHCP reservation that always assigns the same IP address configuration to the MAC address associated with the physical computer's network adapter.

This won't work with Hyper-V VMs in their default configuration because the MAC address may change if you power the VM off and then on. Rather than configure a static IP address using the VM's operating system, you can instead configure a static MAC address on a per-virtual network adapter basis. This will ensure that a VM's virtual network adapter retains the same MAC address whether the VM is restarted or even if the VM is migrated to another virtualization host.

To configure a static MAC address on a per-network adapter basis, edit the network adapter's advanced features. When entering a static MAC address, you will need to select a MAC address manually. You shouldn't use one from the existing MAC address pool because there is no way for the current virtualization hosts or other virtualization hosts on the same subnet to check whether a MAC address that is to be assigned dynamically has already been assigned statically.

## Network isolation

Hyper-V supports VLAN (virtual local area network) tagging at both the network adapter and the virtual switch levels. VLAN tags allow the isolation of traffic for hosts connected to the same network by creating separate broadcast domains. Enterprise hardware switches also support VLANs as a way of partitioning network traffic. To use VLANs with Hyper-V, the virtualization hosts' network adapter must support VLANs. A VLAN ID has 12 bits, which means you can configure 4,095 VLAN IDs.

You configure VLAN tags at the virtual network adapter level by selecting **Enable Virtual LAN Identification** in the Virtual Network Adapter Properties dialog box. VLAN tags applied at the virtual switch level override VLAN tags applied at the virtual network adapter level. To configure VLAN tags at the virtual switch level, select the **Enable Virtual LAN Identification For Management Operating System** option and specify the VLAN identifier.

## Optimizing network performance

You can optimize network performance for VMs hosted on Hyper-V in a number of ways. For example, you can configure the virtualization host with separate network adapters connected to separate subnets. You do this to separate network traffic related to the management of the Hyper-V virtualization host from network traffic associated with hosted VMs. You can also use NIC teaming on the Hyper-V virtualization host to provide increased and fault-tolerant network connectivity. You'll learn more about NIC teaming later in this chapter in the section "Configure NIC teaming."

### BANDWIDTH MANAGEMENT

An additional method of optimizing network performance is to configure *bandwidth management* at the virtual network adapter level. Bandwidth management allows you to specify a minimum and the maximum traffic throughput for a virtual network adapter. The minimum bandwidth allocation is an amount that Hyper-V will reserve for the network adapter. For example, if you set the minimum bandwidth allocation to 10 Mbps for each VM, Hyper-V would ensure that when other VMs needed more, they would be able to increase their bandwidth utilization until they reached a limit defined by the combined minimum bandwidth allocation of all VMs hosted on the server. Maximum bandwidth allocations specify an upper limit for bandwidth utilization. By default, no minimum or maximum limits are set on virtual network adapters.

You configure bandwidth management by selecting the **Enable Bandwidth Management** option on a virtual network adapter and specifying a minimum and maximum bandwidth allocation in megabits per seconds (Mbps).

### SR-IOV

SR-IOV (Single Root I/O Virtualization) increases network throughput by bypassing a virtual switch and sending network traffic straight to the VM. When you configure SR-IOV, the physical network adapter is mapped directly to the VM. As such, SR-IOV requires that the VM's operating system include a driver for the physical network adapter. You can only use SR-IOV if the physical network adapter and the network adapter drivers used with the virtualization host support the functionality. You can only configure SR-IOV for a virtual switch during switch creation. Once you have an SR-IOV enabled virtual switch, you can then enable SR-IOV on the virtual network adapter that connects to that switch.

### DYNAMIC VIRTUAL MACHINE QUEUE

Dynamic Virtual Machine Queue is an additional technology that you can use to optimize network performance. When a VM is connected through a virtual switch to a network adapter that supports Virtual Machine Queue and Virtual Machine Queue is enabled on the virtual network adapter's properties, the physical network adapter can use Direct Memory Access (DMA) to forward traffic directly to the VM. With Virtual Machine Queue, network traffic is processed by the CPU assigned to the VM rather than by the physical network adapter used by the Hyper-V virtualization host. Dynamic Virtual Machine Queue automatically adjusts the number of CPU cores used to process network traffic. Dynamic Virtual Machine Queue is automatically enabled on a virtual switch when you enable Virtual Machine Queue on the virtual network adapter.

## Configure NIC teaming

NIC teaming allows you to aggregate bandwidth across multiple network adapters while also providing a redundant network connection in the event that one of the adapters in the team fails. NIC teaming allows you to consolidate up to 32 network adapters and to use them as a single network interface. You can configure NIC teams using adapters that are from different manufacturers and that run at different speeds (though it's generally a good idea to use the same adapter make and model in production environments).

You can configure NIC teaming at the virtualization host level if the virtualization host has multiple network adapters. The drawback is that you can't configure NIC teaming at the host level if the network adapters are configured to use SR-IOV. If you want to use SR-IOV and NIC teaming, create the NIC team instead in the VM. You can configure NIC teaming within VMs by adding adapters to a new team using the Server Manager console or the New-NetLbfoTeam PowerShell cmdlet.

When configuring NIC teaming in a VM, ensure that each virtual network adapter that will participate in the team has MAC address spoofing enabled.

## Configure Hyper-V switch

Hyper-V virtual switches, called Hyper-V virtual networks in previous versions of Hyper-V, represent network connections to which the Hyper-V virtual network adapters can connect. You can configure three types of Hyper-V virtual switches: external switches, internal switches, and private switches.

## External switches

An external switch connects to a physical or wireless network adapter. Only one virtual switch can be mapped to a specific physical or wireless network adapter or NIC team. For example, if a virtualization host had four physical network adapters configured as two separate NIC teams, you could configure two external virtual switches. If a virtualization host had three physical network adapters that did not participate in any NIC teams, you could configure three external virtual switches. VMs connected to the same external switch can communicate with each other as well as external hosts connected to the network to which the network adapter mapped to the external switch is connected. For example, if an external switch is connected to a network adapter that is connected to a network that can route traffic to the internet, a VM connected to that external virtual switch will also be able to connect to hosts on the internet. When you create an external switch, a virtual network adapter that maps to this switch is created on the virtualization host unless you clear the option that allows the management operating system to share the network adapter. If you clear this option, the virtualization host will not be able to communicate through the network adapter associated with the external switch.

## Internal switches

An internal switch allows communication between the VM and the virtualization host. All VMs connected to the same internal switch are able to communicate with each other and the virtualization host. For example, you could successfully initiate an RDP connection from the virtualization host to an appropriately configured VM or use the `Test-NetConnection` Power-Shell cmdlet from a PowerShell prompt on the virtualization host to get a response from a VM connected to an internal network connection. VMs connected to an internal switch are unable to use that virtual switch to communicate with hosts on a separate virtualization host that are connected to an internal switch with the same name.

## Private switches

VMs connected to the same private switch on a VM host can communicate with one another, but they cannot communicate directly with the virtualization host. Private switches only allow communication between VMs on the same virtualization host. For example, say VM alpha and beta are connected to private switch p_switch_a on virtualization host h_v_one. VM gamma is connected to private switch p_switch_a on virtualization host h_v_ two. VMs alpha and beta will be able to communicate with each other, but they won't be able to communicate with h_v_one or VM gamma.

**EXAM TIP**

The `Validate-DCB` cmdlet allows you to verify that Switch Embedded Teaming (SET) and remote direct memory access (RDMA) are configured properly.

# Skill 3.2: Create and manage containers

A *container* is a portable isolated application execution environment. Containers allow developers to bundle an application and its dependencies in a single image. This image can easily be exported, imported, and deployed on different container hosts, from a developer's laptop computer, to Server Core on bare-metal hardware, and eventually to being hosted and run on Azure. Because an application's dependencies are bundled with the application within a container, IT operations can deploy a container as soon as it is handed off without worrying if an appropriate prerequisite software package has been installed or if a necessary setting has been configured. Because a container provides an isolated environment, a failure that occurs within one container will only impact that container and will not impact other containerized applications running on the container host.

> **This skill covers how to:**
> - Understand container concepts
> - Manage Windows Server container images
> - Manage container instances
> - Configure container networking
> - Create Windows Server container images

## Understand container concepts

Containers can be conceptually challenging. To understand how containers work, you first need to understand some of the terminology involving containers. While some of these concepts will be fleshed out more completely later in this chapter, you should understand the following terms at a high level:

- **Container images**  A container image is a template from which a container is generated. There are two general types of container images, which are usually created for a workload: a base OS image and a specific image. The difference between these containers on Windows Server is as follows:

  - **Container base OS image**  This is an image of the operating system on which other container images are built.

  - **Container image**  A container image stores changes made to a running container base OS image or another container image. For example, you can start a new container from a container base OS image, make modifications such as installing Java or a Windows feature, and then save those modifications as a new container image. The new container image only stores the changes you make, and therefore, it is much smaller than the parent container base OS image. You can then create an additional container image that stores modifications made to the container image that has an installed Java and Windows feature. Each container image only stores the changes made to the image from which it was run.

- **Container instance**   When you run a container, a copy of the container image you are starting is created and runs on the container host. You can make changes to the container instance but they won't be written back to the original container image. Container instances can be thought of as a disposable temporary version of the container. If problems occur with a container instance, you just end that instance and create a new instance to replace it. You can create many instances of a container to run in parallel with each other. The orchestration of large fleets of containers can be accomplished using technologies such as Kubernetes, which is beyond the scope of the AZ-800 exam.

- **Sandbox**   The sandbox is the environment in which you can make modifications to an existing container image before you commit the changes to create a new container image. If you don't commit those changes to a new image, those changes will be lost when the container is removed.

- **Image dependency**   A new container image has the container image from which it was created as a dependency. For example, you can create a container image named WebServer-1.0 that has the IIS role installed from the Server Core base OS image and the Server Core base OS image is a dependency for the WebServer-1.0 image. This dependency is very specific, and you can't use an updated version of the Server Core base OS image as a replacement for the version that you used when creating the WebServer-1.0 image. You can then export this container image that only records the changes made to another container host. You can start the image as long as the dependency container OS base image is present on that container host. You can have multiple images in a dependency chain.

- **Container host**   A container host is a computer that runs containers. A container host can be virtual, physical, or even a cloud-based platform as a service (PaaS) solution.

- **Container registries**   Container registries are central storehouses of container images. Though it's possible to transfer containers or copy them to file shares using tools like FTP, common practice is to use a container registry as a repository for container images. Public container registries, such as the one that hosts the base OS images for Microsoft, also store previous versions of the container base OS images. This allows you to retrieve earlier versions of the container base OS image that other images may depend on. Container registries can be public or private. When working with your own organization's container images, you have the option of creating and maintaining a private container registry.

Windows Server supports two container isolation modes: process isolation mode and Hyper-V isolation mode. In previous versions of Microsoft documentation, these isolation modes were occasionally called "Windows Server containers" and "Hyper-V containers." Windows 10 and Windows 11 support only Hyper-V isolation mode. Windows Server 2016 and later support process isolation and Hyper-V isolation modes.

## Process isolation

Process isolation mode provides a container with process and namespace isolation. Containers running in this isolation mode share a kernel with all other containers running on the container host. This is similar to the manner in which containers run on Linux container hosts. Process isolation is the default mode used when running a container. If you want to ensure that the container is being used, start the container using the `--isolation=process` option.

## Hyper-V isolation

A container running in Hyper-V isolation mode runs in a highly optimized virtual machine that also provides an isolated application execution environment. Hyper-V isolation mode containers don't share the kernel with the container host, nor do they share the kernel with other containers on the same container host. You can only use Hyper-V isolation mode containers if you have enabled the Hyper-V role on the container host. If the container host is a Hyper-V virtual machine, you must enable nested virtualization. By default, a container uses the process isolation mode. You can start a container in Hyper-V isolation mode by using the `--isolation=hyperv` option.

For example, to create a Hyper-V container from the *microsoft/windowsservercore* image, issue this command:

```
Docker run -it --isolation=hyperv mcr.microsoft.com/windows/servercore cmd
```

## Installing and configuring Docker

Containers on Windows Server are managed using the Docker engine. The advantage here is that the command syntax of Docker on Windows is almost identical to the command-line tools in Docker on Linux. Although there is a community-maintained PowerShell module for managing containers on Windows Server available on GitHub, PowerShell is not the primary tool for Windows Server container management, and very few people use PowerShell to manage containers.

For Windows Server administrators unfamiliar with Docker syntax, the commands include extensive help support. Typing **Docker** at the command prompt will provide an overview of the high-level Docker functionality. You can learn more about specific commands by using the `--help` command parameter. For example, the following command will provide information about the Docker Image command:

```
docker image --help
```

### INSTALLING DOCKER

Docker is not included with the Windows Server installation media, and you don't install it as a role or feature. Instead, you have to install Docker from the PowerShell Gallery. Although this is unusual for an important role on a Windows Server operating system, it does have the advantage of ensuring that you have the latest version of Docker.

The simplest way to install Docker is to first ensure that your Windows Server computer has internet connectivity. You then run the following command from an elevated PowerShell prompt:

```
Install-Module -Name DockerMsftProvider -Repository PSGallery -Force
```

Next, install the most recent version of Docker by executing the following command, ensuring that you answer Yes when prompted to install software from a source not marked as trusted:

```
Install-Package -Name docker -ProviderName DockerMsftProvider
```

You'll then need to restart the computer that will function as the container host to complete the installation of Docker. You can update the version of Docker when a new one becomes available by rerunning the following command:

```
Install-Package -Name docker -ProviderName DockerMsftProvider
```

### DAEMON.JSON

If you want to change the default Docker Engine settings, such as whether to create a default NAT network, you need to create and configure the Docker Engine configuration file. This file doesn't exist by default. When it is present, the settings in the file override the Docker Engine's default settings.

You should create this file in the c:\ProgramData\Docker\config folder. Before editing the daemon.json file, stop the Docker service using the following command:

```
Stop-Service docker
```

You only need to add settings that you want to change to the configuration file. For example, if you only want to configure the Docker Engine to accept incoming connections on port 2701, you add the following lines to daemon.json:

```
{
    "hosts": ["tcp://0.0.0.0:2701"]
}
```

The Windows Docker Engine doesn't support all possible Docker configuration file options. The ones that you can configure are shown here:

```
{
    "authorization-plugins": [],
    "dns": [],
    "dns-opts": [],
    "dns-search": [],
    "exec-opts": [],
    "storage-driver": "",
    "storage-opts": [],
    "labels": [],
    "log-driver": "",
    "mtu": 0,
    "pidfile": "",
```

```
    "cluster-store": "",
    "cluster-advertise": "",
    "debug": true,
    "hosts": [],
    "log-level": "",
    "tlsverify": true,
    "tlscacert": "",
    "tlscert": "",
    "tlskey": "",
    "group": "",
    "default-ulimits": {},
    "bridge": "",
    "fixed-cidr": "",
    "raw-logs": false,
    "registry-mirrors": [],
    "insecure-registries": [],
    "disable-legacy-registry": false
}
```

These options allow you to do the following when starting the Docker Engine:

- **authorization-plugins** Specify the authorization plug-ins the Docker Engine should load
- **dns** Specify the DNS server the containers should use for name resolution
- **dns-opts** Specify the DNS options you want to use
- **dns-search** Specify the DNS search domains you want to use
- **exec-opts** Specify runtime execution options
- **storage-driver** Specify the storage driver
- **storage-opts** Specify the storage driver options
- **labels** Specify Docker Engine labels
- **log-driver** Specify the default driver for the container logs
- **mtu** Specify the container network MTU
- **pidfile** Specify the path to use for the daemon PID file
- **group** Specify the local security group that has permissions to run Docker commands
- **cluster-store** Specify cluster store options
- **cluster-advertise** Specify the cluster address you want to advertise
- **debug** Enable debug mode
- **hosts** Specify daemon sockets you want to connect to
- **log-level** Specify level of logging detail
- **tlsverify** Use TLS and perform verification
- **tlscacert** Specify which certificate authorities to trust
- **tlscert** Specify the location of the TLS certificate file
- **tlskey** Specify the location of the TLS key file
- **group** Specify the UNIX socket group

- **default-ulimits**   Specify default ulimits for containers

- **bridge**   Attach containers to network bridge

- **fixed-cidr**   IPv4 subnet for static IP address

- **raw-logs**   Specify the log format you want to use

- **registry-mirrors**   Specify the preferred registry mirror

- **insecure-registries**   Allow insecure registry communication

- **disable-legacy-registry**   Block contacting legacy registries

Once you have made the necessary modifications to the daemon.json file, you should start the Docker service by running this PowerShell command:

```
Start-Service docker
```

## Manage Windows Server container images

Container registries are repositories for the distribution of container images. From the Microsoft Container registry, you can retrieve the following Microsoft published container images:

- **Windows Server Core**   This is the base image for the Windows Server Core container operating system. This image supports traditional .NET Framework applications. You can retrieve this image using the following Docker command:

  ```
  docker pull mcr.microsoft.com/windows/servercore:ltsc2022
  ```

- **Nanoserver**   This is the base image for the Nano Server container operating system. This is a Windows Server image with all unnecessary elements stripped out. It is suitable for hosting .NET Core applications. The Nano Server container image is what became of the Nano Server installation option that was available with the RTM version of Windows Server 2016. Because the image is stripped down to the essentials, it is far smaller than the Windows Server Core image and can be deployed and run more quickly. You can retrieve this image using the following Docker command:

  ```
  docker pull mcr.microsoft.com/windows/nanoserver:ltsc2022
  ```

- **Windows**   This is an image that provides the full Windows API set but doesn't include all the server roles and features that are available in the Server Core image. You should only use this option if the application you are trying to host has a dependency that is not included in the Windows Server Core container image. Use this image with Windows Server 2016 and Windows Server 2019 container hosts, but not with Windows Server 2022 container hosts if you are using process isolation. You can run this image on Windows Server 2022 hosts if you're using Hyper-V isolation. You can retrieve this image using the following Docker command:

  ```
  docker pull mcr.microsoft.com/windows:20H2
  ```

- **Windows Server**   This is an image that provides the full Windows API set but doesn't include all the server roles and features that are available in the Server Core image. You should only use this option if the application you are trying to host has a dependency that is not included in the Windows Server Core container image. This version of the container image only works on Windows Server 2022 container hosts. You can retrieve this image using the following Docker command:

```
docker pull mcr.microsoft.com/windows/server:ltsc2022
```

In cases where multiple images exist, such as Windows Server Core and Nano Server, you can use the -a option with the Docker pull command to retrieve all images. This can be helpful if you don't know the image ID of the specific image that you wish to retrieve.

When you pull an image from a registry, the action will also download any dependency images that are required. For example, if you pull an image that was built on a specific version of the Windows Server Core base image and you don't have that image on the container host, that image will also be downloaded from a container registry.

You can view a list of images that are installed on a Windows Server container host by using the following command:

```
docker image list
```

You can use Windows Admin Center to view a list of container images that are installed on a Windows Server container host. The Windows Admin Center also allows you to delete images that are installed on a Windows Server container host.

## Service accounts for Windows containers

Although containers based on the Server Core and Nano Server operating systems have most of the same characteristics as a virtual machine or a bare-metal deployment of the Server Core or Nano Server versions of Windows Server, one thing that you can't do with containers is to join them to a domain. This is because containers are supposed to be temporary, rather than permanent, and domain-joining them would clog up Active Directory with unnecessary computer accounts.

While containers can't be domain-joined, it is possible to use a group-managed service account (gMSA) to provide one or more containers with a domain identity similar to that used by a device that is realm-joined. Performing this task requires downloading the Windows Server Container Tools and ensuring that the container host is a member of the domain that hosts the gMSA. When you perform this procedure, the container's LocalSystem and Network Service accounts use the gMSA. This gives the container the identity represented by the gMSA.

To configure gMSA association with a container, perform the following steps:

1. Ensure that the Windows Server container host is domain-joined.
2. Add the container host to a specially created domain security group. This domain security group can have any name.
3. Create a gMSA and grant gMSA permission to the specially created domain security group of which the container host is a member.
4. Install the gMSA on the container host.

5. Use the `New-CredentialSpec` cmdlet on the container host to generate the gMSA credentials in a file in JSON format. This cmdlet is located in the CredentialSpec PowerShell module, which is available as a part of the Windows Server Container Tools. For example, if you created a gMSA named MelbourneAlpha, you would run the following command:

```
New-CredentialSpace -Name MelbourneAlpha -AccountName MelbourneAlpha
```

6. You can verify that the credentials have been saved in JSON format by running the `Get-CredentialSpec` cmdlet. By default, credentials are stored in the c:\ProgramData\ Docker\CredentialSpecs\ folder.

7. Start the container using the option `--security-opt "credentialspec="` and specify the JSON file containing the credentials associated with the gMSA. For example, run the following command if the credentials are stored in the file twt_webapp01.json:

```
docker run --security-opt "credentialspec=file://twt_webapp01.json" --hostname
webapp01 -it

mcr.microsoft.com/windows/servercore:ltsc2019 powershell
```

Once you've configured the container to indirectly use the gMSA for its Local System and Network Service accounts, you can give the container permission to access domain resources by providing access to the gMSA. For example, if you want to provide the container with access to the contents of a file share hosted on a domain member, you can configure permissions so that the gMSA has access to the file share.

## Updating images

One of the concepts that many IT operations personnel find challenging is that you don't update a container that is deployed in production. Instead, you create a fresh container from the original container image, update that container, and then save that updated container as a new container image. You then remove the container in production and deploy a new container to production that is based on the newly updated image.

For example, suppose you have a container that hosts a web app deployed from a container image named WebApp1 that is deployed in production. The developers in your organization release an update to WebApp1 that involves changing some existing settings. Rather than modifying the container in production, you start another container from the WebApp1 image, modify the settings, and then create a new container image named WebApp2. You then deploy a new container into production from the WebApp2 container image and remove the original container (that hasn't been updated).

Although you can manually update your container base OS images by applying software updates, Microsoft releases updated versions of the container base images each time a new software update is released. After a new container OS base image is released, you or your organization's developers should update existing images that are dependent on the container OS base image. Regularly updated container base OS images provide an excellent reason for eventually moving toward using Dockerfiles to automate the process of building containers. If you have a Dockerfile configured for each container image used in your organization, updating your container base OS images when a new container base OS image is released is a quick, painless, and automated process.

## Managing container images

To save a Docker image for transfer to another computer, use the docker save command. When you save a Docker image, you save it in TAR format. For example, to export the container image tailwind_app to the c:\archive folder, issue this command:

```
docker save tailwind_app -o c:\archive\tailwind_app.tar
```

You can load a Docker image from a saved image using the docker load command. For example, to load the container image from the c:\archive\tailwind_app.tar file created earlier, use this command:

```
docker load < c:\archive\tailwind_app.tar
```

When you have multiple container images that have the same name, you can remove an image by using the image ID. You can determine the image ID by running the command docker images. You can also use Windows Admin Center to view this information. You can't remove a container image until the last container instance created from that image either directly or indirectly has been deleted.

You then remove the image by using the command docker rmi with the image ID. For example, to remove the container image with the ID a896e5590871, use this command:

```
docker rmi a896e5590871
```

You can also remove a container image by selecting the image in the list of containers in Windows Admin Center and selecting Delete.

While you can transfer container images between hosts by exporting and importing them as TAR files, the usual way to distribute container images is to use a container registry. A *container registry* is a service that allows you to store and distribute container images. Public registries are available for anyone to interact with, and private registries allow you to limit access to authorized individuals.

Before uploading (also termed *pushing*) an image to a registry, it's necessary to tag the container image with the fully qualified name of the registry login server. For example, to tag the image tailwind-app when you are using the Azure Container Registry instance twt-registry.azurecr.io, run the command

```
docker tag tailwind-app twt-registry.azurecr.io/tailwind-app
```

You upload a container image to a container registry using the docker push command. For example, to upload a container image named tailwind-app to registry twt-registry.azurecr.io, use the command

```
docker push twt-registry.azurecr.io /tailwind-app
```

# Manage container instances

Container instances are separate copies of the container image that have their own existence. Although the analogy is far from perfect, each container instance is like a separate virtual machine, with its own IP address and ability to interact with other hosts on the network.

## Starting a container

You create a new container instance by using the `docker run` command and specifying the container image that will form the basis of the container. You can start a container instance by selecting a container image that is present locally or by specifying a container image that is stored in a registry. For example, to start a container from the Microsoft/windowsserver core image stored in the Microsoft container image registry, run this command:

```
docker run mcr.microsoft.com/windows/servercore:ltsc2022
```

You can start a container and run an interactive session either by specifying `cmd.exe` or `PowerShell.exe` by using the `-it` option with `docker run`. Interactive sessions allow you to directly interact with the container through the command line from the moment the container starts. Detached mode starts a container, but it doesn't start an interactive session with that container.

For example, to start a container from the Microsoft/windowsservercore image and to enter an interactive PowerShell session within that container once it's started, use this command:

```
docker run -it mcr.microsoft.com/windows/servercore:ltsc2022 powershell.exe
```

If you want to start an interactive session on a container that you started in detached mode, use the command `docker exec -i <containername> powershell.exe`.

By default, containers use network address translation. This means that if you are running an application or service on the container that you want to expose to the network, you'll need to configure port mapping between the container host's network interface and the container. For example, if you wanted to start a container in detached mode, mapping port 8080 on the container host to port 80 on the container, you would run the following command:

```
docker run -d -p 8080:80 mcr.microsoft.com/windows/servercore:ltsc2022
```

You can verify which containers are running by using the `docker ps` command or by using Windows Admin Center. The problem with the simple `docker ps` command option is that this will only show you the running containers and won't show you any that are in a stopped state. You can see which containers are on a container host, including containers that aren't currently running, by using the `docker ps -a` command. If you have loaded the Containers extension into Windows Admin Center, you can also view the containers that are on a Windows Server container host using Windows Admin Center. In some cases, it will be necessary to start a stopped container. You can start a stopped container using the `docker start <container-name>` command.

One thing that you'll notice about containers is that they appear to be assigned random names, such as sarcastic_hedgehog, fraggle_advocate, dyspeptic_hamster, and sententious_muppet. Docker assigns random names rather than asking you for one because containers are a more ephemeral type of application host than a VM; because they are likely to only have a short life span, it isn't worth assigning any name to them that you'd need to remember. The reason for the structure of the random names is that they are easy to remember in the short term, which makes containers that you must interact with on a short-term basis easier to address than when using hexadecimal container IDs.

### Modifying a running container

After you have a container running, you can enter the container and make the modifications that you want to make to ensure that the application the container hosts will run correctly. This might involve creating directories, using the dism.exe command to add roles, or using the wget PowerShell alias to download and install binaries such as Java. For example, the following code, when run from inside a container, downloads and installs an older version of Java into a container based on the Server Core base OS container:

```
wget -Uri "http://javadl.sun.com/webapps/download/AutoDL?BundleId=107944" -outfile
javaInstall.exe -UseBasicParsing
REG ADD HKLM\Software\Policies\Microsoft\Windows\Installer /v DisableRollback /t REG_
DWORD /d 1 | Out-Null ./javaInstall.exe /s INSTALLDIR=C:\Java REBOOT=Disable | Out-Null
```

Once you are finished modifying the container, you can type **Exit** to exit the container. A container must be in a shutdown state before you can capture it as a container image. You use the docker stop <containername> cmdlet to shut down a container.

## Configure container networking

Each container has a virtual network adapter. This virtual network adapter connects to a virtual switch, through which inbound and outbound traffic is sent. Networking modes determine how network adapters function in terms of IP addressing, meaning whether they use NAT or are connected to the same network as the container host.

Windows containers support the following networking modes:

- **NAT**  Each container is assigned an IP address from the private 172.16.0.0 /12 address range. When using NAT, you can configure port forwarding from the container host to the container endpoint. If you create a container without specifying a network, the container will use the default NAT network. The Docker service creates its own default NAT network. When the container host reboots, the NAT network will not be created until the Docker service has restarted. Any container that was attached to the existing NAT network and that is configured to persist after reboot (for example, because it uses the –restart always option) will reattach to the NAT network that is newly created when the Docker service restarts.

- **Transparent** Each container endpoint connects to the physical network. The containers can have IP addresses assigned statically or through DHCP.
- **Overlay** Use this mode when you have configured the Docker engine to run in swarm mode. Overlay mode allows container endpoints to be connected across multiple container hosts.
- **L2 Bridge** Container endpoints are on the same IP subnet used by the container host. IP addresses must be assigned statically. All containers on the container host have the same MAC address.
- **L2 Tunnel** This mode is only used when you deploy containers in Azure.

You can list available networks using the `docker network ls` command. You can also use the Networks blade of the Windows Admin Center to view available container networks. You can create multiple container networks on a container host, but you need to keep in mind the following limitations:

- If you are creating multiple networks of the transparent or L2 bridge type, you need to ensure that each network has a separate network adapter.
- If you create multiple NAT networks on a container host, additional NAT networks prefixes will be partitioned from the container host's NAT network's address space. (By default, this is 172.16.0.0/12.) For example, these will be 172.16.1.0/24, 172.16.2.0/24, and so on.

## NAT

Network address translation (NAT) allows each container to be assigned an address in a private address space, whereas connecting to the container host's network uses the container host's IP address. The default NAT address range for containers is 172.16.0.0 /16. In the event that the container host's IP address is in the 172.16.0.0 /12 range, you will need to alter the NAT IP prefix.

You can also allow connections to custom NAT networks when a container is run by allowing use of the `--network` parameter and specifying the custom NAT network name. To do so, you need to have the `bridge: none` option specified in the daemon.json file. The command to run a container and join it to the CustomNat network created earlier is:

```
docker run -it --network=CustomNat <ContainerImage> <cmd>
```

Port mappings allow ports on the container host to be mapped to ports on the container. For example, to map port 8080 on the container host to port 80 on a new container created from the windowsservercore image and to run `powershell.exe` interactively on the container, create the container using the following command:

```
docker run -it -p 8080:80 microsoft/windowsservercore powershell.exe
```

Port mappings must be specified when the container is created or when it is in a stopped state. You can specify them using the -p parameter or the EXPOSE command in a Dockerfile when using the -P parameter. If you do not specify a port on the container host but you do specify one on the container itself, a random port will be assigned. For example, run this command:

```
docker run -itd -p 80 mcr.microsoft.com/windows/servercore/windowsservercore: ltsc2022
powershell.exe
```

A random port on the container host can be mapped to port 80 on the container. You can determine which port is randomly assigned by using the docker ps command. When you configure port mapping, firewall rules on the container host will be created automatically that will allow traffic through.

## Transparent

Transparent networks allow each container endpoint to connect to the same network as the container host. You can use the transparent networking mode by creating a container network that has the driver name transparent. The driver name is specified with the -d option, as shown in this command:

```
docker network create -d transparent TransparentNetworkName
```

If the container host is a virtual machine running on a Hyper-V host and you want to use DHCP for IP address assignment, it's necessary to enable MACAddressSpoofing on the VM network adapter. The transparent networking mode supports IPv6. If you are using transparent network mode, you can use a DHCPv6 server to assign IPv6 addresses to containers.

If you want to manually assign IP addresses to containers, when you create the transparent network you must specify the subnet and gateway parameters. These network properties must match the network settings of the network to which the container host is connected.

For example, if your container host is connected to a network that uses the 192.168.30.0/24 network and uses 192.168.30.1 as the default gateway, you would create a transparent network that will allow static address assignment for containers on the network called TransNet by running this command:

```
docker network create -d transparent --subnet=192.168.30.0/24 --gateway=192.168.30.1
TransNet
```

Once the transparent network is created with the appropriate settings, you can specify an IP address for a container by using the --ip option. For example, to start a new container from the microsoft/windowsservercore image, enter the command prompt within the container. To assign it the IP address 192.168.30.101 on the TransNet network, run this command:

```
docker run -it --network:TransNet --ip 192.168.30.101 microsoft/windowsservercore cmd.
exe
```

As when you use transparent network, containers are connected directly to the container host's network; you don't need to configure port mapping into the container.

## Layer 2 Bridge

Layer 2 Bridge (L2 Bridge) networks are similar to transparent networks in that they allow containers to have IP addresses on the same subnets as the container host. They differ in that IP addresses must be assigned statically. This is because all containers on the container host that use an L2 Bridge network have the same MAC address.

When creating an L2 Bridge network, you must specify the network type as **l2bridge**. You must also specify subnet and default gateway settings that match the subnet and default gateway settings of the container host. For example, to create an L2 Bridge network named L2BridgeNet for the IP address range 192.168.88.0/24 and with the default gateway address 192.168.88.1, use the following command:

```
docker network create -d l2bridge –subnet=192.168.88.0/24 --gateway=192.168.88.1
L2BridgeNet
```

# Create Windows Server container images

The key to creating new container images is configuring a running container instance in a desired way and then capturing that instance as a new image. There are a variety of methods you can use to do this, from performing manual configuration tasks interactively within the container instance to automating the build of container instances that are then captured as images.

## Creating a new image from a container

Once the container is in the desired state and shut down, you can capture the container to a new container image. You do this using the docker commit <container_name> <new_image_name> command. For example, to commit the container image elegant_wombat to the image name tailwind_app, run this command:

```
docker commit elegant_wombat tailwind_app
```

After you have committed a container to a container image, you can remove the container using the docker rm command. For example, to remove the elegant_wombat container, issue this command:

```
docker rm elegant_wombat
```

## Using Dockerfiles

Dockerfiles are text files that allow you to automate the process of creating new container images. You use a Dockerfile with the docker build command to automate container creation, which is very useful when you need to create new container images from regularly updated base OS container images.

Dockerfiles have the elements shown in Table 3-1.

**TABLE 3-1** Dockerfile element

| Instruction | Description |
| --- | --- |
| FROM | Specifies the container image used in creating the new image creation. For example:<br><br>`FROM mcr.microsoftcom/windows/servercore:ltsc2022` |
| RUN | Specifies commands to be run and captures them into the new container image.For example:<br><br>`RUN wget -Uri "http://javadl.sun.com/webapps/download/AutoDL?BundleId=107944" -outfile javaInstall.exe -UseBasicParsing`<br><br>`RUN REG ADD HKLM\Software\Policies\Microsoft\Windows\Installer /v DisableRollback /t REG_DWORD /d 1 | Out-Null`<br><br>`RUN ./javaInstall.exe /s INSTALLDIR=C:\Java REBOOT=Disable | Out-Null` |
| COPY | Copies files and directories from the container host filesystem to the filesystem of the container. For Windows containers, the destination format must use forward slashes. For example:<br><br>`COPY example1.txt c:/temp/` |
| ADD | Can be used to add files from a remote source, such as a URL. For example:<br><br>`ADD https://www.python.org/ftp/python/3.9.9/python-3.9.9.exe /temp/python-9.9.9.exe` |
| WORKDIR | Specifies a working directory for the RUN and CMD instructions. |
| CMD | A command to be run when deploying an instance of the container image. |

For example, the following Dockerfile will create a new container from the mcr.microsoft.com/windows/servercore:ltsc2022 image, create a directory named ExampleDirectory, and then install the iis-webserver feature:

```
FROM mcr.microsoftcom/windows/servercore:ltsc2022
RUN mkdir ExampleDirectory
RUN dism.exe /online /enable-feature /all /featurename:iis-webserver /NoRestart
```

To create a container image named example_image, change into the directory that hosts the Dockerfile (no extension) file, and run the following command:

```
docker build -t example_image .
```

 **EXAM TIP**

If you need to create a container image for an application that requires .NET Core, you should choose the Nano Server base image.

# Skill 3.3: Manage Azure Virtual Machines that run Windows Server

This objective deals with managing and configuring Windows Server VMs that run in Azure. In hybrid environments, many organizations treat Azure IaaS VMs in the same manner they would Windows Server instances that are hosted in a traditional remote third-party datacenter. In this section you learn what you need to know about managing Windows Server IaaS VMs in Azure.

> **This skill covers how to:**
> - Administer IaaS VMs
> - Manage data disks
> - Resize Azure VMs
> - Configure continuous delivery for an Azure VM
> - Configure connections to VMs
> - Manage Azure VM network configuration

## Administer IaaS VMs

In your on-premises environment, you would not allow most users of a VM to have access to a VM in Hyper-V Manager and would only allow them to connect directly to the VM using RDP or PowerShell. You should do the same thing in Azure since most people who use IaaS VMs in Azure don't need to interact with them through the Azure console.

Azure IaaS VMs are only visible to users in the Azure portal if they have a role that grants them that right. The default Azure IaaS VM role-based access control (RBAC) roles are as follows:

- **Virtual Machine Contributor**    Users who hold this role can manage virtual machines through the Azure console and perform operations such as restarting and deleting the virtual machine. Membership in this role does not provide the user with access to the VM itself. It also does not provide access to the virtual network or storage account to which the VM is connected.

- **Virtual Machine Administrator Login**    If the VM is configured to allow login using Azure AD accounts, assigning this role grants the user local administrator privileges in the virtual machine. Users who hold this role can view the details of a VM in the portal but cannot change the VM's properties.

- **Virtual Machine User Login**    Users who hold this role are able to view the details of a virtual machine in the Azure portal and can log in using their Azure AD account with user permissions. Users who hold this role cannot change the VM's properties.

Users who aren't members of the Virtual Machine Administrator Login or Virtual Machine User Login roles can still access IaaS VMs if they have a local account on the virtual machine. Put another way, just because you can't see it in the portal doesn't mean you can't RDP to it if you have the IaaS VM's network address and the correct ports are open.

## Manage data disks

Most Azure IaaS VM sizes deploy automatically with an operating system disk and a temporary disk. On Windows Server VMs the operating system disk will be assigned as volume C and the temporary disk will be assigned volume D. You can also add separate data disks to VMs, with the number and type of data disks available dependent on which VM size or SKU you select.

Although data stored on the temporary disk should persist when you perform a simple restart operation on an IaaS VM, data on the temporary disk may be lost during Azure maintenance events or when an IaaS VM is redeployed in a new size. You should assume that the data on a temporary disk may disappear, so make sure you don't use the disk to store anything important that you may need in the future. By default, temporary disks are not encrypted.

You can perform the following actions with a data disk:

- **Attach data disks**  Data disks can be attached to an IaaS VM while the IaaS VM is running. If you have created a new data disk and attached it to a Windows Server IaaS VM, you'll need to initialize and then format the disk before you can start to use it.
- **Detach data disks**  You can detach data disks from an IaaS VM while the IaaS VM is running. Before performing this operation, you should take the disk offline using the Disk Management console, Windows Admin Center, the diskpart.exe command-line utility, or the Set-Disk PowerShell cmdlet.

You can't change the size of a virtual machine data disk attached to a running or shutdown (but not deallocated) IaaS VM. If you want to change the size of a data disk, you need to first detach it. If you don't want to detach the disk, you should stop and deallocate the IaaS VM and then perform the resize operation.

### Shared disks

Shared disks are a managed disk functionality that you can use to attach a single Azure managed disk to multiple IaaS VMs simultaneously. Shared disks allow you to create guest clusters from Azure IaaS VMs where the shared disk functions as shared storage. The functionality of Azure shared managed disks is conceptually similar to the functionality of shared virtual hard disks used with guest clusters on Hyper-V. Only ultra disks, premium SSDs, and standard SSDs can be configured as shared disks for IaaS VMs.

### Disk images and snapshots

Managed disks support images and snapshots. An image of an IaaS VM can be created from a generalized IaaS VM (on Windows Server you would use sysprep.exe to perform the generalization operation) only when that IaaS VM has been deallocated. IaaS VM images include all disks attached to the IaaS VM and can be used to create new IaaS VMs.

Snapshots are point-in-time copies of an IaaS VM virtual hard disk. Snapshots can be used as a point-in-time backup or as a copy of the virtual machine for troubleshooting scenarios. Snapshots can be created of OS and data disks. You should only take snapshots of shutdown IaaS VMs to ensure that data is consistent across the disk since managed disk snapshots do not use Volume Shadow Copy services to ensure point-in-time consistency. Unlike disk images, the IaaS VM does not need to be deallocated for you to take a snapshot. Snapshots exist only at a per-disk level, which means that you shouldn't use them in any situation where data is striped across multiple disks. You can create snapshots of an operating system disk and create a new IaaS VM from that snapshot.

### IaaS VM encryption

Beyond storage service encryption, you can configure BitLocker disk encryption for Windows Server IaaS VMs. To support IaaS VM disk encryption, the Windows Server IaaS VM must be able to do the following. (By default, IaaS VMs do meet these conditions unless you remove the default network security group rules.)

- The server must be able to connect to the key vault endpoint so that the Windows Server IaaS VM can store and retrieve encryption keys.
- The server must be able to connect to an Azure Active Directory endpoint at *login.microsoftonline.com* so that it can retrieve a token that allows it to connect to the key vault that holds the encryption keys.
- The server must be able to connect to an Azure storage endpoint that hosts the Azure extension repository and the Azure storage account that stores the VM's virtual hard disks.
- If the Windows Server IaaS VM is domain-joined, do not configure BitLocker-related Group Policies other than the Configure User Storage Of BitLocker Recovery Information: Allow 256-Bit Recovery Key policy. This policy is usually configured automatically during the encryption process, and the encryption process will fail if a Group Policy conflict in any TPM- or BitLocker-related policies exists.

## Resize Azure VM

Azure allows you to resize an IaaS VM. Resizing an IaaS VM allows you to change the IaaS VM's processor and memory allocation. Resizing an IaaS VM might also alter the number of disks that can be associated with an IaaS VM; cheaper SKUs will be limited to less storage, and in some cases, they will be limited to standard rather than premium storage types. If the Azure IaaS VM is running, the only drawback is that the IaaS VM will need to restart for the resize to occur.

To resize an Azure IaaS VM, perform the following steps:

1. Open the VM's page in the Azure portal under Virtual Machines.
2. In the left menu under Settings, select Size.
3. Select the new size that you wish to apply to the IaaS VM.
4. Click Resize.

The virtual machine will then restart, and the new size will apply.

> **NEED MORE REVIEW?**  **RESIZE AZURE VM**
>
> You can learn more about resizing an Azure VM at *https://docs.microsoft.com/azure/virtual-machines/windows/resize-vm*.

## Configure continuous delivery for an Azure VM

The most common method of configuring continuous delivery for Windows Server IaaS VMs is to use ARM templates with specific IaaS VM configurations stored in Git repositories. When you deploy a new IaaS VM using the Azure portal, you can choose to create an ARM template with the deployment options that you can use later. There also exist many sample Azure IaaS Windows Server IaaS VM configurations that you can deploy or modify at *https://azure.microsoft.com/resources/templates*.

> **NEED MORE REVIEW?**  **CONTINUOUS DELIVERY FOR AZURE VMS**
>
> You can learn more about continuous delivery for Azure VMs at *https://docs.microsoft.com/azure/architecture/solution-ideas/articles/cicd-for-azure-vms*.

## Configure connections to VMs

Once an IaaS VM is deployed, you need to consider how to allow administrative connections to the IaaS VM. You'll need to ensure that any network security groups and firewalls between your administrative host and the target IaaS VM are configured to allow the appropriate administrative traffic, though tools such as Just-in-Time VM access and Azure Bastion can automate that process. As a general rule, you shouldn't open the Remote Desktop port (TCP port 3389) or a remote PowerShell port (HTTP port 5985, HTTPS port 5986) so that any host from any IP address on the internet has access. If you must open these ports on a network security group applied at the IaaS VM's network adapter level, try to limit the scope of any rule to the specific public IP address or subnet that you will be initiating the connection from.

### Connecting with an Azure AD Account

When you deploy an IaaS VM, you usually configure a username and password for a local Administrator account. If the computer is standalone and not AD DS or Azure AD DS joined, you have to decide whether you want to limit access to the accounts that are present that you have configured on the IaaS VM itself or if you also want to allow local sign-on using Azure AD accounts.

Sign-on using Azure AD is supported for IaaS VMs running Windows Server 2019 and Windows Server 2022. The IaaS VMs need to be configured on a virtual network that allows access to the following endpoints over TCP port 443:

- *https://enterpriseregistration.windows.net*—For device registration
- *http://169.254.169.254*—Azure Instance Metadata Service endpoint
- *https://login.microsoftonline.com*—For authentication flows
- *https://pas.windows.net*—For Azure RBAC flows

You can enable Azure AD logon for a Windows Server IaaS VM when creating the IaaS VM using the Azure portal or when creating an IaaS VM using Azure Cloud Shell. When you do this, the AADLoginForWindows extension is enabled on the IaaS VM. If you have an existing VM Windows Server IaaS VM, you can use the following Azure CLI command to install and configure the AADLoginForWindows extension (where ResourceGroupName and VMName are unique to your deployment):

```
Az vm extension set --publisher Microsoft.Azure.ActiveDirectory --name
AADLoginForWindows --resource-group ResourceGroupName --vm-name VMName
```

Once the IaaS VM has the AADLoginForWindows extension configured and enabled, you can determine what permissions the Azure AD user account has on the IaaS VM by adding them to the following Azure roles:

- **Virtual Machine Administrator Login**   Accounts assigned this role are able to sign on to the IaaS VM with local administrator privileges.
- **Virtual Machine User Login**   Accounts assigned this role are able to sign on to the VM with regular user privileges.

## Remote PowerShell

You can initiate a remote PowerShell session from hosts on the internet. Another option is to run a Cloud Shell session in a browser and perform PowerShell remote administration in this manner. Cloud Shell is a browser-based CLI and a lot simpler to use than adding the Azure CLI to your local computer. There is a Cloud Shell icon on the top panel of the Azure console.

You can enable Remote PowerShell on an Azure IaaS Windows VM by performing the following steps from Cloud Shell:

1. Ensure that Cloud Shell has PowerShell enabled by running the pwsh command.
2. At the PowerShell prompt in Cloud Shell, type the following command to enter local Administrator credentials for the Azure IaaS Windows VM:

   ```
   $cred=get-credential
   ```

3. At the PowerShell prompt in Cloud Shell, type the following command to enable PowerShell remoting on the Windows Server IaaS VM, where the VM name is 2022-IO-A and the resource group that hosts the VM is 2022-IO-RG:

   ```
   Enable-AzVMPSRemoting -Name 2022-IO-A -ResourceGroupName 2022-IO-RG -Protocol
   https -OSType Windows
   ```

4. Once this command has completed executing, you can use the `Enter-AzVM` cmdlet to establish a remote PowerShell session. For example, run this command to connect to the IaaS VM named 2022-IO-A in resource group 2022-IO-RG:

```
Enter-AzVM -name 2022-IO-A -ResourceGroupName 2019-22-RG -Credential $cred
```

## Azure Bastion

Azure Bastion allows you to establish an RDP session to a Windows Server IaaS VM through a standards-compliant browser such as Microsoft Edge or Google Chrome rather than having to use a remote desktop client. You can think of Azure Bastion as "jumpbox as a service" because it allows access to IaaS VMs that do not have a public IP address. Before the release of Azure Bastion, the only way to gain access to an IaaS VM that didn't have a public IP address was either through a VPN to the virtual network that hosted the VM or by deploying a jumpbox VM with a public IP address from which you then created a secondary connection to the target VM. If you have configured an SSH server on the IaaS VM, Bastion also supports creating SSH connections to Linux IaaS VMs or Windows Server configured with the SSH server service.

Prior to deploying Azure Bastion, you need to create a special subnet named AzureBastion-Subnet on the virtual network that hosts your IaaS VMs. Once you deploy Azure Bastion, the service will manage the network security group configuration to allow you to successfully make connections.

## Just-in-Time VM access

Rather than have management ports, such as the port used for Remote Desktop Protocol, TCP port 3389, open to hosts on the internet all the time, Just-in-Time (JIT) VM access allows you to open a specific management port for a limited duration of time and only open that port to a small range of IP addresses. You only need to use JIT if you require management port access to an Azure IaaS VM from a host on the internet. If the IaaS VM only has a private IP address or you can get by using a browser-based RDP session, then Azure Bastion is likely a better option. JIT also allows an organization to log on that has requested access, so you can figure out exactly which member of your team was the one who signed in and messed things up, which led to you writing up a report about the service outage. JIT VM access requires that you use the Azure Security Center, although doing so incurs an extra monthly cost per IaaS VM. Keep that in mind if you are thinking about configuring JIT.

## Windows Admin Center in Azure Portal

Windows Admin Center, available in the Azure portal, allows you to manage Windows Server IaaS VMs. When you deploy Windows Admin Center in the Azure portal, WAC will be deployed on each Azure IaaS VM that you wish to manage. Once this is done, you can navigate directly to an Azure portal blade containing the WAC interface instead of loading Windows Admin Center up directly on your administrative workstation or jumpbox server.

## Azure Serial Console

Azure Serial Console allows you to access a text-based console to interact with IaaS VMs through the Azure Portal. The serial connections connect to the COM1 serial port of the Windows Server IaaS VM and allow access independent of the network or operating system state. This functionality replicates the Emergency Management Services (EMS) access that you can configure for Windows Server, which you are most likely to use in the event that an error has occurred that doesn't allow you to access the contents of the server using traditional administrative methods.

You can use the Serial Console for an IaaS VM as long as the following prerequisites have been met:

- Boot diagnostics are enabled for the IaaS VM.
- The Azure account accessing the Serial Console is assigned the Virtual Machine Contributor role for the IaaS VM and the boot diagnostics storage account.
- A local user account is present on the IaaS VM that supports password authentication.

> **NEED MORE REVIEW?** **SERIAL CONSOLE**
>
> You can learn more about the Serial Console at *https://docs.microsoft.com/en-us/troubleshoot/ azure/virtual-machines/serial-console-overview.*

# Manage Azure VM network configuration

IaaS VMs connect to virtual networks. An IaaS virtual network is a collection of subnets that share a common private IP address space in the RFC 1918 range. For example, you might create a virtual network that uses the 192.168.0.0/16 address space and create subnets, such as 192.168.10.0/24. Azure IaaS virtual machines connect to the subnets in an Azure virtual network.

## IaaS virtual networks

Azure IaaS VMs can only use virtual networks that are in the same location as the IaaS virtual machine. For example, if you are deploying an IaaS VM to Australia South East, you'll only be able to connect the IaaS VM directly to a virtual network in Australia South East.

Once you have deployed the virtual network, you can configure the following properties for the virtual network using the Azure console:

- **Address Space** This property allows you to add additional address spaces to the Azure virtual network. You partition these address spaces using subnets.
- **Connected Devices** This property lists the current devices that are connected to the Azure virtual network. The property includes a list of VM network adapters and the internal IP address to which those adapters are assigned.

- **Subnets**   This property shows subnets that you create within the address space and allows you to put different Azure virtual machines on separate subnets within the same virtual network.

- **DNS Servers**   This property allows you to configure the IP address of the DNS servers assigned by the DHCP server used by the Azure virtual network. Use this to configure DNS settings when you deploy a domain controller on an Azure IaaS VM or when you deploy Azure AD DS for an Azure virtual network.

- **Properties**   This property allows you to change which subscription the Azure virtual network is associated with.

- **Locks**   This setting allows you to apply configuration locks, which block changes being made to the settings of the resource unless the lock is first removed.

- **Automation Script**   This setting allows you to access the JSON template file that you can use to reproduce and redeploy virtual networks with similar settings.

By default, hosts that are located on one subnet in a virtual network will automatically be able to communicate with other subnets on a virtual network. You can modify this behavior by configuring user-defined routes, network security groups, Azure Firewall, or network virtual appliances, which allow you to configure the subnets within a virtual network in a manner similar to the way you might segment traffic on an on-premises network.

## IP addressing

A virtual machine on an Azure network will have an internally assigned IP address in the range specified by the virtual network it is associated with. You can configure this assignment to be static or dynamic. It is important to remember that you assign an IP address as dynamic or static on the network adapter object within Azure—you don't manage IP address configuration from within the IaaS virtual machine operating system.

You may also assign a public IP address to the IaaS VM, but you should only do this in the event that the VM needs to be directly accessible to hosts on the internet. An IaaS VM with an internally assigned IP address can perform outbound communication to hosts on the internet without a public IP address, so a public address is necessary only if hosts on the internet need to directly communicate with the IaaS VM.

Even VMs that do need to be accessible to hosts on the internet can avoid having a public IP address if they are sitting behind a load balancer, web application, or network virtual appliance. A network virtual appliance (NVA) is similar to a traditional perimeter firewall or application gateway device and mediates traffic flow to a web application or VM running in the cloud.

You can determine which IP addresses are assigned to an Azure virtual machine on the Network Interfaces blade of the IaaS VM's properties. You can also use this blade to apply a region-specific DNS name to the network interface so that you can connect to the IaaS VM using a fully qualified domain name (FQDN) rather than an IP address. If you have a DNS server or you have configured an Azure DNS zone, you can then create a CNAME record that points to the region-specific DNS name for future connections. This saves you from always connecting to a cloudapp.azure.com address, and by using a CNAME, the FQDN will also remain pointing to the IaaS VM if the IaaS VM changes IP address.

## Network security groups

A network security group (NSG) is a packet filter for mediating traffic at the virtual network subnet level and also at the level of an IaaS VM's network adapter. When you create a virtual machine, an NSG is automatically applied to the IaaS VM's network adapter interface, and you can choose whether you want to allow traffic on management ports, such as TCP port 3389 and to the IaaS VM.

An NSG rule has the following elements:

- **Priority** NSG rules are processed in order, with lower numbers processed before higher ones. The moment traffic meets the conditions of a rule, that rule is enforced, and no further rules are processed.
- **Source** Specifies the source address or subnet of traffic. Can also include a service tag, which allows you to specify a particular Azure service or an application security group (a way of identifying the network identity of a series of workloads that make up an application).
- **Destination** Specifies the destination address or subnet of traffic. Can also include a service tag, which allows you to specify a particular Azure service or an application security group.
- **Protocol** Can be configured to TCP, UDP, ICMP, or Any.
- **Port Range** Allows you to specify either an individual port or a range of ports.
- **Direction** Specifies whether the rule applies to inbound or outbound traffic.
- **Action** Allows you to specify whether you want to allow or deny the traffic.

Network security groups are fairly basic in that they only work on the basis of IP address information and cannot be configured on the basis of an FQDN. Azure offers more advanced ways of mediating traffic flow, including Azure Firewall and network virtual appliances, which can be used in conjunction with NSGs; however, these topics are beyond the scope of the AZ-800 exam.

## VPNs and IaaS virtual networks

You can configure IaaS virtual networks to support VPN connections by configuring a VPN gateway. IaaS virtual network VPN gateways support site-to-site connections. A site-to-site connection allows you to connect an IaaS virtual network to an existing network, just as you might connect a branch office network to a head office network in your on-premises environment. IaaS virtual network VPN gateways also support point-to-site VPN connections. This allows you to connect individual host computers to IaaS virtual networks. Windows Server 2022 includes simplified setup of a point-to-site VPN connection through deployment of Azure Network Adapter, covered in more detail in Chapter 4, "Implement and manage an on-premises and hybrid networking infrastructure."

**EXAM TIP**

You can't resize a data disk that is attached to a running IaaS VM. You either have to detach the disk, perform the resize operation, and reattach the disk or you'll need to shut down the IaaS VM.

# Chapter summary

- VM enhanced session mode allows local devices to be connected to remote VMs. It requires either local admin access on the VM or that the account used to connect be a member of the Remote Desktop Users group.
- You can connect directly from a Hyper-V host to a VM by using PowerShell Direct or HVC.exe even if the VM does not have network connectivity.
- VMs can be configured with static or dynamic memory, with dynamic memory only consuming memory resources that the VM requires.
- Hyper-V integration services allow VMs to synchronize time with the Hyper-V host, volume checkpoints for backup, data exchange, and the ability to use the Copy-VMFile cmdlet.
- Discrete Device Assignment allows you to directly assign GPUs or NVMe storage to a VM.
- VM resource and CPU groups allow you to configure CPU resources to be used only by specific VMs.
- Hyper-V Replica lets you replicate a VM from one Hyper-V host to another.
- Hyper-V failover clusters ensure that VMs keep running with minimal disruption in the event a Hyper-V host fails. These clusters require some form of shared storage for the virtual machine files.
- Virtual hard disks in VHDX format can be up to 64 TB in size.
- NIC teaming allows you to combine multiple network adapters to improve network throughput.
- Container images are created by running and modifying a container instance and then saving that instance as a new image.
- If you want to run Windows and Linux container images simultaneously, you will need to use the Hyper-V isolation mode.
- You can attach and detach data disks to IaaS VMs while the VMs are running, but new data disks must still be initialized and formatted in the Windows Server operating system.
- Resizing an Azure IaaS VM always requires that the VM restart.
- You can connect an Azure IaaS VM to multiple virtual networks as long as you have multiple network adapters.

# Thought experiment

In this thought experiment, demonstrate your skills and knowledge of the topics covered in this chapter. You can find answers to this thought experiment in the next section.

You are responsible for the Windows Server hybrid deployment at Tailwind Traders. For your on-premises deployment, you have several clusters of Windows Server 2022 servers hosting the Hyper-V role. These servers are deployed using the Server Core installation option. Several VMs running on these Hyper-V hosts need to be configured from a PowerShell prompt, but they do not currently have their network configuration set.

Developers at Tailwind are using .NET Core for a new application that they will host in Windows containers. They wish to ensure that container images are as small as possible to make transferring them between developer workstations, container hosts, and Azure as simple as possible.

Several Windows Server IaaS VMs have been deployed in the Australia East datacenter. These IaaS VMs host workloads that can only be configured and managed directly, so it will be necessary every two weeks to make an RDP connection to these hosts. Unless the IaaS VMs are in the process of being managed by authorized users, it should not be possible to initiate an RDP connection to these hosts.

1. What tool can you use from the command prompt of the Server Core Hyper-V hosts to create a PowerShell connection to VMs that are not configured to interact with the network?

2. Which container image should you use as the basis for the .NET Core applications?

3. Which Azure service can you use to provide time-limited RDP access to the Windows Server IaaS VMs in the Australia East datacenter?

# Thought experiment answers

This section contains the solution to the thought experiment. Each answer explains why the answer choice is correct.

1. You can use PowerShell Direct to establish a connection from the Server Core Hyper-V hosts to VMs that are not configured to interact with the network.

2. You should use the Nano Server container image as the basis for the .NET core applications.

3. You can use Just-in-Time VM access to provide time-limited RDP access to the Windows Server IaaS VMs in the Australia East datacenter.

# CHAPTER 4

# Implement and manage an on-premises and hybrid networking infrastructure

The key to a successful hybrid deployment is ensuring that hosts connected to on-premises networks can communicate securely and reliably with workloads hosted in the cloud. To solve problems related to hybrid networking infrastructure effectively, you need to understand how to reliably implement on-premises and hybrid name resolution, ensure that IP address spaces across on-premises and cloud environments support coexistence, and determine which technologies will best facilitate communication between on-premises and cloud workloads.

## Skills covered in this chapter:

- Skill 4.1: Implement on-premises and hybrid name resolution
- Skill 4.2: Manage IP addressing in on-premises and hybrid scenarios
- Skill 4.3: Implement on-premises and hybrid network connectivity

## Skill 4.1: Implement on-premises and hybrid name resolution

This objective deals with ensuring that name resolution occurs properly across workloads running both in Azure and on-premises in hybrid configurations. To master this objective you'll need to understand how to integrate Domain Name System (DNS) with Active Directory Domain Services (AD DS), how to manage zones and records, how to configure forwarding and conditional forwarding, how to integrate Windows Server DNS with Azure DNS, and how to implement DNSSEC.

# Integrate DNS with AD DS

At the most basic level, DNS servers translate host names to IP addresses and translate IP addresses to host names. By querying special records on DNS servers, it's possible to locate mail servers and name servers, verify domain ownership, and locate servers such as domain controllers. While DNS servers are usually deployed on a domain controller on a Windows Server network, it's also possible to deploy them on standalone computers.

## DNS zone types

Zones store DNS resource record information. The DNS Server role in Windows Server supports several zone types, each of which is appropriate for a different set of circumstances. These zone types include primary, secondary, stub, and GlobalNames zones. You can integrate zones into Active Directory, or you can use the traditional primary or secondary architecture.

### ACTIVE DIRECTORY–INTEGRATED ZONES

Active Directory–integrated zones provide high availability for DNS as any DNS server that hosts an Active Directory–integrated primary zone can process updates to that zone. In traditional DNS, if the primary server becomes unavailable, secondary servers cannot process updates to the zone. Both primary and stub zones can be configured as Active Directory–integrated zones.

You can create an Active Directory–integrated zone only on a writable domain controller. When you choose to make a zone Active Directory–integrated , you have the option to configure a replication scope. You can configure the zone to be replicated so that it is present on all domain controllers in the domain, in the forest, or within the scope of a custom Active Directory partition. When determining the appropriate replication scope, consider which clients need regular, direct access to the zone and which clients require only occasional, indirect access.

You can use custom directory partitions to replicate a zone to some, but not all, domain controllers. You can select this option only if there is an existing custom DNS application directory partition. You can use the `Add-DNSServerDirectoryPartition` cmdlet to create a directory partition. You can also use ntdsutil.exe and dnscmd.exe to create custom partitions to host DNS zones. For example, to create a DNS Server directory partition called Tasmania on a subset of your organization's domain controllers using PowerShell, execute this command:

```
Add-DNSServerDirectoryPartition -Name Tasmania
```

Active Directory–integrated zones use multimaster replication, meaning any domain controller that hosts the DNS zone can process updates to the zone. When creating a DNS zone, you must specify whether the zone supports dynamic updates, which allow clients to update DNS records. This is useful in environments in which clients change IP addresses on a regular basis. When a client gets a new IP address, it can update the record associated with its host name in the appropriate DNS zone. There are three dynamic update configuration options:

- **Allow Only Secure Dynamic Updates**   You can use this option only with Active Directory–integrated zones. Only authenticated clients can update DNS records.

- **Allow Both Non-Secure And Secure Dynamic Updates**   With this option, any client can update a record. Although this option is convenient, it is also insecure because any client can update the DNS zone, which could potentially redirect clients that trust the quality of the information stored on the DNS server.

- **Do Not Allow Dynamic Updates**   When you choose this option, all DNS updates must be performed manually. This option is very secure, but it is also labor-intensive.

An Active Directory–integrated zone can replicate to a read-only domain controller (RODC). With this configuration, the RODC-hosted zone is read only and the RODC cannot process updates to the zone, which is also the case with a traditional writable domain controller. When you replicate an Active Directory–integrated zone to an RODC, the RODC forwards any client that wants to update the zone to a writable domain controller.

You can create an Active Directory–integrated primary zone by using the `Add-DnsServerPrimaryZone` cmdlet with the `ReplicationScope` parameter. For example, to create the Active Directory–integrated zone tailwindtraders.com so that it replicates to all domain controllers in the forest, issue this command:

```
Add-DnsServerPrimaryZone -Name tailwindtraders.com -ReplicationScope Forest
```

When you first install Active Directory, the installation process ensures that the DNS zone associated with the root domain is automatically configured as an Active Directory–integrated zone. This root domain zone is automatically replicated to all domain controllers in the forest.

---

***NEED MORE REVIEW?***   **ACTIVE DIRECTORY–INTEGRATED DNS**

You can learn more about Active Directory–integrated DNS at *https://docs.microsoft.com/windows-server/identity/ad-ds/plan/active-directory-integrated-dns-zones*.

# Create and manage zones and records

In traditional DNS implementations, a single server hosts a primary zone, which processes all zone updates, and a collection of secondary servers replicate zone data from the primary zone. One drawback to this model is that if the primary server fails, no zone updates can occur until the primary zone is restored. Azure DNS servers function as highly available primary servers.

Windows Server supports two types of primary zones: Active Directory–integrated zones and standard primary zones. Active Directory–integrated zones can only be hosted on computers that also function as domain controllers. Computers running Windows Server that do not function as domain controllers can host standard primary zones.

The DNS server service on a domain controller supports all zone types. This means that you can choose to deploy a standard or Active Directory–integrated primary zone, a stub zone, a reverse lookup zone, or a secondary zone on a domain controller.

## Secondary zones

A secondary zone is a read-only copy of a primary zone. Secondary zones cannot process updates and retrieve updates from a primary zone. Also, secondary zones cannot be Active Directory–integrated zones, but you can configure a secondary zone for an Active Directory–integrated primary zone. Before configuring a secondary zone, you need to configure the primary zone that you want it to replicate from to enable transfers to that zone. You can do this on the Zone Transfers tab of the Zone Properties dialog box. Secondary zones work best when the primary zone that they replicate from does not update frequently. If the primary zone does update frequently, it is possible that the secondary zone might have out-of-date records.

Use the Add-DNSServerSecondaryZone cmdlet to create a secondary zone. For example, to create a secondary zone for the australia.contoso.com zone, where a DNS server hosting the primary zone is located at 192.168.15.100, issue the following command:

```
Add-DnsServerSecondaryZone -Name "australia.contoso.com" -ZoneFile "australia.contoso.
com.dns" -MasterServers 192.168.15.100
```

## Reverse lookup zones

Reverse lookup zones translate IP addresses into FQDNs. You can create IPv4 or IPv6 reverse lookup zones, and you can also configure reverse lookup zones as Active Directory–integrated zones, standard primary zones, secondary zones, or stub zones. The domain controller promotion process automatically creates a reverse lookup zone based on the IP address of the first domain controller promoted in the organization.

Reverse lookup zones are dependent on the network ID of the IP address range that they represent. IPv4 reverse lookup zones can only represent /8, /16, or /24 networks, which are the old Class A, Class B, and Class C networks. You can't create a single reverse lookup zone for IP subnets that doesn't fit into one of these categories, and the smallest reverse lookup zone you can create is for subnet mask /24, or 255.255.255.0.

Use the `Add-DNSPrimaryZone` cmdlet and the `NetworkID` parameter to create a reverse lookup zone. For example, to create an Active Directory–integrated reverse lookup zone for the 192.168.15.0/24 subnet, issue the following command:

```
Add-DnsServerPrimaryZone -NetworkID "192.168.15.0/24" -ReplicationScope "Forest"
```

Few applications actually require that you configure reverse lookup zones. In most organizations, the only reverse lookup zone is the one that is automatically created when Active Directory is installed. One of the few times where reverse lookup zones seem necessary is when you configure Simple Mail Transfer Protocol (SMTP) gateways. This is because some anti-SPAM checks perform a reverse IP address lookup to verify the identity of the SMTP gateway. Often, the SMTP gateway's IP address, being a public address, belongs to the ISP, which means creating the reverse lookup zone entry is beyond your direct control as a systems administrator.

## GlobalNames zones

GlobalNames zones are a single-label, name-resolution replacement for WINS (Windows Internet Naming System) that can utilize existing DNS infrastructure. Deploying GlobalNames zones enables organizations to retire their existing WINS servers. If your organization still needs WINS (and apparently some do), you can still deploy the service on computers running Windows Server 2022.

Your organization should consider deploying GlobalNames zones instead of WINS in the following situations:

- Your organization is transitioning to IPv6. WINS does not support IPv6, and you need to support single-label name resolution.
- Single-label name resolution is limited to a small number of hosts that rarely change. GlobalNames zones must be updated manually.
- You have a large number of suffix search lists because of a complex naming strategy or disjoined namespace.

Entries in the GlobalNames zones must be populated manually. GlobalNames zone entries are alias (CNAME) records to existing DNS A or AAAA records. The existing DNS A and AAAA records can be dynamically updated, with these updates flowing on to records in the GlobalNames zone.

To deploy a GlobalNames zone in a forest, perform the following steps:

1. On a domain controller that is configured as a DNS server, create a new Active Directory–integrated forward lookup zone and configure it to replicate to every domain controller in the forest using the New Zone Wizard

2. On the **Zone Name** page, enter **GlobalNames** as the zone name. You can also accomplish the same task by running the following PowerShell command:

```
Add-DnsServerPrimaryZone -Name GlobalNames -ReplicationScope Forest
```

3. Next, activate the GlobalNames zone on each authoritative DNS server hosted on a domain controller in the forest. To do this, execute the following PowerShell command (where DNSServerName is the name of the domain controller hosting DNS):

```
Set-DnsServerGlobalNameZone -ComputerName DNSServerName -Enable $True
```

4. To populate the GlobalNames zone, create alias (CNAME) records in the GlobalNames zone that point to A or AAAA records in existing zones.

## Zone delegation

Zone delegations function as pointers to the next subordinate DNS layer in the DNS hierarchy. For example, if your organization uses the contoso.com DNS zone and you want to create a separate australia.contoso.com DNS zone, you can perform a zone delegation so that the DNS servers for the contoso.com DNS zone point to the DNS servers for the australia.contoso.com DNS zone. When you create a new child domain in an Active Directory forest, zone delegation occurs automatically. When you're performing a manual delegation, create the delegated zone on the target DNS server before performing the delegation from the parent zone.

Although you can delegate several levels, remember that the maximum length of an FQDN is 255 bytes and the maximum length of an FQDN for an Active Directory Domain Services domain controller is 155 bytes.

Use the Add-DnsServerZoneDelegation cmdlet to add a delegation. For example, to add a delegation for the australia.contoso.com zone to the contoso.com zone pointing at the name server ausdns.australia.contoso.com, which has the IP address 192.168.15.100, use the following command:

```
Add-DnsServerZoneDelegation -Name "contoso.com" -ChildZoneName "australia" -NameServer
"ausdns.australia.contoso.com" -IPAddress 192.168.15.100 -PassThru
```

### RESOURCE RECORDS

DNS supports a large number of resource records. The most basic resource record maps an FQDN to an IP address. More complex resource records provide information about the location of services, such as SMTP servers and domain controllers.

### HOST RECORDS

Host records are the most common form of record and can be used to map FQDNs to IP addresses. There are two types of host records:

- The A record, which is used to map FQDNs to IPv4 addresses
- AAAA records, which are used to map FQDNs to IPv6 addresses

You can add a new host record to a zone by right-clicking the zone in DNS Manager and then selecting New Host (A or AAAA). You also have the option of creating a pointer (PTR) record in the appropriate reverse lookup zone, if one exists. You can add host records with the Add-DnsServerResourceRecordA cmdlet and AAAA records with the Add-DnsServer ResourceRecordAAAA cmdlet.

### ALIAS (CNAME)

An alias, or CNAME, record enables you to provide an alternate name when there is an existing host record. You can create as many aliases for a particular record as you need. To create a new alias in a zone, right-click the zone in DNS Manager and then select **New Alias** (CNAME). When you create an alias, you must point the alias to an existing host record. You can use the Browse button to navigate to the target host record or enter it manually. You can also add an alias record to a zone from PowerShell by using the Add-DnsServerResourceRecordCName cmdlet.

### MAIL EXCHANGER

Mail exchanger (MX) records are used to locate mail gateways. For example, when a remote mail gateway wants to forward an email message to an email address associated with your organization's DNS zone, it performs an MX lookup to determine the location of the mail gateway. After that determination has been made, the remote mail gateway contacts the local gateway and transmits the message. MX records must map to existing host records. To create an MX record, right-click the zone in DNS Manager, select **New Mail Exchanger (MX)**, and enter information in the **New Resource Record** dialog box. The **Mail Server Priority** field is available to allow for the existence of more than one MX record in a zone and is often used when organizations have multiple mail gateways. This is done so that if an organization's primary mail gateway fails, remote mail servers can forward message traffic to other mail gateways. You can add MX records using the Add-DnsServerResourceRecordMX PowerShell cmdlet.

### POINTER RECORD

Pointer (PTR) records enable you to connect IP addresses to FQDNs and are hosted in reverse lookup zones. When you create a host record, a PTR record is automatically created by default, if an appropriate reverse lookup zone exists. To create a PTR record, right-click the reverse lookup zone in **DNS Manager**, select **New Pointer (PTR)**, and enter the PTR record information in the **New Resource Record** dialog box. You can create a PTR record from PowerShell by using the Add-DnsServerResourceRecordPtr cmdlet.

### UNKNOWN RECORDS

Windows Server 2016 and later DNS supports "unknown records," which are resource records whose RDATA format is unknown to the DNS server. "Unknown records" are defined in RFC 3597 and can be added to Windows Server DNS zones when they are hosted on computers running the Windows Server 2016 or later operating system.

## Zone aging and scavenging

Aging and scavenging provide a technique to reduce the incidence of stale resource records in a primary DNS zone. Stale records are records that are out of date or no longer relevant. If your organization has zones that relate to users with portable computers, such as laptops and tablets, those zones might end up accumulating stale resource records. This can lead to the following problems:

- DNS queries return stale rather than relevant results.

- Large zones can cause DNS server performance problems.
- Stale records might prevent DNS names being reassigned to different devices.

To resolve these problems, you can configure the DNS server service to do the following:

- Time stamp resource records that are dynamically added to primary zones. This occurs when you enable aging and scavenging.
- Age resource records based on a refresh time period.
- Scavenge resource records that are still present beyond the refresh period.

After you configure the DNS server service, aging and scavenging occur automatically. It is also possible to trigger scavenging by right-clicking the DNS server in **DNS Manager** and then selecting **Scavenge Stale Resource Records**. You can also configure aging and scavenging using the Set-DnsServerScavenging cmdlet. For example, to enable stale resource record scavenging on all zones of a DNS server and to set the Scavenging and Refresh Intervals to 10 days, issue this command:

```
Set-DnsServerScavenging -ApplyOnAllZones -RefreshInterval 10.0:0:0 -ScavengingInterval
10.0:0:0 -ScavengingState $True
```

## Configure DNS forwarding/conditional forwarding

Forwarders and conditional forwarders enable your DNS server to forward traffic to specific DNS servers when a lookup request cannot be handled locally. For example, you might configure a conditional forwarder to forward all traffic for resource records in the *tailspintoys.com* zone to a DNS server at a specific IP address. If you don't configure a forwarder or if a configured forwarder can't be contacted, the DNS Server service forwards the request to a DNS root server and the request is resolved normally.

### Forwarders

When you want to have a specific DNS server on the internet handle your organization's DNS resolution traffic, you are likely to use a DNS forwarder, rather than have your DNS server just use the root servers. Most organizations configure their ISP's DNS server as a forwarder. When you do this, the ISP's DNS server performs all the query work, returning the result to your organization's DNS server. Your organization's DNS server then returns the result of the query back to the original requesting client.

You configure forwarders on a per-DNS server level. You can configure a forwarder using the DNS Manager. You can do this by editing the properties of the DNS server and then configuring the list of forwarders on the Forwarders tab.

You can create a DNS forwarder by using the Add-DnsServerForwarder cmdlet. For example, to create a DNS forwarder for a DNS server with 10.10.10.111 as the IP address, issue this command:

```
Add-DnsServerForwarder 10.10.10.111
```

You can't create a forwarder on one DNS server and then have it replicate to all other DNS servers in the forest or the domain; however, this is possible with conditional forwarders and stub zones.

## Conditional forwarders

Conditional forwarders only forward address requests from specific domains rather than forwarding all requests that can't be resolved by the DNS server. When configured, a conditional forwarder takes precedence over a forwarder. Conditional forwarders are useful when your organization has a trust relationship or partnership with another organization or you need to have resolution occur in an Azure DNS private zone that can be connected to through site-to-site VPN or ExpressRoute. You can configure a conditional forwarder that directs all traffic to host names within that organization instead of having to resolve those host names through the standard DNS-resolution process.

You can create conditional forwarders using the Add-DnsServerConditionalForwarderZone PowerShell cmdlet. For example, to create a conditional forwarder for the DNS domain tailspintoys.com that forwards DNS queries to the server at IP address 10.10.10.102 and also replicates that conditional forwarder to all DNS servers within the Active Directory forest, issue this command:

```
Add-DnsServerConditionalForwarderZone -MasterServers 10.10.10.102 -Name tailspintoys.com
-ReplicationScope Forest
```

## Stub zones

A *stub zone* is a special zone that stores authoritative name server records for a target zone. Stub zones have an advantage over forwarders when the address of a target zone's authoritative DNS server changes on a regular basis. Stub zones are often used to host the records for authoritative DNS servers in delegated zones. Using stub zones in this way ensures that delegated zone information is up to date. If you create the stub zone on a writable domain controller, it can be stored with Active Directory and replicated to other domain controllers in the domain or forest.

You can add a stub zone using the Add-DnsServerStubZone cmdlet. For example, to add a DNS stub zone for the fabrikam.com zone using the DNS server at 10.10.10.222 and to also replicate that stub zone to all DNS servers in the forest, execute this command:

```
Add-DnsServerStubZone -MasterServers 10.10.10.222 -Name fabrikam.com -ReplicationScope
Forest -LoadExisting
```

# Integrate Windows Server DNS with Azure DNS private zones

Azure DNS is a highly available DNS service that runs in the Microsoft cloud. Rather than deploy the DNS server service on an IaaS virtual machine to host a public zone and have to perform all the administrative tasks for the care and maintenance of that IaaS VM, Azure DNS allows you to just deploy and manage DNS zones and records. When you configure Azure

DNS, you are provided with the IP address of the DNS servers within Azure that can be used to resolve records in the configured zones. You can use these addresses when configuring DNS delegation from your chosen domain registrar. You can also use these addresses when configuring forwarders and stub zones from on-premises DNS servers.

Azure DNS private zones allow you to host private DNS zones that host records that can only be queried by hosts on specific virtual networks and connected networks. For example, records in an Azure DNS private zone could be queried by hosts on an on-premises network connected using a site-to-site VPN but not hosts on an on-premises network that connect to Azure DNS servers over the internet.

Azure DNS does not support zone transfers from primary to secondary or from secondary to primary zones. This means that you cannot directly integrate an Active Directory–integrated zone with an Azure DNS zone functioning as a secondary zone.

The best method of integrating Azure DNS with on-premises DNS is to use conditional forwarders and stub zones. When configuring a conditional forwarder or a stub zone for an Azure AD DS zone, use the DNS server addresses that are configured for the Azure AD DS virtual network.

> **NEED MORE REVIEW?** **HYBRID DNS ARCHITECTURE**
>
> You can learn more about hybrid DNS architecture at *https://docs.microsoft.com/en-us/azure/ architecture/hybrid/hybrid-dns-infra*.

## Implement DNSSEC

Domain Name System Security Extensions (DNSSEC) add security to DNS by enabling DNS servers to validate the responses given by other DNS servers. DNSSEC enables digital signatures to be used with DNS zones. When the DNS resolver issues a query for a record in a signed zone, the authoritative DNS server provides both the record and a digital signature, enabling validation of that record.

To configure DNSSEC, perform the following steps:

1. Right-click the zone in **DNS Manager**, select **DNSSEC**, and then select **Sign the Zone**.
2. On the Signing Options page, select Use default settings to sign the zone.

When you configure DNSSEC, three new resource record types are available. These records have the following properties:

- **Resource Record Signature (RRSIG) record**   This record is stored within the zone, and each is associated with a different zone record. When the DNS server is queried for a zone record, it returns the record and the associated RRSIG record.
- **DNSKEY**   This is a public key resource record that enables the validation of RRSIG records.

- **Next Secure (NSEC/NSEC3) record** This record is used as proof that a record does not exist. For example, the contoso.com zone is configured with DNSSEC. A client issues a query for the host record tasmania.contoso.com and if there is no record for tasmania.contoso.com, the NSEC record returns, which informs the host making the query that no such record exists.

In addition to the special resource records, a DNSSEC implementation has the following components:

- **Trust anchor** This is a special public key associated with a zone. Trust anchors enable a DNS server to validate DNSKEY resource records. If you deploy DNSSEC on a DNS server hosted on a domain controller, the trust anchors can be stored in the Active Directory forest directory partition. This replicates the trust anchor to all DNS servers hosted on domain controllers in the forest.
- **DNSSEC Key Master** This is a special DNS server that you use to generate and manage signing keys for a DNSSEC-protected zone. Any computer running Windows Server 2012 or later that hosts a primary zone, whether standard or integrated, can function as a DNSSEC Key Master. A single computer can function as a DNSSEC Key Master for multiple zones. The DNSSEC Key Master role can also be transferred to another DNS server that hosts the primary zone.
- **Key Signing Key (KSK)** You use the KSK to sign all DNSKEY records at the zone root. You create the KSK by using the DNSSEC Key Master.
- **Zone Signing Key (ZSK)** You use the ZSK to sign zone data, such as individual records hosted in the zone. You create the ZSK by using the DNSSEC Key Master.

You can configure Group Policy to ensure that clients only accept records from a DNS server for a specific zone if those records have been signed using DNSSEC. You do this by configuring the Name Resolution Policy Table, which is located in the Computer Configuration\Policies\Windows Settings\Name Resolution Policy node of a GPO. You create entries in the table; for example, requiring that all queries against a specific zone require DNSSEC validation. You can configure the NRPT by using Group Policy or through PowerShell.

DNSSEC is appropriate for high-security environments, such as those where IPsec and authenticating switches are in use. DNSSEC protects against attacks where clients are fed false DNS information. In many small to medium-sized environments, the likelihood of such an attack is minimal; however, in high-security environments, enabling DNSSEC is a prudent precaution.

## Manage Windows Server DNS

Managing DNS on Windows Server also includes understanding how to maintain the DNS event logs and how to configure advanced DNS options.

## DNS event logs

The DNS server log is located in the Applications And Services Logs folder in Event Viewer. Depending on how you configure event logging on the Event Logging tab of the DNS server's properties, this event log can record information, including the following:

- Changes to the DNS service, such as when the DNS server service is stopped or started
- Zone loading and signing events
- Modifications to the DNS server configuration
- DNS warning and error events

By default, the DNS server records all these events. It's also possible to configure the DNS server to only log errors, or you can have it log errors and warning events. The key with any type of logging is that you should only enable logging for information that you might need to review at some point in time. Many administrators log everything "just in case," even though they're only ever interested in a specific type of event.

In the event that you need to debug how a DNS server performs, you can enable **Debug Logging** on the **Debug Logging** tab of the DNS server's **Properties** dialog box. Debug logging is resource intensive, and you should only use it when you have a specific problem related to the functionality of the DNS server. You can configure debug logging to use a filter so that only traffic from specific hosts is recorded, instead of recording traffic from all hosts that interact with the DNS server.

## DNS options

In high-security environments, you can take a number of steps to make a DNS server more secure from attackers who attempt to spoof it. *Spoofing* can cause the server to provide records that redirect clients to malicious sites. While DNSSEC provides security for zones hosted on the server, most DNS server traffic involves retrieving information from remote DNS servers and passing that information on to clients. In this section, you learn about settings that you can configure to ensure that the information relayed to clients retains its integrity in the event that a nefarious third party attempts to spoof your organization's DNS servers.

### DNS SOCKET POOL

DNS socket pool is a technology that makes cache-tampering and spoofing attacks more difficult by using source port randomization when issuing DNS queries to remote DNS servers. To spoof the DNS server with an incorrect record, the attacker needs to guess which randomized port was used as well as the randomized transaction ID that was issued with the query. By default, one DNS server running on Windows Server uses a socket pool of 2,500. You can use the dnscmd command-line tool to change the socket pool size to a value between 0 and 10,000. For example, to set the socket pool size to 4,000, issue the following command:

```
Dnscmd /config /socketpoolsize 4000
```

You must restart the DNS service before you can use the reconfigured socket pool size.

## DNS CACHE LOCKING

DNS cache locking provides you with control over when information stored in the DNS server's cache can be overwritten. For example, when a recursive DNS server responds to a query for a record that is hosted on another DNS server, it caches the results of that query so that it doesn't have to contact the remote DNS server if the same record is queried again within the Time to Live (TTL) value of the resource record. DNS cache locking prevents record data in a DNS server's cache from being overwritten until a configured percentage of the TTL value has expired. By default, the cache-locking value is set to 100 percent, but you can reset it by using the Set-DNSServerCache cmdlet with the LockingPercent option. For example, to set the cache-locking value to 80 percent, issue the following command and then restart the DNS server service:

```
Set-DNSServerCache -LockingPercent 80
```

## DNS RECURSION

By default, DNS servers on Windows Server perform recursive queries on behalf of clients. This means when the client asks the DNS server to find a record that isn't stored in a zone hosted by the DNS server, the DNS server then goes out and finds the result of that query and passes it back to the client. It's possible, however, for nefarious third parties to use recursion as a denial-of-service attack vector, which could slow a DNS server to the point where it becomes unresponsive. You can disable recursion on the **Advanced** tab of the DNS server's properties, or you can configure it by using the Set-DNSServerRecursion cmdlet. For example, to configure the recursion retry interval to 3 seconds, use the following command:

```
Set-DNSServerRecursion -RetryInterval 3 -PassThru
```

## NETMASK ORDERING

Netmask ordering ensures that the DNS server returns the host record on the requesting client's subnet, if such a record exists. For example, imagine that the following host records exist on a network that uses 24-bit subnet masks:

- 10.10.10.105 wsus.contoso.com
- 10.10.20.105 wsus.contoso.com
- 10.10.30.105 wsus.contoso.com

If netmask ordering is enabled and a client with the IP address 10.10.20.50 performs a lookup of wsus.contoso.com, the lookup always returns the record 10.10.20.105 because this record is on the same subnet as the client. If netmask ordering is not enabled, the DNS server returns records in a round-robin fashion. If the requesting client is not on the same network as any of the host records, the DNS server also returns records in a round-robin fashion. Netmask ordering is useful for services, such as WSUS, that you might have at each branch office. When you use netmask ordering, the DNS server redirects the client in the branch office to a resource on the local subnet when one exists. Netmask ordering is enabled by default on Windows Server. You can verify that netmask ordering is enabled by viewing the Advanced Properties of the DNS server.

## RESPONSE RATE LIMITING

Distributed denial-of-service attacks against DNS servers are becoming increasingly common. One method of ameliorating such attacks is by configuring response rate limiting. Response rate limiting determines how a DNS server responds to clients sending an unusually high number of DNS queries. You can configure the following response rate limiting settings:

- **Responses Per Second**  Determines the maximum number of times an identical response can be returned to a client per second.
- **Errors Per Second**  Determines the maximum number of error responses returned to a client per second.
- **Window**  The timeout period for any client that exceeds the maximum request threshold.
- **Leak Rate**  Determines how often the DNS server responds to queries if a client is in the suspension window. The leak rate is the number of queries it takes before a response is sent. A leak rate of 42 means that the DNS server only responds to one query out of every 42 when a client is in the suspension window period.
- **TC Rate**  Tells the client to try connecting with TCP when the client is in the suspension window. The TC rate should be below the leak rate to give the client the option of attempting a TCP connection before a leak response is sent.
- **Maximum Responses**  The maximum number of responses that a DNS server issues to a client during the timeout period.
- **White List Domains**  Domains that are excluded from response rate limiting settings.
- **White List Subnets**  Subnets that are excluded from response rate limiting settings.
- **White List Server Interfaces**  DNS server interfaces that are excluded from response rate limiting settings.

## DANE

DNS-based Authentication of Named Entities (DANE) allows you to configure records that use Transport Layer Security Authentication (TLSA) to inform DNS clients of which certificate authorities (CAs) they should accept certificates from for your organization's domain name DNS zone. DANE blocks attackers from using attacks where a certificate is issued from a rogue CA and is used to provide validation for a rogue website when a DNS server is compromised. When DANE is implemented, a client requesting a TLS connection to a website, such as *www.tailspintoys.com*, knows that it should only accept a TLS certificate from a specific CA. If the TLS certificate for *www.tailwindtraders.com* is from a different CA, the client knows that the website that appears to be at *www.tailwindtraders.com* might have been compromised or that the client might have been redirected by an attacker corrupting a DNS cache.

## DNS POLICIES

You use DNS policies to control how DNS servers respond to queries based on the properties of that query. You can configure DNS policies to achieve the following:

- **Application load balancing**   Allows you to weight which endpoint is returned when multiple endpoints exist for an address—for example, returning one IP address 75 percent of the time and another IP address 25 percent of the time. This differs from DNS round-robin, where multiple IP addresses associated with a specific address would be returned to clients on an equal basis (netmask ordering is the exception).

- **Traffic management**   The DNS server provides a response to the client that directs them to the datacenter closest to them. For example, clients making DNS requests from Australia are redirected to an application endpoint in Australia and clients making DNS requests from Canada are redirected to an application endpoint in Canada.

- **Split-brain DNS**   DNS records can be segmented into zone scopes. Records can be placed in different scopes. This allows external clients to query the DNS zone and be only able to access a specific number of DNS records that are members of a scope designed for external clients. Internal clients have access to a more comprehensive internal scope.

- **Filtering**   Allows you to block DNS queries from specific IP addresses, IP address ranges, or FQDNs.

- **Forensics**   Redirects malicious clients to a sinkhole host rather than to the host they are trying to reach. For example, if clients appear to be attempting a denial-of-service attack, redirect them to a static page rather than the site they are attempting to attack.

- **Time of day–based redirection**   Allows you to configure a policy where clients are redirected to specific hosts based on the time of day when the query is received.

To accomplish most of these tasks, you create a *zone scope*, which is a collection of records within a zone. For example, in a split-brain scenario, you'd create a zone scope for the internal records. You'd then use the `Add-DNSServerQueryResolutionPolicy` cmdlet to create a policy that allowed all queries from the DNS server's internal network interface to have access to records in the internal zone scope; queries that came through any other interface on the DNS server would only have access to the Default scope, which would consist only of those records in the zone to which you wanted public clients to have access. Similarly, in the time-of-day-based redirection scenario, you'd create scopes for each period of time and then create policies that were triggered based on the time of day that would direct clients to records within the particular scope associated with that period of time.

**EXAM TIP**

Remember that you can allow hosts on an on-premises network to query records in an Azure DNS private zone if the on-premises network is connected to Azure using a site-to-site VPN or ExpressRoute and you have configured the appropriate forwarder or stub zone.

# Skill 4.2: Manage IP addressing in on-premises and hybrid scenarios

This objective deals with how to manage IP addressing on-premises and in hybrid environments. To master this objective you'll need to understand how you can use IPAM to manage the DHCP and DNS server roles, how to configure the DHCP server role separately, how to ensure you minimize the chance of IP address issues in hybrid environments, how you can manage DHCP scopes, and how you make sure that the DHCP server service remains available even if an individual DHCP server fails.

> **This skill covers how to:**
> - Implement and manage IPAM
> - Implement and configure the DHCP server role
> - Resolve IP address issues in hybrid environments
> - Create and manage scopes
> - Create and manage IP reservations
> - Implement DHCP high availability

## Implement and manage IPAM

IPAM allows you to centralize the management of DHCP and DNS servers. Rather than manage each server separately, you can use IPAM to manage them from a single console. You can use a single IPAM server to manage up to 150 separate DHCP servers and up to 500 individual DNS servers. Also, it can manage 6,000 separate DHCP scopes and 150 separate DNS zones. You can perform tasks such as creating address scopes, configuring address reservations, and managing DHCP and DNS options globally, instead of having to perform these tasks on a server-by-server basis. IPAM supports both Active Directory and file-based DNS zones.

### Deploy IPAM

You can install the IPAM feature only on a computer that is a member of an AD DS domain. You can have multiple IPAM servers within a single AD DS forest. You are likely to do this if your organization is geographically dispersed and you have separate support teams in the different geographic locations.

It's important to note that IPAM cannot manage a DHCP or DNS server if the role is installed on the same computer that hosts IPAM. For this reason, you should install the IPAM server feature on a server that doesn't host the DNS or DHCP roles. IPAM is also not supported on computers that host the AD DS domain controller server role. Additionally, if you want to use the IPAM server to manage IPv6 address ranges, you need to ensure that IPv6 is enabled on the computer hosting the IPAM server. IPAM can use the Windows Internal Database or a dedicated SQL server instance to host data.

## Configure server discovery

Server discovery is the process where the IPAM server checks with Active Directory to locate domain controllers, DNS servers, and DHCP servers. You select which domains to discover in the Configure Server Discovery dialog box. After you've completed server discovery, you need to run a PowerShell cmdlet that creates and provisions Group Policy objects (GPOs) that allow these servers to be managed by the IPAM server. When you set up the IPAM server, you choose a GPO name prefix. Use this prefix when executing the `Invoke-IpamGpoProvisioning` PowerShell cmdlet that creates the appropriate GPOs.

If you use the GPO prefix IPAM, the three GPOS are named:

- IPAM_DC_NPS
- IPAM_DHCP
- IPAM_DNS

Until these GPOs apply to the discovered servers, these servers are listed as having an IPAM Access status of Blocked. After the GPOs are applied to the discovered servers, the IPAM Access status is set to Unblocked. After the discovered service has an IPAM Access status set to Unblocked, you can edit the properties of the server and set it to Managed. After you do this, you are able to use IPAM to manage the selected services on the server.

IPAM supports managing DNS and DHCP servers in forests where a two-way trust relationship has been configured. You perform DHCP and DNS server discovery in a trusted forest on a per-domain basis.

## IPAM administration

You can delegate administrative permissions by adding user accounts to one of five local security groups on the IPAM server. By default, members of the Domain Admins and Enterprise Admins groups are able to perform all tasks on the IPAM server. The five following local security groups are present on the IPAM server after you deploy the role, and they allow you to delegate the following permissions:

- **DNS Record Administrator** Members of this role can manage DNS resource records.
- **IP Address Record Administrator** Members of this role can manage IP addresses, but not address spaces, ranges, subnets, or blocks.
- **IPAM Administrators** Members of this role can perform all tasks on the IPAM server, including viewing IP address tracking information.
- **IPAM ASM Administrators** ASM stands for Address Space Administrator. Users added to this group can perform all tasks that can be performed by members of the IPAM Users group, but they are also able to manage the IP address space. They cannot perform monitoring tasks and are unable to perform IP address tracking tasks.

- **IPAM DHCP Administrator** Members of this role can manage DHCP servers using IPAM.
- **IPAM DHCP Reservations Administrator** Members of this role can manage DHCP reservations using IPAM.
- **IPAM DHCP Scope Administrator** Members of this role can manage DHCP scopes.
- **IPAM MSM Administrators** MSM stands for Multi-Server-Management. Members of this role can manage all DNS and DHCP servers managed by IPAM.
- **IPAM DNS Administrator** Members of this role can manage DHCP servers using IPAM.

## Managing the IP address space

The benefit of IPAM is that it allows you to manage all the IP addresses in your organization. IPAM supports the management of IPv4 public and private addresses, whether they are statically or dynamically assigned. IPAM allows you to detect whether there are overlapping IP address ranges defined in DHCP scopes on different servers; determine IP address utilization and whether there are free IP addresses in a specific range; create DHCP reservations centrally without having to configure them on individual DHCP servers; and create DNS records based on IP address lease information.

IPAM separates the IP address space into blocks, ranges, and individual addresses. An IP address block is a large collection of IP addresses that you use to classify the address space that your organization uses at the highest level. An organization might only have one or two address blocks: one for its entire internal network and another smaller block that represents the public IP address space used by the organization. An IP address range is part of an IP address block. An IP address range cannot map to multiple IP address blocks. Generally, an IP address range corresponds to a DHCP scope. An individual IP address maps to a single IP address range. IPAM stores the following information with an IP address:

- Any associated MAC (Media Access Control) addresses
- How the address is assigned (static/DHCP)
- Assignment date
- Assignment expiration
- Which service manages the IP address
- DNS records associated with the IP address

## IP address tracking

One of the most important features of IPAM is its ability to track IP addresses by correlating DHCP leases with user and computer authentication events on managed domain controllers and Network Policy Servers (NPSs). IP address tracking allows you to figure out which user was associated with a specific IP address at a particular point in time, which can be important when trying to determine the cause of unauthorized activity on the organizational network.

You can search for IP address records using one of the following four parameters:

- **Track by IP address**   You can track by IPv4 address, but IPAM does not support tracking by IPv6 address.
- **Track by client ID**   You can track by client ID in IPAM, which allows you to track IP address activity by MAC address.
- **Track by host name**   You can track by the computer's name as registered in DNS.
- **Track by username**   You can track a username, but to do this, you must also provide a host name.

Naturally, you can only track data that has been recorded since IPAM has been deployed. So, while it is possible to store several years of data in the Windows Internal Database that IPAM uses, you are limited to only being able to retrieve events recorded after IPAM was configured.

Microsoft estimates that the Windows Internal Database IPAM uses is able to store three years of IP address utilization data for an organization that has 100,000 users before data must be purged.

You can use IPAM to locate free subnets and free IP address ranges in your existing IP address scheme. For example, if you need 50 consecutive free IP addresses for a project, you can use the Find-IpamFreeRange PowerShell cmdlet to determine whether such a range is present in your current environment.

## Implement and configure the DHCP server role

DHCP is a network service that most administrators barely pay attention to after they've configured it. The main concern that most administrators have with DHCP is up until the release of Windows Server 2012, it had been difficult to configure as a highly available service. While DNS became highly available through its ability to be hosted on any domain controller, the problem with making DHCP highly available was ensuring that, when multiple DHCP servers were in play, duplicate addresses were not being assigned to separate clients. Windows Server 2012 introduced highly available DHCP servers, allowing two servers to share a scope, rather than having to split the scope according to the old 80/20 rule.

DHCP servers need to be authorized in Active Directory before they start leasing addresses. DHCP servers on Microsoft operating systems must always be authorized before they start working, simply because this reduces the chance that a rogue DHCP server might start leasing IP addresses. Only the following can authorize DHCP servers:

- Members of the Enterprise Admins group
- Members of the Domain Admins group in the forest root domain
- Accounts delegated the ability to add, modify, or delete new objects of the DHCP class type on the NetServices folder in Active Directory

When you deploy the DHCP server role, the following local groups are created. You can use membership of these groups to delegate DHCP server management permissions to users or groups:

- **DHCP Administrators**   Members of this group can view or modify any DHCP server settings, including configuring DHCP options, failover, and scopes.

- **DHCP Users**   Members of this group have only read-only access to the DHCP server. They can view, but not modify, DHCP server settings, including scope information and data.

## Resolve IP address issues in hybrid environments

Any organization that's merged with another knows the challenges involved in resolving overlapping IP address spaces. Many organizations choose default private IP address ranges for their on-premises networks and do the same with their resources in the cloud. This does not cause problems until an attempt is made to connect the two environments and the duplicate ranges are discovered.

Common IP address issues in hybrid environments are:

- **Overlapping IP address ranges**   Many cloud environments suffer from unplanned sprawl of IP address spaces. Developers spin up new virtual networks for each new workload. This is especially likely to occur in environments where different parts of an organization maintain separate Azure subscriptions. It can also happen when organizations have multicloud deployments with IaaS resources in Azure and third-party clouds and connect those resources using VPNs.

- **IP address conflicts**   This issue occurs when hosts on-premises and in the cloud are assigned the same IP address. You can avoid this problem by ensuring that no overlapping IP address ranges are used.

- **Routing problems**   Without clear and differentiated IP address ranges on-premises and in Azure, routing problems can occur. One simple solution is to use a completely different IP address range for on-premises networks and cloud networks. For example, on-premises networks can use IP addresses in the 10.0.0.0/8 range and private IP addresses on cloud networks.

- **Public versus private traffic**   In many environments it's necessary to ensure that all traffic that passes between the on-premises network and Azure passes across VPN or ExpressRoute. If routes are not configured properly, traffic that should pass across an encrypted private link may instead travel across the internet.

## Create and manage scopes

A *DHCP scope* is a collection of IP address settings that a client uses to determine its IP address configuration. You configure a DHCP scope for every separate IPv4 subnet to which you want the DHCP servers to provide IP address configuration information. When configuring an IPv4 scope, specify the following information:

- **Scope Name**   The name of the scope. The name should be descriptive enough that you recognize which hosts the scope applies to—for example, Level 2, Old Arts Building.
- **IP Address Range**   This is the range of IP addresses encompassed by the scope, and it should be a logical subnet.
- **IP Address Exclusions**   This includes which IP addresses within the IP address range you do not want the DHCP server to lease. For example, you could configure exclusions for several computers that have statically assigned IP addresses.
- **Delay**   This setting determines how long the DHCP server waits before offering an address. This provides you with a method of DHCP server redundancy, with one DHCP server offering addresses immediately and another offering addresses only after a certain period of time has elapsed.
- **Lease Duration**   The lease duration determines how long a client has an IP address before the address returns to the lease pool.
- **DHCP Options**   There are 61 standard options that you can configure. These include settings, such as DNS server address and default gateway address, that apply to leases in the scope.

You can add a DHCP server scope using the Add-DHCPServer4Scope or Add-DHCPServer6 Scope PowerShell cmdlet. For example, to create a new scope for the 192.168.10.0/24 network named MelbourneNet, issue the following PowerShell command:

```
Add-DHCPServerv4Scope -Name "MelbourneNet" -StartRange 192.168.10.1 -Endrange
192.168.10.254 -SubnetMask 255.255.255.0
```

Most organizations are still using IPv4 with their DHCP server. For the sake of brevity, all PowerShell examples are for IPv4.

## Server and scope options

DHCP options include additional configuration settings, such as the address of a network's default gateway or the addresses of DNS servers. You can configure DHCP options at two levels: the scope level and the server level. Options configured at the scope level override options configured at the server level.

Common scope options include:

- **003 Router**   The address of the default gateway for the subnet.
- **006 DNS Servers**   The address of DNS servers that the client should use for name resolution.
- **015 DNS Domain Name**   This is the DNS suffix assigned to the client.
- **058 Renewal time**   This determines how long after the lease is initially acquired that the client waits before it attempts to renew the lease.

You can configure IPv4 scope options using the `Set-DHCPServer4OptionValue` cmdlet. For example, to configure the scope with ID 192.168.10.0 on DHCP server dhcp.contoso.com with the value for the DNS server set to 192.168.0.100, issue the following command:

```
Set-DHcpServerv4OptionValue -Computername dhcp.contoso.com -ScopeID 192.168.10.0
-DNSServer 192.168.0.100
```

## Superscopes

A *superscope* is a collection of individual DHCP scopes. You might create a superscope when you want to bind existing scopes for administrative reasons. For example, imagine that you have a subnet in a building that is close to fully allocated. You can add a second subnet to the building and then bind them into a superscope. The process of binding several separate logical subnets on the same physical network is known as *multinetting*.

At least one existing scope must be present on the DHCP server before you can create a superscope. After you have created a superscope, you can add new subnets or remove subnets from that scope. It's also possible to deactivate some subnets within a scope while keeping others active. You might use this technique when migrating clients from one IP address range to another. For example, you could have both the source and destination scopes as part of the same superscope and activate the new scope and deactivate the original scope as necessary when performing the migration. You can create superscopes using the Add-DHCPServerv4 Superscope cmdlet. For example, to add the scopes with ID 192.168.10.0 and 192.168.11.0 to a superscope named MelbourneCBD, run the following command:

```
Add-DhcpServerv4Superscope -SuperscopeName "MelbourneCBD" -ScopeId 192.168.10.0,
192.168.11.0
```

## Multicast scopes

A *multicast address* is an address that allows one-to-many communications on a network. When you use multicast, multiple hosts on a network listen for traffic on a single multicast IP address. Multicast addresses are in the IPv4 range of 224.0.0.0 to 239.255.255.255. Multicast scopes are collections of multicast addresses. You can configure a Windows Server 2016 DHCP server to host multicast scopes. Multicast scopes are also known as Multicast Address Dynamic Client Allocation Protocol (MADCAP) scopes because applications that require access to multicast addresses support the MADCAP API.

The most common use for multicast addresses using the default Windows Server 2016 roles is for Windows Deployment Services (WDS). You can, however, configure the WDS server with its own set of multicast addresses, and you don't need to configure a special multicast scope in DHCP to support this role.

## Split scopes

A split scope is one method of providing fault tolerance for a DHCP scope. The idea behind a split scope is that you host one part of the scope on one DHCP server and a second, smaller part of the scope on a second DHCP server. Usually, this split has 80 percent of the addresses on the first DHCP server and 20 percent of the addresses on the second server. In this scenario, the DHCP server that hosts the 20 percent portion of the address space is usually located on a remote subnet. In the split-scope scenario, you also use a DHCP relay agent configured with a delay so that most addresses are leased from the DHCP server that hosts 80 percent of the address space. Split scopes are most likely to be used in scenarios where your DHCP servers aren't running on Windows Server 2012 or later operating systems. If you want to provide fault tolerance for scopes hosted on servers running Windows Server 2012 or later, you should instead implement DHCP failover.

## Name protection

DHCP name protection is a feature that allows you to ensure that the host names a DHCP server registers with a DNS server are not overwritten in the event that a non-Windows operating system has the same name. DHCP name protection also protects names from being overwritten by hosts that use static addresses that conflict with DHCP-assigned addresses.

For example, imagine that in the tailwindtraders.com domain there is a computer running the Windows 11 operating system that has the name Auckland and receives its IP address information from a Windows Server DHCP server. The DHCP server registers this name in DNS and creates a record in the contoso.com DNS zone that associates the name Auckland.tailwindtraders.com with the IP address assigned to the computer running Windows 11. A newly installed computer running a custom distribution of Linux is also assigned the name Auckland. Because name protection has been enabled, this new computer is unable to overwrite the existing record with a new record that associates the name Auckland.tailwindtraders.com with the Linux computer's IP address. If name protection had not been enabled, it is possible that the record would have been overwritten.

You can enable name protection on a scope by selecting Configure on the DNS tab of the IPv4 or IPv6 Properties dialog box. You can also do this by using the `Set-DhcpServerv4 DnsSetting` or the `Set-DhcpServerv6DnsSetting` cmdlet. For example, to configure the DHCP server on computer MEL-DC so that name protection is enabled on all IPv4 scopes, issue the following command:

```
Set-DhcpServerv4DnsSetting –Computer MEL-DC –NameProtection $true
```

## DHCP relay

The DHCP relay agent allows you to relay DHCP requests from a logical network or VLAN that does not have a DHCP server to a subnet that does. Windows Server supports the deployment of a DHCP relay agent as part of the Routing and Remote Access role. When configuring the

DHCP relay agent component of Routing and Remote Access, you specify the IP address of the DHCP server that is used to provision IP addresses. Because configuring Routing and Remote Access to support a DHCP relay agent is more complicated than deploying a new DHCP server, some organizations simply opt to deploy a new DHCP server and manage the relevant scopes through IPAM. Alternatively, most organizations configure routers to forward DHCP requests, and in those environments, it is not necessary to configure a DHCP relay agent. Other aspects of the Routing and Remote Access role are covered later in this chapter.

## DHCP policies

DHCP policies allow you to group DHCP clients based on information contained with that client's DHCP request packet. For example, if you had a collection of Microsoft Teams phones that had a specific range of MAC addresses connected to a subnet serviced by a specific DHCP scope, you could configure a DHCP policy to assign separate scope options to those clients that differed from those assigned normally.

# Create and manage IP reservations

Reservations allow you to ensure that a particular computer always receives a specific IP address. You can use reservations to allow servers to always have the same address, even when they are configured to retrieve that address through DHCP. If you don't configure a reservation for a computer, it can be assigned any available address from the pool. Although you can configure DHCP to update DNS to ensure that other hosts can connect using the client's host name, it is generally a good idea to ensure that a server retains the same IP address.

## Configuring reservations

There are two ways to configure a DHCP reservation. The simplest way is to locate an existing IP address lease in the DHCP console, right-click it, and then select **Add To Reservation**. This then ties that specific network adapter address to that IP address. The only drawback of this method is that the reservation is for the assigned IP address, and you cannot customize it.

If you know the network adapter address, also known as a MAC address, of the computer for which you want to configure a reservation, you can right-click the Reservations node under the scope that you want to configure the reservation under, and then select **New Reservation**. In the New Reservation dialog box fill out the Reservation Name, IP Address, and Network Adapter Address fields, and then select **Add** to create the reservation. You can also configure a reservation using the Add-DhcpServerv4Reservation cmdlet. For example, to configure a reservation, issue the following command:

```
Add-DhcpServerv4Reservation -ScopeId 192.168.10.0 -IPAddress 192.168.10.8 -ClientId
A0-FE-C1-7A-00-E5 -Description "A4 Printer"
```

## DHCP filtering

You can configure DHCP filtering on the Filters tab of the IPv4 Properties dialog box in the DHCP console. DHCP filtering is used in high-security environments to restrict the network adapter addresses that can utilize DHCP. For example, you can have a list of all network adapter addresses in your organization and use the **Enable Allow List** option to lease only IP addresses to this list of authorized adapters. This method of security is not entirely effective because it is possible for unauthorized people to fake an authorized adapter address as a way of gaining network access. You can add a specific network adapter to the allowed list of MAC addresses using the Add-DHCPServerv4Filter cmdlet. For example, to allow a laptop with the MAC address D1-F2-7C-00-5E-F0 to the authorized list of adapters, issue this command:

```
Add-DhcpServerv4Filter -List Allow -MacAddress D1-F2-7C-00-5E-F0 Description "Rooslan's
Laptop"
```

## Implement DHCP high availability

DHCP failover allows you to configure DHCP to be highly available without using split scopes. You have two options when configuring DHCP failover:

- **Hot Standby mode**   This relationship is a traditional failover relationship. When you configure this relationship, the primary server handles all DHCP traffic unless it becomes unavailable. You can configure DHCP servers to be in multiple separate relationships, so it's possible that a DHCP server can be the primary server in one relationship and a hot standby server in another relationship. When configuring this relationship, you specify a percentage of the address ranges to be reserved on the standby server. The default value is 5 percent. These 5 percent of addresses are instantly available after the primary server becomes unavailable. The hot standby server takes control of the entire address range when the figure specified by the state switchover interval is reached. The default value for this interval is 60 minutes.

- **Load balance mode**   This is the default mode when you create a DHCP failover relationship. In this mode, both servers provide IP addresses to clients according to the ratio defined by the load balance percentage figure. The default is for each server to share 50 percent of the load. The maximum client lead time figure enables one of the partners to take control of the entire scope in the event that the other partner is not available for the specified time.

Before configuring DHCP failover, you need to remove any split scopes between the potential partners. You can also choose a shared secret to authenticate replication traffic, but you don't have to enter this secret on the partner DHCP server.

**EXAM TIP**

Remember that you should deploy IPAM on a server that is not a domain controller, DNS server, or DHCP server.

# Skill 4.3: Implement on-premises and hybrid network connectivity

Hybrid environments require some type of bridge between on-premises workloads and those hosted in the cloud. To build these connections you will need to configure a VPN or ExpressRoute connection. When choosing a VPN, you'll need to chose between a point-to-site or site-to-site VPN. Connecting an organization with multiple on-premises sites to Azure also provides you the option of using the cloud as a central hub for routing organizational traffic. The final element to implementing hybrid network connectivity is selecting the appropriate technology to connect on-premises applications and workloads to front end services and clients in the cloud.

---

**This skill covers how to:**

- Implement and manage the Remote Access role
- Implement and manage Azure Network Adapter
- Implement and manage Azure Extended Network
- Implement and manage Network Policy Server role
- Implement Web Application Proxy
- Implement Azure Relay
- Implement Site-to-Site VPN
- Implement Azure Virtual WAN
- Implement Azure AD Application Proxy
- Use Azure App Service Hybrid Connections

---

## Implement and manage the Remote Access role

The Remote Access role service enables you to provide network access and routing functionality using a computer running Windows Server that you might otherwise provision using a dedicated hardware device. The Remote Access role enables you to provide the following services to computers:

- Access to trusted networks (such as an organization's internal network) for clients on untrusted networks (such as the internet) through VPNs or DirectAccess.
- Network routing using the Routing Information Protocol (RIP) and static routes, enabling you to connect separate IPv4 and IPv6 networks. It also enables you to configure encrypted site-to-site tunnels that can be used as wide area network (WAN) links between branch offices across the internet.

## RADIUS servers

The Network Policy Server (NPS) role is Microsoft's implementation of a RADIUS server. A RADIUS server performs authentication, authorization, and accounting for VPN, 802.1x wireless access point and authenticating switches, and dial-up connections.

Given that NPS is an implementation of the RADIUS protocol, you can use NPS with other third-party products that support the RADIUS protocol, as well as other versions of Microsoft products that support RADIUS. The NPS role's support for the RADIUS protocol means that you can integrate it with most third-party remote and network access products. Active Directory functions as the user account database when a server with the NPS role installed is a member of an Active Directory Domain Services (AD DS) domain. You configure whether the local server performs RADIUS authentication when creating a connection request policy, or by editing the properties of a connection request policy.

### RADIUS PROXIES

A RADIUS proxy forwards traffic from RADIUS clients to other RADIUS servers based on the properties of the connection request. When you configure a server with the NPS role installed as a RADIUS proxy, information about messages passed on to RADIUS servers from RADIUS clients is recorded in the accounting log. A server configured as a RADIUS proxy functions as a RADIUS client from the perspective of the RADIUS server performing authentication.

You deploy a RADIUS proxy when you need to provide authentication and authorization for users who have accounts in other Active Directory forests. For example, if there are three forests in your organization in which no forest trusts have been configured, but only one VPN server, you can use a RADIUS proxy to forward authentication traffic to RADIUS servers in the other forests. If a forest trust has been configured, you don't need to use a RADIUS proxy. You can also use a RADIUS proxy when you need authentication to occur against an account database running on a third-party operating system.

To configure a server with the NPS role installed to function as a RADIUS proxy, you need to have configured a remote RADIUS server group. A remote RADIUS server group is a collection of RADIUS servers to which a RADIUS proxy can forward authentication traffic. You configure the priority and weight of each server in the group to determine the balance of traffic forwarded from the proxy. Weight is for load balancing allocation and priority is used in high availability situations. You can add additional servers to the group if the current RADIUS servers can't cope with the current traffic load.

### RADIUS CLIENTS

When many IT professionals are first introduced to the term RADIUS client, they assume that it is something similar to a laptop computer on the internet trying to make a remote access connection. A RADIUS client is a device that forwards authentication and authorization traffic to a RADIUS server. A RADIUS client can be one of the following:

- **Another RADIUS server** In this case, the RADIUS server is acting as a proxy. The response from the RADIUS server is forwarded back to the client through the proxy.

- **A wireless access point that uses 802.1x authentication**   Rather than have the wireless access point perform authentication and authorization, the wireless access point functions as a RADIUS client and forwards authentication and authorization traffic to the RADIUS server. The response from the RADIUS server determines whether the connection is allowed or denied.

- **A switch that uses 802.1x authentication**   Rather than have the authenticating switch perform authentication and authorization, the authenticating switch functions as a RADIUS client and forwards authentication and authorization traffic to the RADIUS server. The response from the RADIUS server determines whether the connection is allowed or denied.

- **A VPN server**   The VPN server handles the setup of the VPN connection. The authentication and authorization is handled by another server. The response from the RADIUS server determines whether the connection is allowed or denied. This configuration is more secure because the account database is not hosted on the VPN server. If the VPN server is on a perimeter network, you configure a firewall to allow RADIUS authentication and authorization traffic between the VPN server and the RADIUS server on the protected network.

- **A dial-up server**   Although dial-up is less likely to be used today, dial-up servers can function as RADIUS clients. In this configuration, they forward authentication and authorization traffic to a RADIUS server and then allow or deny the connection based on the response.

### RADIUS ACCOUNTING

RADIUS accounting is a function that you can configure on a server that hosts the NPS role that enables you to record successful and failed connection attempts through devices that participate in your organization's RADIUS infrastructure. You can use the RADIUS accounting function available in NPS to record the following information:

- User authentication requests
- Access-Accept messages
- Access-Reject messages
- Accounting requests and responses
- Periodic status updates

You can configure RADIUS accounting on a server with the NPS role installed in one of the following three ways:

- **Event logging**   This method is the least sophisticated. You use this method to audit and troubleshoot connection attempts. The events are written to the event log.

- **Logging user authentication and accounting requests to a local file**   Enables logs to be written in Internet Authentication Service (IAS) and database-compatible format. This type of logging is appropriate when there are only a small number of remote access clients.

- **Logging user authentication and accounting requests to a Microsoft SQL Server XML-compliant database**   Logging onto an SQL Server database has the advantage of enabling multiple servers with the NPS role installed to write accounting data to a single location. Because the data is stored on an SQL Server instance, it can be queried using Microsoft SQL Server syntax. In large environments in which RADIUS accounting data needs to be regularly examined, administrators can write a web application to query and extract data from this database.

When configuring logging, you can enable an option that will block connection requests if logging fails. When considering whether to implement this option, you should balance the inconvenience of disallowing network access, which could be substantial if you have deployed NAP, against the security impact of having connections that would otherwise be authenticated and authorized being denied because a log entry cannot be written.

## VPN server

After you install the Remote Access role on a computer running Windows Server, you can configure the server as a VPN server. Before you deploy Windows Server as a VPN server, ensure that you have met the following requirements:

- The computer that functions as the VPN server must have two network adapters. Prior to configuring the VPN server, you must determine which interface accepts incoming traffic from untrusted networks. You specify this network interface during VPN setup.

- Determine how clients from untrusted networks receive IP addresses on the trusted network. You can configure the VPN server to interact with an existing DHCP server on the trusted network. When you do this, the VPN server leases blocks of 10 IP addresses and assigns them to remote clients. You also have the option of manually configuring an address pool from which the VPN server can lease IP addresses. When you do this, you must ensure that the manually selected IP addresses are not already in use and are not used in the future by clients other than those that connect using the VPN server.

- Decide whether you want the VPN server to authenticate connections or pass authentication requests on to a server with the NPS role installed. You might choose to configure the VPN server to pass authentication requests on to a server with the NPS role installed if you have multiple servers or if you have configured a stand-alone server as a VPN server as a way of enhancing security.

### VPN AUTHENTICATION

When planning to allow clients to remotely connect to trusted networks, consider the authentication protocols that can be used to establish those connections. Although Windows Server supports many protocols that have been in use for some time, these protocols are often less secure than more recently developed protocols. Windows Server supports the following protocols, listed from most secure to least secure:

- **Extensible Authentication Protocol-Transport Level Security (EAP-TLS)**   You use this protocol with smart cards or digital certificates. You can use this protocol only if you are using RADIUS authentication or if the remote access server performing authentication is domain-joined.

- **Microsoft Challenge Handshake Authentication Protocol version 2 (MS-CHAPv2)**    Provides mutual authentication. This means that not only is the user authenticated but the service that the user is connecting to is also authenticated. Allows for the encryption of the authentication process and the session.

- **Extensible Authentication Protocol-Message Digest 5 Challenge Handshake Authentication (EAP-MD5 CHAP)**    Supports encryption of authentication data through MD5 hashing and also uses the EAP framework. Used to support third-party clients.

- **Challenge Handshake Authentication Protocol (CHAP)**    Authentication data is encrypted through MD5 hashing. The data is not encrypted.

- **Password Authentication Protocol (PAP)**    This protocol does not encrypt authentication data, meaning that if the authentication is captured, the username and password data can be read directly without having to be decrypted.

### VPN PROTOCOLS

A Windows Server VPN server supports four VPN tunneling protocols. In most organizations, you leave the protocols enabled. Clients attempt to negotiate a connection using the most secure protocol available to them. VPN servers on computers running Windows Server support the following protocols:

- IKEv2
- SSTP
- L2TP/IPsec
- PPTP

### IKEV2

IKEv2 has the following features:

- Supports IPv6
- Enables VPN reconnect
- Supports EAP and Computer certificates for client authentication
- Does not support PAP or CHAP
- Only supports MS-CHAPv2 with EAP
- Supports data origin authentication, data integrity, replay protection, and data confidentiality
- Uses UDP port 500

VPN Reconnect enables the automatic reconnection of VPN connections without requiring users to perform manual authentication. VPN Reconnect works across different connections, so a VPN connection can remain active when a user switches between hotspots or a wired and wireless connection. VPN Reconnect allows for automatic reconnection without authentication for periods of disruption for up to 8 hours.

### SSTP

SSTP functions by encapsulating PPTP traffic over the Transport Layer Security (TLS) (formerly Secure Sockets Layer [SSL]) channel of the Secure Hypertext Transfer Protocol (HTTPS). The advantage of SSTP is that it uses TCP port 443, which means that it is likely to work in locations in which other protocols, such as IKEv2, L2TP/IPsec, and PPTP, do not work because of intervening firewalls.

SSTP has the following requirements:

- Requires that the client trusts the certification authority (CA) that issued the VPN server's SSL certificate.
- The SSL certificate must be configured with a name that matches the FQDN of the IP address of the external interface of the VPN server.
- Can't be used to create VPN connections if there is a web proxy that requires authentication.

### L2TP/IPSEC

Although L2TP/IPsec usually requires the deployment of digital certificates, it is possible, with special configuration, to get L2TP/IPsec to work with preshared keys. When used with digital certificates, L2TP/IPsec VPN clients must trust the CA that issued the certificate to the VPN server, and the VPN server must trust the CA that issued the certificates to the clients. The simplest way to implement L2TP/IPsec is by also deploying an Enterprise CA on the trusted network. L2TP/IPsec supports all authentication protocols that are supported with Windows Server, which means you can use the protocol with advanced authentication methods such as smart cards.

### PPTP

PPTP is the oldest VPN protocol supported by Windows Server. It is also the least secure. It is most often used by organizations that need to support clients running legacy operating systems or that haven't deployed the certificate infrastructure required to implement L2TP/IPsec. PPTP connections provide data confidentiality but do not provide data integrity or data origin protection. That means captured data can't be read, but you can't be sure that the transmitted data was the same data sent by the client.

## LAN routing

You can configure Windows Server to function as a network router in the same way that you configure traditional hardware devices to perform this role. LAN routing is often used with virtual machines to connect private or internal virtual machine networks with an external network. To perform the LAN routing function, Windows Server must have two or more network adapters. Windows Server supports using Routing Information Protocol (RIP) v2 for route discovery. You can also use the Routing and Remote Access console to configure static routes.

## Network address translation

Network address translation (NAT) enables you to share an internet connection with computers on an internal network. In a typical NAT configuration, the NAT server has two network interfaces, where one network interface is connected to the internet and the second network interface connects to a network with a private IP address range. Computers on the private IP address range can then establish communication with computers on the internet. It is also possible to configure port forwarding so all traffic that is sent to a particular port on the NAT server's public interface is directed to a specific IP address/port combination on a host on the private IP address range.

## DirectAccess

DirectAccess is an always-on remote access solution, which means that if a client computer is configured with DirectAccess and connects to the internet, a persistent connection is established between that computer and the organization's internal network. One big advantage of DirectAccess is that it does not require users to directly authenticate. The client computer determines that it is connected to the internet by attempting to connect to a website that is only accessible from the internal network. If the client determines that it is on a network other than the internal network, it automatically initiates a connection to the internal network.

When determining its network connection status, the client first attempts to determine whether it is connected to a native IPv6 network. If the client has been assigned a public IPv6 address, it can make a direct connection to the organization's internal DirectAccess servers. If the client determines that it is not connected to a native IPv6 network, it attempts to create an IPv6 over IPv4 tunnel using the 6to4 and then Teredo technologies. If connections cannot be established using these technologies, it attempts to use IP-HTTPS, which is similar to the SSTP protocol discussed earlier, except that it encapsulates IPv6 traffic within the HTTPS protocol.

When a connection is established, authentication occurs using computer certificates. These computer certificates must be preinstalled on the client, but the benefit of this requirement is that user intervention is not required. Authentication occurs automatically and the connection occurs seamlessly.

DirectAccess supports remote client management through a feature named Manage Out. Manage Out enables remote management functionality for DirectAccess clients, allowing administrative tasks, including tasks that in the past could only be performed on computers on a local area network, to be performed on clients without requiring a connection to cloud-hosted solutions such as Intune.

The primary drawback of DirectAccess is that it requires a domain-joined computer. Direct Access clients are configured through GPOs. The configuration GPO is automatically created through the DirectAccess setup process. This GPO is filtered so that it only applies to the security group you've designated to host the DirectAccess clients.

### DIRECTACCESS TOPOLOGIES

DirectAccess supports multiple deployment topologies. You don't have to deploy the DirectAccess server with a network adapter directly connected to the internet. Instead, you can integrate the DirectAccess server with your organization's existing edge topology. During your DirectAccess server deployment, the Remote Access Server Wizard asks you which of the topologies reflects your server configuration. The difference between them is as follows:

- **Edge**  This is the traditional DirectAccess deployment method. The computer hosting the server has two network adapters. The first network adapter is connected directly to the internet and has been assigned one or more public IPv4 addresses. The second network adapter connects directly to the internal trusted network.

- **Behind An Edge Device (With Two Network Adapters)**  In this type of deployment, the DirectAccess server is located behind a dedicated edge firewall. This configuration includes two network adapters. One of the network adapters on the DirectAccess server is connected to the perimeter network behind the edge firewall. The second network adapter connects directly to the internal trusted network.

- **Behind An Edge Device (With A Single Network Adapter)**  In this type of deployment, the DirectAccess server has a single network adapter connected to the internal network. The edge firewall passes traffic to the DirectAccess server.

### DIRECTACCESS SERVER

The DirectAccess server is a domain-joined computer running Windows Server 2012 or later that accepts connections from DirectAccess clients on untrusted networks, such as the internet, and provides access to resources on trusted networks. The DirectAccess server performs the following roles:

- Authenticates DirectAccess clients connecting from untrusted networks

- Functions as an IPsec tunnel mode endpoint for DirectAccess traffic from untrusted networks

Before you can configure a computer running Windows Server 2012 or later to function as a DirectAccess server, you must ensure that it meets the following requirements:

- The server must be a member of an Active Directory Domain Services domain.

- If the server is connected directly to the internet, it must have two network adapters: one that has a public IP address and one that is connected to the trusted internal network.

- The DirectAccess server can be deployed behind a NAT device, which limits DirectAccess to using IP over HTTPS (IP-HTTPS).

- A server connected to the internet only requires a single public IPv4 address. Two-factor authentication, using either a smart card or a one-time password (OTP), however, requires two consecutive public IPv4 addresses.

- The DirectAccess server can also host a VPN server. This functionality was not present in the Windows Server 2008 R2 version of DirectAccess.

- You can configure DirectAccess in a network load-balanced configuration of up to eight nodes.

- The TLS certificate installed on the DirectAccess server must contain an FQDN that resolves through DNS servers on the internet to the public IP address assigned to the DirectAccess server or to the gateway through which the DirectAccess server is published.

- The TLS certificate installed on the DirectAccess server must have a Certificate Revocation List (CRL) distribution point that is accessible to clients on the internet.

You should strongly consider obtaining the TLS certificate for your organization's DirectAccess server from a public CA. If you obtain the certificate this way, you don't have to worry about publishing the CRL from your internal certificate services deployment to a location that is accessible to the internet. Using a trusted third-party CA ensures that the CRL is available to clients on the internet.

A DirectAccess implementation also relies on the following infrastructure being present:

- **Active Directory domain controller**   DirectAccess clients and servers must be members of an Active Directory domain. By necessity, when you deploy a domain controller, you also deploy a DNS server. Active Directory, due to its basic nature, also makes Group Policy available.

- **Group Policy**   When you configure DirectAccess, the setup wizard creates a set of Group Policy objects (GPOs) that are configured with settings you choose in the wizard. They apply to DirectAccess clients, DirectAccess servers, and servers that you use to manage DirectAccess.

Prepare DNS servers by removing the ISATAP name from the global query block list. You must take this step on all DNS servers that are hosted on computers running Windows Server operating systems.

You can remove ISATAP from the DNS global query block list by issuing the following command on each DNS server and restarting the DNS server service:

```
Dnscmd /config /globalqueryblocklist wpad
```

Alternatively, you can remove ISATAP from the GlobalQueryBlockList value on the Computer\HKEY_LOCAL_MACHINE\SYSTEM\CurrentControlSet\Services\DNS\Parameters hive of the registry so that it contains only the wpad entry. After making this configuration change, you must restart the DNS server.

### NETWORK LOCATION SERVER

The Network Location Server (NLS) is a specially configured server that enables clients to determine whether they are on a trusted network or an untrusted network. The NLS server's only function is to respond to specially crafted HTTPS requests. When the client determines that it has a connection to any network, it sends this specially crafted HTTPS request. If there is a response to this request, the client determines that it is on a trusted network and disables the DirectAccess components. If there is no response to this request, the client assumes that it is connected to an untrusted network and initiates a DirectAccess connection.

DirectAccess clients are informed of the NLS's location through Group Policy. You don't have to configure these policies manually because they are created automatically when you use the DirectAccess Setup Wizard. Any server that hosts a website and has an SSL certificate installed can function as the NLS. You should ensure that the NLS is highly available because if this server fails, it causes all clients that are configured for DirectAccess on the trusted network to assume they are on an untrusted network.

## Implement and manage Azure Network Adapter

Azure Network Adapter allows you to create a point-to-site VPN connection to an Azure virtual network directly from Windows Admin Center on a computer running Windows Server 2019 or Windows Server 2022. Because it is a point-to-site VPN, the computer that you're configuring with Azure Network Adapter only needs a connection to the internet; it does not need to have a public IP address.

While it's possible to create point-to-site VPN connections from the Azure console, as is the case with creating an Azure VM from Windows Admin Center, this allows you to perform all the necessary tasks from the primary tool that you use to manage Windows Server. Windows Admin Center will also assist in the creation of Azure VPN gateways if one isn't already present on the virtual network to which you are creating a connection.

Once you have configured Azure Network Adapter, you'll be able to connect to and manage IaaS VMs running Windows Server operating systems connected to the virtual network the adapter connects to. You can configure multiple Azure virtual network adapters, each of which connects to a different Azure virtual network.

Azure Network Adapter is appropriate if you only need to connect one or more individual Windows Server computers to an Azure virtual network. If you need to connect your entire on-premises network to an Azure virtual network, you should use a site-to-site VPN or ExpressRoute, which are covered later in this chapter.

> **NEED MORE REVIEW?** **AZURE NETWORK ADAPTER**
>
> You can learn more about Azure Network Adapter at *https://docs.microsoft.com/azure/architecture/hybrid/azure-network-adapter.*

## Implement and manage Azure Extended Network

Extended Network for Azure, alternatively named Azure Extended Network, allows your organization to extend an on-premises subnet with a private IP address range into an Azure virtual network. This allows you to have existing on-premises hosts retain their private IP address when migrating or configuring coexistence with Azure.

Network extension is enabled through a bidirectional VXLAN tunnel between two Windows Server computers hosting virtual appliances. One virtual appliance is deployed on the on-premises subnet you wish to extend and one is deployed using nested virtualization in Azure on the network to which you wish to extend the IP address range. You can extend up to 250 addresses from an on-premises network to Azure. Extended Network, for Azure supports an aggregate throughput of approximately 700 Mbps with performance depending on the CPU capacity of the VXLAN tunnel endpoint appliances. If a firewall exists between your on-premises network and Azure, you will need to configure it to allow asymmetric routing traffic. This involves enabling TCP state bypass and disabling sequence number randomization.

Deployment occurs by adding the Extended Network extension to Windows Admin Center that is connected to an Azure subscription. You will need a virtual network in Azure that has a minimum of two subnets as well as an additional subnet for the gateway connection. One of the subnets will need the same address range as the on-premises private address range that you wish to extend into Azure. You'll also need to deploy a Windows Server VM in Azure configured for nested virtualization. This server will host the cloud instance of the virtual appliance. Once you have connected Windows Admin Center to your on-premises and Azure Windows Server virtual machine hosts and installed the Extended Network extension, you will be able to deploy and configure Extended Network for Azure. You need to configure each IP address that you wish to extend from on-premises to Azure, ensuring that there are no con-flicts with the same address being present both on-premises and in Azure. Once the address has been extended to Azure, it can be assigned to a VM connected to the appropriate Azure subnet.

> **NEED MORE REVIEW?** **EXTENDED NETWORK FOR AZURE**
>
> You can learn more about this topic at *https://docs.microsoft.com/windows-server/manage/windows-admin-center/azure/azure-extended-network*.

## Implement and manage Network Policy Server role

NPS enables you to configure network access policies. These policies can be related to remote connection requests, such as through a VPN or an RD gateway server. You can also configure a Windows Server with the NPS role as a RADIUS proxy. A RADIUS proxy forwards remote access connection requests to another RADIUS server that can authorize or deny that request.

You can configure the NPS role on Windows Server to function in one or more of the following capacities:

- NAP policy server
- RADIUS server
- RADIUS proxy

### Connection request policies

A connection request policy is a set of conditions that enable you to specify which RADIUS server performs the authorization and authentication process for specific RADIUS clients. You can configure multiple connection request policies on a server with the NPS role installed. When multiple policies are present, policies are processed according to the policy processing order. The first policy where conditions are met is used.

## Network access server type

One of the first steps you take when creating a connection request policy is to specify the type of network access server that will be sending traffic to the NPS server. When configuring the policy, you can choose from the following connection types:

- **Remote Desktop Gateway**  Use this option when you are configuring the NPS server to perform authentication for an RD Gateway server.

- **Remote Access Server (VPN-Dial Up)**  Use this option when you are configuring the NPS server to perform authentication for remote access. You can use this method with both VPN and dial-up servers.

- **Unspecified**  Use this type if you are configuring NPS to perform authentication for an 802.1x authenticating switch or wireless access point.

You can also configure a vendor-specific network access server and use the vendor-specific ID if you are configuring NPS to perform authentication from a third-party access server.

## Request policy conditions

When you configure multiple policies, the policies are evaluated in numerical order, with the first policy that matches the specified conditions being used. You add conditions on the Specify Conditions page of the New Connection Request Policy wizard. Although at least one condition must exist, you can also use multiple conditions when you create a connection request policy. You can select from the following conditions:

- **Username**  The username as specified in the RADIUS message. This name includes both the user account name and the RADIUS realm name. You can use wildcards when configuring this condition.

- **Access Client IPv4 Address**  The IPv4 address of the client requesting access.

- **Access Client IPv6 Address**  The IPv6 address of the client requesting access.

- **Framed Protocol**  Use this condition when you want to apply the policy to clients using a specific framing protocol such as PPP.

- **Service Type**  Enables you to create a condition that depends on the type of service.

- **Tunnel Type**  Use this condition to create a policy that applies only to a specific type of tunnel, such as an LT2P/IPsec tunnel.

- **Day and Time Restrictions**  Enables you to create a condition determining when connection attempts will be accepted or denied. Day and time restrictions are based on the time zone set on the NPS server.

- **Calling Station ID**  This RADIUS client property enables the policy to match the telephone number of the network access server to which the client connected. For example, if the dial-up server had the phone number 555-5555, it could be used as the calling station ID.

- **Client Friendly Name** This RADIUS client property enables the policy to match the identity of the RADIUS client that forwarded the connection request to the NPS server. For example, if the VPN server were named VPN-ALPHA, it could be used as the client friendly name.

- **Client IPv4 Address** This RADIUS client property enables the policy to match the IPv4 address of the RADIUS client that forwarded the connection request to the NPS server. For example, you could use the IPv4 address of a VPN server as the client IPv4 address.

- **Client IPv6 Address** This RADIUS client property enables the policy to match the IPv6 address of the RADIUS client that forwarded the connection request to the NPS server. For example, you could use the IPv6 address of a VPN server as the client IPv6 address.

- **Client Vendor** Enables you to use the name of the RADIUS client vendor that is forwarding connection requests to the NPS server.

- **Called Station ID** Similar to the RADIUS client property, this property enables you to specify the telephone number of the network access server. In this and the following property items, the network access server is not using RADIUS but is forwarding authentication traffic to the server with the NPS role installed.

- **NAS Identifier** In this scenario, NAS is the acronym of Network Access Server rather than Network Attached Storage. This property enables you to specify a character string representing the name of the network access server.

- **NAS IPv4 Address** This property enables you to specify the IPv4 address of the network access server.

- **NAS IPv6 Address** Use this property to specify the IPv6 address of the network access server.

- **NAS Port Type** Use this property to specify the types of access media, including ISDN, VPN, Ethernet, or Cable.

RADIUS terminology can be confusing. It is important to remember that RADIUS clients are not the same as remote access clients. For example, a VPN or dial-up server that forwards authentication requests to an NPS server is a RADIUS client. The remote computer making the connection to the VPN or dial-up server is not a RADIUS client.

## Connection request forwarding

By configuring a connection request forwarding setting, you can specify whether the local server performs authentication or forwards authentication traffic to a remote RADIUS server group. You can also configure connection request forwarding so that users are automatically accepted without any credential validation. You can also configure accounting on the Specify Connection Request Forwarding page. Accounting enables you to record RADIUS traffic.

## Authentication methods

The Specify Authentication Methods page enables you to configure which authentication method or methods clients can use. These settings override any authentication methods specified in the network policy. When you specify multiple methods, the NPS server attempts the most secure method, and then the next most secure method, until it reaches the least secure specified method. The most secure authentication types are the Extensible Authentication Protocols (EAPs), which include the following:

- Microsoft: Smart Card or Other Certificate
- Microsoft: Protected EAP (PEAP)
- Microsoft: Secured Password (EAP-MSCHAP v2)

You can also configure NPS to support less secure authentication protocols. The less secure authentication protocols, from most secure to least secure, are the following:

- **Microsoft Encrypted Authentication Version 2 (MS-CHAP-v2)**   When enabling this authentication method, you can also allow users to change passwords after that password has expired. MS-CHAP-v2 was first introduced with Windows NT 4.0 Service Pack 4.

- **Microsoft Encrypted Authentication (MS-CHAP)**   A less secure version of MS-CHAP-v2. You can also allow users to change passwords after the password expiration date.

- **Encrypted Authentication (CHAP)**   Unless there is an excellent reason otherwise, don't use this authentication protocol. You should use this protocol only if you need to support old clients that don't support more secure authentication protocols.

- **Unencrypted Authentication (PAP, SPAP)**   You use these protocols only if you need to support old clients that don't support more secure authentication protocols. Use these protocols with care because they pass credentials in cleartext format.

- **Allow Clients To Connect Without Negotiating An Authentication Method**   This option enables clients to connect without requiring a specific authentication method.

## Realm and RADIUS attributes

You can apply a realm name as well as RADIUS attributes to a connection request policy. This is often done when the computer with the NPS server role installed is functioning as a RADIUS proxy. When functioning as a proxy, the server with the NPS role installed can alter attributes that were passed to it by a RADIUS client. This process enables the RADIUS server providing authentication to use the altered attributes instead of the ones sent by the client. When functioning as a RADIUS proxy, the server with the NPS role installed can also add additional attributes to the traffic forwarded to the RADIUS server that provides authentication services.

## Default connection request policy

Windows Server creates a default connection request policy when you deploy the NPS role. The name of this policy is Use Windows Authentication For All Users, and it is assigned the processing order of 999999. The NPS server uses this policy as a last resort. The policy has the following properties, with all other properties not configured:

- Authentication Methods: Unspecified
- Authentication: Authenticate Requests On This Server
- Conditions: Sunday To Saturday, 00:00 To 24:00

## Creating a connection request policy

You can create a connection request policy from the NPS console. To create a connection request policy, perform the following steps:

1. Open the NPS console from the Tools menu in Server Manager, expand the Policies node, and select **Connection Request Policies**. In the Action menu, select **New**.

2. On the **Specify Connection Request Policy Name And Connection Type** page, provide a policy name and specify the type of network access server to which the policy applies.

3. On the **Specify Conditions** page, add at least one condition that differentiates the policy from any other policies on the server with the NPS role installed.

4. On the **Specify Connection Request Forwarding** page, specify whether the local server will perform authentication, or whether the server with the NPS role installed will function as a RADIUS proxy and forward requests to a remote server. You can also configure accounting on this page.

5. On the **Specify Authentication Methods** page, choose whether to override network policy authentication settings. If you do, you must specify which authentication methods you will use in place of the ones specified in the network policy.

6. If the server with the NPS role installed is functioning as a RADIUS proxy, you can configure additional attributes as well as replace existing attributes forwarded by a RADIUS client on the **Configure Settings** page.

7. You then complete the New Connection Request Policy Wizard. The policy will be assigned the next available processing order number. You can right-click the policy and select **Move Up** or **Move Down** to change the policy processing order.

## IP filters

IP filters enable you to control incoming and outgoing traffic based on source and destination IP address, as well as port and protocol. You use IP address filters to limit communication between clients and specific hosts and services on the network. You can configure IP filters on the **Settings** page of the **Network Policy properties** or when creating a network policy.

## Encryption

When configuring network policies, you can select which types of encryption the connection can use on the **Configure Settings** page of the **New Network Policy Wizard** or by editing the properties of an existing network policy. If you want to force network connections to use strong encryption, ensure that the **No Encryption** and **Basic Encryption** settings are not selected in the network policy. The key length determines the strength of the encryption. Although increased key length does improve security, it also comes at the cost of increased processor overhead.

## IP settings

IP settings, which you can configure when creating a network policy or by editing the properties of a policy, enable you to configure how a client receives an IP address. You can configure the following settings:

- Server Must Supply An IP Address
- Client May Request An IP Address
- Server Settings Determine IP Address Assignment
- Assign A Static IPv4 Address

You can configure an IPv6 address on the **Standard** page of the RADIUS attributes section.

## Creating network policies

Network policies determine which users and computers are authorized to connect to the network. The process of creating network policies is similar to creating connection request policies. Both sets of policies share many of the same elements. To create a network policy, perform the following steps:

1. In the NPS console, select **Network Policies** under the **Policies** node and on the **Action** menu, select **New**.

2. On the **Specify Network Policy Name And Connection Type** page, enter a policy name and specify the type of network access server. The options are the following:

   - Remote Desktop Gateway
   - Remote Access Server (VPN-Dial Up)

3. On the **Specify Conditions** page, select one or more conditions that determine whether the policy applies.

   - **Windows Groups**    The user or computer must belong to a Windows security group.
   - **Machine Groups**    The computer must belong to a Windows security group.
   - **User Groups**    The user must belong to a Windows security group.
   - **Day And Time Restrictions**    Policy applies only at specific dates and times.
   - **Access Client IPv4 Address**    The client's IPv4 address, not the RADIUS client's IP address.
   - **Access Client IPv6 Address**    The client's IPv6 address.
   - **Authentication Type**    Authentication method used, which includes CHAP, EAP, MS-CHAP v1, MS-CHAP v2, PAP, PEAP, and Unauthenticated.

- **Allowed EAP Types** Allowed EAP types, which includes Microsoft: Smart Card or other certificate, Microsoft PEAP, and Microsoft: EAP-MSCHAP v2.
- **Framed Protocol** Policy applies only to clients using the specified framed protocol, such as PPP or SLIP.
- **Service Type** Applies when the client uses a particular service type.
- **Tunnel Type** Applies when the client uses a particular tunnel type.
- **Calling Station ID** RADIUS calling station ID.
- **Client Friendly Name** RADIUS client name.
- **Client IPv4 Address** RADIUS IPv4 address.
- **Client IPv6 Address** RADIUS IPv6 address.
- **Client Vendor** RADIUS client vendor.
- **MS-RAS Vendor** RADIUS vendor ID.
- **Called Station ID** Number of the network access server.
- **NAS Identifier** Network access server name.
- **NAS IPv4 Address** Network access server IPv4 address.
- **NAS IPv6 Address** Network access server IPv6 address.
- **NAS Port Type** Network access server media type, including ISDN, wireless, VPN, or tunnel.

4. On the **Specify Access Permission** page, choose whether access is granted or denied to computers or users that meet the specified conditions.

5. On the **Configure Authentication Methods** page, specify which authentication methods the client can use to authenticate.

6. On the **Configure Constraints** page, you can configure the following properties:
   - Idle Timeout
   - Session Timeout
   - Called Station ID
   - Day and Time Restrictions
   - NAS Port Type

7. On the **Configure Settings** page of the **New Network Policy Wizard**, you can configure the following:
   - RADIUS Attributes
   - Multilink and Bandwidth Allocation Protocol
   - IP Filters
   - Encryption
   - IP Settings

8. Clicking Next enables you to complete the wizard. You can then alter the position of the policy by moving it up and down. Clients use the first policy for which they meet the conditions.

### NPS templates

NPS templates enable you to save a specific NPS component configuration so that it can be reused or exported to another server with the NPS role installed. You can apply the template to multiple policies to ensure uniform configuration. You can configure the following templates:

- Shared Secrets
- RADIUS Clients
- Remote RADIUS Servers
- IP Filters

To configure a template, select the type of template that you want to configure in the NPS console. Then, from the Action menu, select New. Configure the template in the same way that you would configure the associated properties in a policy.

## Implement Web Application Proxy

Web Application Proxy is a remote access role that allows you to configure a reverse proxy to publish applications and services hosted on protected networks to hosts on untrusted networks, such as the internet. When you publish an application through Web Application Proxy, you can choose to use Active Directory Federation Services (AD FS) to perform preauthentication and configure pass-through mode. When you configure pass-through mode, the Web Application Proxy passes all authentication traffic to the server hosting the published application.

To deploy Web Application Proxy, you need to already have deployed AD FS on a server in the domain. When you deploy the Web Application Proxy, you specify the address of the AD FS server. You also need to import a copy of the web server certificate used with AD FS, including the private key, onto the server that will host the Web Application Proxy. As the server that hosts the Web Application Proxy will be responsible for proxying traffic from hosts on untrusted networks to applications hosted on protected networks, it should be configured as a standalone server rather than a server that is domain-joined.

## Implement Azure Relay

Azure Relay (previously named Service Bus Relay) allows you to securely connect services that run on on-premises networks to Azure. Azure Relay can be scoped to a single application endpoint on a specific computer. This allows you to connect a single application to Azure without creating a broader tunnel for traffic as is the case with a VPN or ExpressRoute connection.

Azure Relay supports the following scenarios between on-premises services and workloads running in Azure:

- Uni-directional, request/response, and peer-to-peer communication
- Unbuffered socket communication across network boundaries
- Event distribution used in publish/subscribe scenarios

Azure Relay has the following features:

- **Hybrid Connections**   Hybrid Connections uses the open standard web sockets. It supports .NET Core, .NET Framework, JavaScript/Node.JS, standards-based open protocols, and remote procedure call (RPC) programming models.
- **WCF Relays**   This uses Windows Communication Foundation (WCF) to enable remote procedure calls. WCF Relays also supports the .NET Framework.

> **NEED MORE REVIEW?**   **AZURE RELAY**
>
> You can learn more about Azure Relay at *https://docs.microsoft.com/azure/azure-relay/relay-what-is-it.*

## Implement site-to-site VPN

An Azure site-to-site VPN allows you to connect your on-premises network to Azure by using a secure VPN tunnel across the public internet. Azure VPN connections are like traditional VPN connections that might exist between a branch office and a head office location except in this case, the connection is between an on-premises network and an Azure virtual network. When deploying a site-to-site VPN, you deploy an Azure VPN gateway on an Azure virtual network. The Azure VPN gateway functions as the Azure VPN endpoint. Your on-premises VPN endpoint, which can be a Windows Server computer with RRAS installed but is usually a specific device, functions as the VPN on-premises endpoint.

Each Azure virtual network can only have a single VPN gateway, but each VPN gateway supports multiple connections. Windows Server's Azure Network Adapter functions as a point-to-site VPN rather than a site-to-site VPN.

> **NEED MORE REVIEW?**   **SITE-TO-SITE VPN**
>
> You can learn more about Azure site-to-site VPNs at *https://docs.microsoft.com/en-us/azure/vpn-gateway/tutorial-site-to-site-portal.*

## Azure ExpressRoute

ExpressRoute allows your organization to have a dedicated private high-speed connection from an on-premises network to Azure. As the connection is dedicated and the equipment is managed by the ExpressRoute provider, ExpressRoute connections have a higher SLA than VPN connections to Azure and also provide guaranteed bandwidth speed. Another difference between ExpressRoute and Azure VPN traffic is that ExpressRoute traffic does not pass across the public internet. As well as connecting on-premises workloads to Azure, ExpressRoute can be used for on-premises traffic to all of Microsoft's clouds, including Microsoft 365 and Dynamics.

> ***NEED MORE REVIEW?*** **AZURE EXPRESSROUTE**
>
> You can learn more about Azure ExpressRoute at *https://docs.microsoft.com/en-au/azure/expressroute/expressroute-introduction*.

## Implement Azure Virtual WAN

Many organizations have branch offices connected to each other using site-to-site VPNs. Azure Virtual WAN allows your organization to use Azure's network as a hub-and-spoke architecture, with Azure functioning as the hub and connections out to branch offices functioning as spokes. For example, if an organization with branch offices in Melbourne, Auckland, Seattle, and Dubai adopted Azure Virtual WAN, any traffic that was passing from Melbourne to Dubai or from Seattle to Auckland would pass across that site's connection to Azure, across Azure's backbone and then back down to the destination site.

Azure Virtual WAN allows geographically distributed organizations with multiple branch offices to remove existing cross-site VPN connections and instead route everything through Azure. As most organizations that adopt hybrid cloud topologies are likely to centralize resources and workloads in Azure rather than host them at a specific branch office, it's likely that whatever remaining inter-branch-office site communication does occur would be minimal and unlikely to justify the need for separate VPN or dedicated connections between those remote on-premises sites.

> ***NEED MORE REVIEW?*** **AZURE VIRTUAL WAN**
>
> You can learn more about Azure Virtual WAN at *https://docs.microsoft.com/azure/virtual-wan/virtual-wan-about*.

## Implement Azure AD Application Proxy

You can use Azure AD Application Proxy to provide users on the internet with access to applications and workloads running on on-premises networks that use Active Directory authentication. You can use Azure AD Application Proxy with the following application types:

- Web applications that use Integrated Windows Authentication
- Web applications that use header-based or form-based authentication

- Applications hosted through Remote Desktop Gateway
- Rich client applications that are integrated with Microsoft Authentication Library (MSAL)

Azure AD Application Proxy requires less administrative effort to configure than Web Application Proxy because you only need to deploy the Application Proxy Service in Azure and the Application Proxy connector on-premises. The Application Proxy connector can be deployed on a Windows Server computer running on a perimeter network and makes outbound connections to Azure. You can also deploy the Application Proxy connector directly on an internal network if you choose. The computer hosting the Application Proxy connector must be able to directly connect to the backend application. You do not need to open any port on the perimeter firewall to allow inbound communication to the Application Proxy connector. You can deploy multiple Application Proxy connectors to ensure they remain highly available.

> **NEED MORE REVIEW?** **AZURE AD APPLICATION PROXY**
>
> You can learn more about Azure AD Application Proxy at *https://docs.microsoft.com/azure/active-directory/app-proxy/what-is-application-proxy*.

## Use Azure App Service Hybrid Connections

Azure App Service Hybrid Connections allow connections between any on-premises workload that communicate with a relay agent that is able to send outbound requests to Azure on port 443 and workloads in Azure. For example, you can use Azure App Service Hybrid Connections to allow a web app running in Azure to connect to an SQL Server database running on-premises through a relay agent deployed on a perimeter network. Azure App Service Hybrid Connections provide access from an app running in Azure to a Transmission Control Protocol (TCP) endpoint. App Service Hybrid Connections are not limited to workloads running on Windows Server platforms, and you can configure App Service Hybrid Connections to access any resource provided it functions as a TCP endpoint, regardless of which application protocol is being used.

Hybrid Connections use a relay agent usually deployed on a perimeter network that can establish connectivity to the TCP endpoint on an internal on-premises network and establish a connection outbound on TCP port 443 to Azure. This connection is secured by using Transport Layer Security (TLS) 1.2, and shared access signature (SAS) keys are used for authentication and authorization.

App Service Hybrid Connections have the following functionality:

- Workloads running in Azure can access on-premises systems and services in a secure manner.
- The on-premises system or service doesn't need to be directly accessible to hosts on the internet but only accessible to the relay agent on the perimeter network.

- All communication is initiated in an outbound manner from the relay agent on TCP port 443 and it is not necessary to open an inbound firewall port on the perimeter firewall.

App Service Hybrid Connections have the following limitations:

- Cannot connect to UDP endpoints
- Cannot connect to TCP-based services that use dynamic ports
- Does not support Lightweight Directory Access Protocol (LDAP)

---

**NEED MORE REVIEW?**   **AZURE APP SERVICE HYBRID CONNECTIONS**

You can learn more about Azure App Service Hybrid Connections at *https://docs.microsoft. com/azure/app-service/app-service-hybrid-connections*.

---

**EXAM TIP**

Use Azure Relay instead of App Service Hybrid Connections when there is no front-end web app running in Azure. Use Azure Relay instead of Azure AD Application Proxy when the application doesn't require Azure AD Authentication.

---

# Chapter summary

- Active Directory–integrated zones can replicate to any domain controller in a domain or a forest, or can be replicated only to domain controllers with a specific custom partition.
- DNS forwarders can be used to forward traffic from on-premises DNS servers to DNS servers in Azure that host Azure private zones as long as the on-premises network is connected to a specially configured Azure virtual network.
- DNSSEC allows for cryptographic verification of DNS records.
- IPAM can be used to manage DNS and DHCP servers in on-premises environments.
- Azure Network Adapter can connect a single Windows Server computer to an Azure virtual network.
- Azure Extended Network allows an IP address range to span an on-premises network and an Azure virtual network.
- There are a variety of methods you can use to allow Azure workloads to access on-premises workloads and whether you use Azure Relay, Application Proxy, or App Service Hybrid Connections depends on the nature of the on-premises workload.

# Thought experiment

In this thought experiment, demonstrate your skills and knowledge of the topics covered in this chapter. You can find answers to this thought experiment in the next section.

You are in the process of updating the network infrastructure of your existing on-premises network. You have four physical local area networks, each of which you expect will host around 230 hosts. Each local area network is connected to the others by routers. You have deployed Active Directory Domain Controllers hosting the DNS role on Subnet_Alpha and Subnet_Delta. You have also deployed member servers with the DHCP role service on Subnet_Alpha and Subnet_Delta. You want to manage all DHCP scopes and DNS zones centrally using IPAM. You have configured the Active Directory–integrated DNS zone tailwindtraders.com with DNSSEC. With this information in mind, answer the following questions:

1. What type of computer should you deploy the IPAM role on?

2. Instead of deploying DHCP servers on Subnet_Beta and Subnet_Gamma, what other role could you deploy to allow clients on those networks to get addresses from an authorized DHCP server?

3. How can you ensure that clients only accept digitally signed DNS records from the tailwindtraders.com DNS zone?

# Thought experiment answers

This section contains the solution to the thought experiment. Each answer explains why the answer choice is correct.

1. You should deploy the IPAM service on a Windows Server domain member that does not function as a domain controller, DHCP server, or DNS server.

2. You could deploy a DHCP relay on Subnet_Beta and Subnet_Gamma to allow clients on those networks to get addresses from an authorized DHCP server.

3. Configure the Name Resolution Policy Table to allow digitally signed records only from the tailwindtraders.com zone.

# CHAPTER 5

# Manage storage and file services

The most common workload for Windows Server is as a file server. This is because ultimately most organizations create documents that need to be stored somewhere and often shared even if their primary business does not involve document creation. Windows Server provides a number of technologies that address the problems that occur related to the reliable storage and sharing of files. These include the humble file shares themselves, synchronization technologies to replicate file share contents across hybrid environments, and technologies that improve the performance and reliability of underlying storage technologies.

## Skills covered in this chapter:

- Skill 5.1: Configure and manage Azure File Sync
- Skill 5.2: Configure and manage Windows Server File Shares
- Skill 5.3: Configure Windows Server Storage

## Skill 5.1: Configure and manage Azure File Sync

Azure File Sync is one of the most useful hybrid technologies available for Windows Server. Anyone who has managed a file server knows the challenges they pose, from having to remove disused files on a regular basis to ensure that there is enough space for new files, to challenges around ensuring that files are regularly backed up, and even to being able to restore a file that you might have removed at some point to save space because someone actually needs it now. Azure File Sync helps you address all these problems, reducing the amount of time you need to spend maintaining file servers so you can get on with the million other things on your to-do list. This objective deals with how to set up and use Azure File Sync.

**This skill covers how to:**

- Create Azure File Sync Service
- Create sync groups
- Create cloud endpoints
- Register servers
- Create server endpoints
- Configure cloud tiering
- Monitor File Sync
- Migrate DFS to Azure File Sync

## Create Azure File Sync Service

The backbone of Azure File Sync is the Storage Sync Service. The storage sync service is the service that runs in Azure that manages Azure. You should deploy as few storage sync services as necessary since a Windows Server file server can only be registered with one sync service and file servers that are connected to different storage sync services are unable to synchronize with each other.

You should plan to deploy the storage sync service and the Azure File Share endpoints used by each sync group in the same Azure region and resource group. To deploy a storage sync service, perform the following steps:

1. In the Azure portal select **Create a resource** and then search for Azure File Sync. In the list of results select **Azure File Sync** and then select **Create**.

2. On the Deploy Storage Sync page, provide the following:

    - **Name**  A name for the storage sync service. This name only needs to be unique on a per-region basis, but it's a good idea to have it unique for your organization.

    - **Subscription**  The name of the subscription that will host the storage sync service. This will be the subscription where costs accrue for the service.

    - **Resource Group**  The resource group that will host the storage sync service. You should also plan to host the storage account used with the sync service in the same resource group.

    - **Location**  The location where you will deploy Azure File Sync. This location should be geographically proximate to where your server endpoints are. Remember that clients will be accessing files through the file server endpoints close to them. Bandwidth and latency between the server endpoint and the file share is generally only an issue when there is a substantive delay between a file that is tiered being requested and it synchronizing back to the endpoint.

# Create sync groups

A sync group allows you to replicate a specific folder and file structure across server and Azure File Share endpoints. Each sync group has a single Azure file share endpoint but can have multiple server endpoints. An Azure file storage sync service can host multiple sync groups, and a Windows Server endpoint can participate in multiple sync groups as long as those sync groups belong to the same storage sync service. To create a sync group, you need to specify a sync group name, which is separate from the sync service name; the name of the storage account that will be used; and the name of the Azure File Share that will be used. You should create the storage account and Azure File Share before creating the sync group.

# Create cloud endpoints

The back end of Azure File Sync is an *Azure File Share*, also termed a *cloud endpoint*. This is a cloud file share that will store any file that is written to an Azure File Sync endpoint. The back-end Azure File Share stores the entire contents of what appears to be on the file share that is the front end for Azure File Sync. Creating a file share involves creating a storage account and then creating the file share within the storage account.

To create an Azure File Share, consider the following:

- **Performance requirements**   In most cases, the only computers interacting with the file share in an Azure File Sync deployment are the server endpoints. This means that you are unlikely to require the higher I/O performance capabilities of a premium file share that is hosted on solid-state disk (SSD)-based hardware.

- **Redundancy requirements**   Standard file shares can use locally redundant, zone-redundant, or geo-redundant storage. Large file shares of the type you are likely to use with Azure File Sync are only available with locally redundant and zone-redundant storage.

- **File share size**   Local and zone redundant storage accounts allow for file shares that span up to 100 TiB. The file share size will need to be able to hold all the tiered data from your file share endpoints and should be substantially larger than the storage on any on-premises server. The amount of storage you allocate to a file share will depend on the amount of data you need to tier and how much storing that data costs. Storage and transfer costs are billed separately, and even if you create a file share that is larger than you need, your organization will only be billed by the storage capacity actually used.

You can configure Azure Backup to back up this file share endpoint. The advantage of this is that in the event of data corruption or deletion, you can just recover data to the Azure File Share in the cloud from the Azure console, and it will replicate down to all the Azure File Sync endpoints.

# Register servers

The Azure File Sync agent allows you to register a server with a storage sync service. To register a server, download and install the Azure File Sync agent from the Microsoft Download Center.

As part of the installation process, you can configure the agent to be automatically updated through Microsoft Update. When the installation completes, you perform registration with a storage sync service. To register a server, you need local Administrator privileges on the server you want to register and you need an Azure account that is a member of the Owner or Contributor management role for the storage sync service in Azure. You can delegate these roles to an Azure AD account under **Access Control (IAM)** on the Storage Sync Service properties page in the Azure console. During the registration process, you must specify the Azure subscription, resource group, and storage sync service that will be used with the server endpoint.

Registration will use Azure credentials to create a trust relationship between the storage sync service and the Windows Server computer. The Windows Server instance will then create an identity separate from the user account used to create the registration that will function as long as the server remains registered and the current share Access Signature token associated with the storage account remains valid.

## Create server endpoints

An Azure File Sync endpoint consists of a server and a path that are enrolled in an Azure File Sync service. A Windows Server can host multiple endpoints, each of which has a different path, as long as those endpoints are in different sync groups associated with the same sync service. An Azure File Sync endpoint functions as the folder structure that underlies a normal file share. Administrators create a traditional shared folder and point it at the path that the Azure File Sync endpoint replicates to. You can also point a Distributed File System (DFS) namespace at this path, replacing Distributed File System Replication (DFSR) with Azure File Sync replication while still keeping the navigational advantages of the DFS way of identifying shared folders.

Create a server endpoint by adding the server that you registered with the storage sync service and specifying the local path to the files that you want to replicate using Azure File Sync. When creating the server endpoint, you also specify the cloud tiering settings in terms of how much free space should always be available on the local volume that hosts the files and how many days after a file was last accessed should pass before the file is tiered. After the endpoint is created, any files in the path specified will be replicated up to the Azure File Share that functions as the cloud endpoint. If you create an endpoint that points to the system volume of the registered server, you cannot enable cloud tiering on that endpoint.

File shares that serve as front ends for Azure File Sync endpoints should have the same share permissions. If you are using Azure File Sync with a failover cluster, ensure that the agent is installed on each node in the cluster and that each node in the cluster is registered to the same storage sync service.

> **NEED MORE REVIEW?** **DEPLOY AZURE FILE SYNC**
>
> You can learn more about deploying Azure File Sync at *https://docs.microsoft.com/en-us/azure/storage/file-sync/file-sync-deployment-guide*.

# Configure cloud tiering

Azure File Sync uses a process called *cloud tiering* to ensure that there is capacity on the volume that hosts the share. Cloud tiering means that you don't need to worry about constantly freeing up space for new files. You can configure Azure File Sync on a per-file share basis to tier files based on when the file was last accessed, how much free space there is on the volume that hosts the share, or both. For example, you might configure Azure File Sync so that any file that hasn't been accessed in 14 days on a particular share is automatically tiered to Azure. You could also specify that the least recently accessed files be automatically tiered to Azure in the event that the volume has only 30 percent free space remaining. If you have both a policy to tier files that exceed a certain age and a requirement that a certain amount of space still be available on the volume, Azure File Sync will ensure that requirement for free space is met by tiering least recently accessed files until the free space requirement is met.

From the users' perspective, a tiered file still appears as though it's on the file server that they are accessing. If users try to open the file, it syncs down from the back-end Azure File Share to the Azure File Sync file share endpoint and then opens normally. Cloud tiering can be configured on a per-server endpoint basis in the Azure console.

# Monitor File Sync

You can monitor Azure File Sync using Azure Monitor, the Storage Sync Service, and Windows Server. Azure Monitor provides the following data:

- Bytes synced
- Cloud tiering cache hit rate
- Cloud tiering recall size
- Cloud tiering recall size by application
- Cloud tiering recall success rate
- Cloud tiering recall throughput
- Files not syncing
- Files synced
- Server cache size
- Server online status
- Sync session results

The Storage Sync Service in the Azure portal provides you with the following data:

- Registered server health
- Server endpoint health
    - Files not syncing
    - Sync activity
    - Cloud tiering efficiency

- Files not tiering
- Recall errors
- Metrics

You can also view the Telemetry event log in Event Viewer on a server endpoint under Applications and Services\Microsoft\FileSync\Agent to view sync health information. Azure File Sync performance counters are available in Performance Monitor that allow you to view bandwidth utilization and performance of the Azure File Sync agent.

> **NEED MORE REVIEW?**   **MONITOR AZURE FILE SYNC**
>
> You can learn more about monitoring Azure File Sync at *https://docs.microsoft.com/en-us/azure/storage/file-sync/file-sync-monitoring*.

## Migrate DFS to Azure File Sync

When you migrate DFS to Azure File Sync, you replace the older DFS file replication technology with Azure File Sync. You'll learn about both these technologies in more detail later in the chapter. The technology that is relevant to Azure File Sync is the namespace technology.

When you use DFS Namespaces, you can configure a single UNC path to map to multiple SMB shares. For example \\adatum\shares\hovercraft can map to \\Adelaide-fs01\hovercraft as well as \\Melbourne-fs01\hovercraft. When a client attempts to access the DFS UNC path, they are directed by DFS to the closest SMB endpoint. When used with DFS replication, it meant that a user attempting to access a share would be connected to the closest DFS endpoint. When you use DFS Namespaces with Azure File Sync, a client that navigates to the DFS address will be directed to the closest Azure File Sync endpoint.

To migrate from DFS replication to Azure File Sync replication, perform the following steps:

1. Create a new sync group that will be used as the substitute for the DFS replication topology you are replacing.
2. Start on the server that has the full set of data in your DFS replication topology to migrate. Install Azure File Sync on that server.
3. Register that server and create a server endpoint for the first server to be migrated. Do not enable cloud tiering.
4. Let all the data on that server sync to your Azure File Share cloud endpoint.
5. Install and register the Azure File Sync agent on each of the remaining servers that host DFS replicas.
6. Disable DFS replication on each server.
7. Create an Azure File Sync server endpoint on each of the previous servers that participated in DFS replication. Do not enable cloud tiering.
8. Ensure that the sync process completes and test your topology.

9.    Retire DFS-R.

10.   Enable cloud tiering on any server endpoint as desired.

> **NEED MORE REVIEW?    USING DFS NAMESPACES WITH AZURE FILES**
>
> You can learn more about using DFS Namespaces with Azure files at *https://docs.microsoft.com/en-us/azure/storage/files/files-manage-namespaces*.

> **EXAM TIP**
>
> Remember what steps you need to take to configure a new server to sync with an Azure storage account's file share.

# Skill 5.2: Configure and manage Windows Server File Shares

Traditionally, the most common use for Windows Servers has been as a file server. No matter how advanced technology gets, people who work in an organization need a way to share files with one another that is less chaotic than emailing them or handing them over on USB drives. Even with cloud storage options such as Teams, SharePoint Online, and OneDrive, many organizations still make use of the humble file server as a way of storing and sharing documents.

> **This skill covers how to:**
> - Configure Windows Server File Share access
> - Configure file screens
> - Configure File Server Resource Manager quotas
> - Use additional FSRM functionality
> - Configure BranchCache
> - Implement and configure Distributed File System

## Configure Windows Server File Share access

The basic idea with shared folders is that you create a folder and assign permissions to a group, such as a department within your organization, and the people in that group use that space on the file server to store files to be shared with the group.

For example, you create a shared folder named Managers on a file server named FS1. Next, you set share permissions on the shared folder and file system permissions on the files and folders within the shared folder. Permissions allow you to control who can access the shared folder and what users can do with that access. For example, permissions determine whether they are limited to just read-only access or whether they can create and edit new and existing files.

When you set share permissions and file system permissions for a shared folder, the most restrictive permissions apply. For example, if you configure the share permission so that the Everyone group has Full Control and then configure the file permission so that the Domain Users group has Read Access, a user who is a member of the Domain Users group accessing the file over the network has Read Access.

Things get a little more complicated when a user is a member of multiple groups; in this case, the most cumulative permission applies. For example, in a file where the Domain Users group has Read Access, but the Managers group has Full Control, a user who is a member of both Domain Users and Managers who accesses the file over the network has the Full Control permission. This is great for a certification exam question, but it can be needlessly complex when you're trying to untangle permissions to resolve a service desk ticket.

You can create shared folders in a variety of ways. The way that many administrators do it, often out of habit, is by using the built-in functionality of File Explorer. If you are using File Explorer to share folders, you have two general options when it comes to permissions:

- **Simple Share Permissions.** When you use the Simple Share Permissions option, you specify whether a user or group account has Read or Read/Write permissions to a shared folder. When you use Simple Share Permissions, both the share permissions and the file and folder level permissions are set at the same time. It is important to note that any files and folders in the shared folder path have their permissions reset to match those configured through the File Sharing dialog box. This, however, doesn't happen with other forms of share permission configurations.

- **Advanced Share Permissions.** Advanced Share Permissions are what administrators who have been managing Windows file servers since the days of Windows NT 4 are likely to be more familiar with. With Advanced Permissions, you configure share permissions separately from file system permissions. You configure Advanced Share Permissions through the Advanced Sharing button on the Sharing tab of a folder's Properties dialog box. When you configure Advanced Sharing Permissions, permissions are only set on the share and are not reset on the files and folders within the share. If you are using Advanced Sharing Permissions, you set the file system permissions separately.

You can manage shares centrally through the Shares area of the Server Manager console. An advantage of the Server Manager console is that you can use it to connect to manage shares on remote servers, including servers running the Server Core installation option. When you edit the properties of a share through Server Manager, you can also edit share permissions. This functions in the same way as editing Advanced Share Permissions through File Explorer in that it won't reset the permissions on the file system itself; permissions are only reset on the share.

You can also use the Server Manager's share properties interface when File Server Resource Manager is installed to edit the following settings:

- **Enable Access-Based Enumeration.** Enabled by default, this setting ensures that users can only see files and folders to which they have access.

- **Allow Caching of Share.** Allows files to be used offline. An additional setting, Enable BranchCache on the file share, allows use of BranchCache if the appropriate group policies are applied. You'll learn more about BranchCache later in this chapter. You can configure this option when the Settings tab is selected.

- **Encrypt Data Access.** When you enable this option, traffic to and from the shared folder is encrypted if the client supports SMB 3.0 (Windows 8 and later). You can configure this option when the Settings tab is selected.

- **Folder Owner Email.** Setting the folder owner's email addresses can be useful when resolving access-denied assistance requests. You can configure this when the Permission tab is selected.

- **Folder Usage.** Folder-usage properties allow you to apply metadata to the folder that specifies the nature of the files stored there. You can choose between User Files, Group Files, Application Files, and Backup and Archival Files. You can use folder usage properties with data classification rules.

Windows Admin Center (WAC) also provides basic file share configuration functionality, though this is not currently as sophisticated as what can be accomplished through Server Manager or File Explorer.

## Configure file screens

File screens allow you to block users from writing files to file shares based on file name extension. For example, you can use a file screen to stop people from storing video or audio files on file shares. File screens are implemented based on file name. Usually, this just means file screens are implemented by file extension, but you can configure file screens based on a pattern match of any part of a file name. You implement file screens using file groups and file screen templates.

A file screen doesn't block files that are already there; file screens just stop new files from being written to the share. File screens also only work based on file name. If you have users who are especially cunning, they might figure out that it's possible to get around a file screen by renaming files, so they don't get blocked by the screen.

### File groups

A file group is a pre-configured collection of file extensions related to a specific type of file. For example, the Image Files file group includes file name extensions related to image files, such as .jpg, .png, and .gif. While file groups are usually fairly comprehensive in their coverage, they aren't always complete. Should you need to, you can modify the list to add new file extensions.

The file groups included with FSRM include the following:

- **Audio And Video Files**   Blocks file extensions related to audio and video files, such as .avi and .mp3s
- **Backup Files**   Blocks file extensions related to backups, including .bak and .old files
- **Compressed Files**   Blocks file extensions related to compressed files, such as .zip and .cab
- **E-mail Files**   Blocks file extensions related to email storage, including .pst and .mbx files
- **Executable Files**   Blocks file extensions related to executable files and scripts, such as .exe or .ps1 extensions
- **Image Files**   Blocks file extensions related to images, such as .jpg or .png extensions
- **Office Files**   Blocks file extensions related to Microsoft Office files, such as .docx and .pptx files
- **System Files**   Blocks file extensions related to system files, including .dll and .sys files
- **Temporary Files**   Blocks file extensions related to temporary files, such as .tmp. Also blocks files starting with the ~ character
- **Text Files**   Blocks file extensions related to text files, including .txt and .asc files
- **Web Page Files**   Blocks file extensions related to web page files, including .html and .htm files

To edit the list of files in a file group, right-select the file group and select Edit File Group Properties. Using the dialog box you can modify the list of files to include and exclude files based on file name pattern. For example, you can do a simple exclusion or inclusion based on the file name suffix, such as *.bak. You also have the option of creating a more complex exclusion or inclusion based on the file name, such as backup *.*, which would exclude all files with the word backup at the start of any extension.

Exclusions allow you to add exceptions to an existing block rule. For example, you could configure a file screen to block all files that have the extension .vhdx. You might then create an exception for the name server2022.vhdx. When implemented, all files with the .vhdx extension would be blocked from being written to the share, except for files with the name server2022.vhdx.

While the NTFS and ReFS file systems are case sensitive, file screens are not case sensitive.

To create a new file group, right-select the File Groups node in the File Server Resource Manager console and select Create File Group. Provide the following information:

- **File Group Name**   The name for the file group.
- **Files To Include**   Provide patterns that match the names of files you want to block from being written to the file server.
- **Files To Exclude**   Provide patterns that match the names of files you want to exclude from the block.

### File screen templates

File screen templates are made up of a screening type, a collection of file groups, and a set of actions to perform when a match is found. File screen templates support the following screening types:

- **Active Screening**   An active screen blocks users from writing files to the file share that have names that match those patterns listed in the file group.

- **Passive Screening**   A passive screen doesn't block users from writing files to the file share that have names that match patterns listed in the file group. Instead, you use a passive screen to monitor such activity.

The actions you can configure include sending an email, writing a message to the event log, running a command, or generating a report.

After you have configured the appropriate file screen template, create the file screen by applying the template to a specific path. You can also create file screen exceptions, which exempt specific folders from an existing file screen. For example, you might apply a file screen at the root of a shared folder that blocks audio and video files from being written to the share. If you wanted to allow users to write audio and video files to one folder in the share, you could configure a file screen exception and apply it to that folder.

## Configure File Server Resource Manager quotas

Quotas are important. If you don't use them, file shares tend to end up consuming all available storage unless you have a solution such as Azure File Sync deployed. Some users dump as much as possible onto a file share unless quotas are in place and unless you are monitoring storage; the first you'll hear about it is when the service desk gets calls about people being unable to add new files to the file share.

NTFS has had rudimentary quota functionality since the Windows NT days. The reason that most Windows Server administrators don't bother with quota functionality is that it applies at the volume level and can't be applied to individual user accounts. Needless to say, if you have 500 users for whom you want to configure quotas, you don't want to have to individually configure a quota for each one. Even with command-line utilities, you still need to create an entry for each user.

File Server Resource Manager (FSRM) provides far more substantial quota functionality that makes quotas more practical to implement as a way of managing storage utilization on Windows Server file servers. Quotas in FSRM can be applied on a per-folder basis and are not cumulative across a volume. You can also configure quotas in FSRM so that users are sent warning emails if they exceed a specific quota threshold but before they are blocked from writing files to the file server. You manage quotas using FSRM by creating a quota template and then applying that quota template to a path.

Creating a quota template involves setting a limit, specifying a quota type, and then configuring notification thresholds. You can choose between the following quota types:

- **Hard Quota. Do Not Allow Users To Exceed Limit**   A hard quota blocks users from writing data to the file share after the quota value is exceeded.

- **Soft Quota. Allow Users To Exceed Limit (Use For Monitoring)**   A soft quota allows you to monitor when users exceed a specific storage utilization value, but it doesn't block users from writing data to the file share after the quota value is exceeded.

Notification thresholds allow you to configure actions to be taken after a certain percentage of the assigned quotas are reached. You can configure notifications via email, get an item written to an event log, run a command, or have a report generated.

After you've created the quota template, you can apply it to a folder. To do this, select the Quotas node under Quota Management, and from the Action menu, select **Create Quota**. In the Create Quota dialog box, select the path to which the quota applies and the quota template you want to apply. You then choose between applying the quota to the whole path or setting up an auto-apply template. Auto-apply templates allow separate quotas to be applied to any new and existing quota path subfolders. For example, if you applied a quota to the C:\Example path using the 2 GB template, the quota would apply cumulatively for all folders in that path. If you chose an auto-apply template, a separate 2 GB quota would be configured for each new and existing folder under C:\Example.

# Use additional FSRM functionality

File Server Resource Manager includes advanced functionality that you can use to manage file servers in on-premises and hybrid environments.

## Storage reports

The Storage Reports functionality of FSRM allows you to generate information about the files that are being stored on a particular file server. You can use FSRM to create the following storage reports:

- **Duplicate Files**   This report locates multiple copies of the same file. If you've enabled deduplication on the volume hosting these files, these additional copies do not consume additional disk space because they are deduplicated.

- **File Screening Audit**   This report allows you to view which users or applications are triggering file screens—for example, which users have tried to save music or video files to a shared folder.

- **Files By File Group**   This report allows you to view files sorted by file group. You can view files by all file groups, or you can search for specific files—for example, a report on ZIP files stored on a shared folder.

- **Files By Owner**   This report allows you to view files by owner. You can search for files by all owners or run a report that provides information on files by one or more specific users.

- **Files By Property**   Use this report to find out about files based on a classification. For example, if you have a classification named Top_Secret, you can generate a report about all files with that classification on the file server.
- **Folders By Property**   Similar to Files By Property, use this report to find out about folders based on a classification.
- **Large Files**   This report allows you to find large files on the file server. By default, it finds files larger than 5 MB, but you can edit this setting to locate all files that are larger.
- **Least Recently Accessed Files**   This report allows you to identify files that have not been accessed for a certain number of days. By default, this report identifies files that have not been accessed in the last 90 days, but you can configure this setting to any number that is appropriate for your organization.
- **Most Recently Accessed Files**   Use this report to determine which files have been accessed most recently. The default version of this report finds files that have been accessed in the last seven days.
- **Quota Usage**   Use this report to view how a user's storage usage compares against the assigned quota. For example, you could run a report to determine which users have exceeded 90 percent of their quota.

You can configure storage reports to run and then to be stored locally on file servers. You also have the option of configuring storage reports to be emailed to one or more email addresses. You can generate storage reports in DHTML, HTML, XML, CSV, and text formats.

## File classification

File classification allows you to apply metadata to files based on file properties. For example, you can apply the tag Top_Secret to a file that has specific properties, such as who authored it and whether a particular string of characters appeared in the file.

The first step to take when configuring file classification is to configure classification properties. After you've done this, you can create a classification rule to assign the classification property to a file. You can also allow users to manually assign classification properties to a file. By specifying the values allowed, you limit which classification properties the user can assign.

You can configure the following file classification properties:

- **Yes/No**   Provide a Boolean value.
- **Date-Time**   Provide a date and time.
- **Number**   Provide an integer value.
- **Multiple Choice List**   Allow multiple values to be assigned from a list.
- **Ordered List**   Provide values in a specific order.
- **Single Choice**   Select one of a selection of options.
- **String**   Provide a text-based value.
- **Multi-string**   Assign multiple text-based values.

Classification rules allow you to assign classifications to files based on the properties of a file. You can use one of three methods to classify a file:

- **Content Classifier** When you choose this method of classification, you configure a regular expression to scan the contents of a file for a specific string or text pattern. For example, you could use the content classifier to automatically assign the Top_Secret classification to any file that contained the text *Project_X*.

- **Folder Classifier** When you choose this method of classification, all files in a particular path are assigned the designated classification.

- **Windows PowerShell Classifier** When you choose this method of classification, a PowerShell script is run to determine whether a file is assigned a particular classification.

You can configure classification rules to run against specific folders. You can also choose to recheck files each time the rule is run. That way, you can change a file's classification in the event that the properties that triggered the initial classification change. When configuring reevaluation, you can also choose to remove user-assigned classification in case there is a conflict.

## File management tasks

File management tasks are automated tasks that FSRM performs on files according to a schedule. FSRM supports three types of file management tasks:

- **File Expiration** This moves all files that match the conditions to a specific directory. The most common usage of a file expiration task is to move files that haven't been accessed by anyone for a specific period, such as 365 days, to a specific directory.

- **Custom** Allows you to run a specific executable against a file. You can specify which executable is to be run, any special arguments to be used when running the executable, and the service account permissions, which can be Local Service, Network Service, or Local System.

- **RMS Encryption** Allows you to apply an RMS template or a set of file permissions to a file based on conditions. For example, you might want to automatically apply a specific set of file permissions to a file that has the Top_Secret classification or apply a specific RMS template to a file that has the Ultra_Secret classification.

When configuring a file management task, you also need to provide the following information:

- **Scope** The path where the task is run.

- **Notification** Any notification settings that you want to configure, such as sending an email, running a command, or writing an event to an event log. With file expiration, you can configure an email to be sent to each user who has files that are subject to the expiration task.

- **Report** Generating a report each time that the task is run. A notification is sent to the user who owns the file, and reports are sent to administrators.

- **Schedule** Specify when you want the file management task to be run.

- **Condition** Specify the condition that triggers the management task.

## Access-denied assistance

Access-denied assistance allows users to be informed why they don't have access to a specific file. Access-denied assistance gives you the option of allowing the user to send an email message to the file owner so that the owner can, if appropriate, grant access to the file. You can configure access-denied assistance using FSRM or by configuring Group Policy. You configure access-denied assistance for a single server in FSRM by editing the FSRM options.

If you want to use access-denied assistance across all file servers in your organization, you can use Group Policy. To do so, edit the policies located in the Computer Configuration\Policies\Administrative Templates\System\Access-Denied Assistance node. This node contains the following policies:

- **Customize Message For Access Denied Errors**  Use this policy to specify the message users see when they are blocked from accessing a file.
- **Enable Access-Denied Assistance On Client For All File Types**  When enabled, access-denied assistance functions for all file types where the user is blocked from accessing the file.

# Configure BranchCache

BranchCache speeds up access to files stored on shared folders that are accessed across medium-to high-latency WAN links. For example, suppose several users in a company's Auckland, New Zealand branch office need to regularly access several files stored on a file server in the Sydney, Australia head office. The connection between the Auckland and Sydney office is low bandwidth and high latency. The files are also fairly large and need to be stored on the Sydney file server. Additionally, the Auckland branch office is too small for a Distributed File System (DFS) replica to make sense. In a scenario such as this, you would implement BranchCache.

BranchCache creates a locally cached copy of files from remote file servers that can be accessed by other computers on the local network, assuming the file hasn't been updated at the source. In the example scenario, after one person in the Auckland office accesses the file, the next person to access the same file in the Auckland office accesses a copy that is cached locally, rather than retrieving it from the Sydney file server. The BranchCache process performs a check to verify that the cached version is up to date. If it isn't, the updated file is retrieved and stored in the Auckland network's BranchCache.

You add BranchCache to a file server by using the following PowerShell command:

```
Install-WindowsFeature FS-BranchCache
```

After installing BranchCache, you need to configure Group Policies that apply to file servers in your organization that allow them to support BranchCache. To do this, you need to configure the Hash Publication for BranchCache policy, located in the Computer Configuration\Policies\Administrative Templates\Network\Lanman Server node.

You have three options when configuring this policy:

- **Allow Hash Publication Only For Shared Folders On Which BranchCache is enabled**   This option allows you to selectively enable BranchCache.

- **Disallow Hash Publication On All Shared Folders**   Use this option when you want to disable BranchCache.

- **Allow Hash Publication For All Shared Folders**   Use this option if you want to enable BranchCache on all shared folders.

Generally, there's rarely a great reason not to enable BranchCache on all shared folders, but should you want to be selective, you do have that option. If you choose to be selective and only enable BranchCache on some shares, you need to edit the properties of the share and enable BranchCache. You do so by selecting Caching on the Advanced Sharing page and then using the Offline Settings options.

After you've configured your file server to support BranchCache, you need to configure client computers to support BranchCache. You do so by configuring Group Policy in the Computer Configuration\Policies\Administrative Templates\Network\BranchCache node of a GPO. Which policies you configure depends on how you want BranchCache to work at each branch office. You can choose between the following options:

- **Distributed Cache Mode**   When client computers are configured for Distributed Cache mode, each Windows 7 or later computer hosts part of the cache.

- **Hosted Cache Mode**   When you configure Hosted Cache mode, a server at the branch office hosts the cache in its entirety. Any server running Windows Server 2008 R2 or later can function as a hosted cache mode server.

To configure a branch office server to function as a hosted cache mode server, run the following PowerShell commands:

```
Install-WindowsFeature BranchCache
Start-Service BranchCache
Enable-BCHostedServer
```

# Implement and configure Distributed File System

Distributed File System (DFS) has two advantages over a traditional file share. The first is that DFS automatically replicates to create copies of the file share and its content on one or more other servers. The second is that clients connect to a single UNC address, with the client directed to the closest server and redirected to the next closest server in the event that a server hosting a DFS replica fails. Azure File Sync provides most of the first functionality but does not provide the second functionality.

Using DFS, you can push a single shared folder structure out across an organization that has multiple branch offices. Changes made to files on one file share replica propagate across to the other file share replicas, with a robust and built-in conflict-management system present to ensure that problems do not occur when users are editing the same file at the same time.

## DFS namespace

A DFS namespace is a collection of DFS shared folders. It uses the same UNC pathname structure, except instead of \\ServerName\FileShareName with DFS, it is \\domainname with all DFS shared folders located under this DFS root. For example, instead of

```
\\FS-1\Engineering
\\FS-2\Accounting
\\FS-3\Documents
```

you could have

```
\\Contoso.com\Engineering
\\Contoso.com\Accounting
\\Contoso.com\Documents
```

In this scenario, the Engineering, Accounting, and Documents folders could all be hosted on separate file servers and you could use a single namespace to locate those shared folders, rather than needing to know the identity of the file server that hosts them.

DFS supports the following types of namespaces:

- **Domain-Based Namespace**   Domain-based namespaces store configuration data in Active Directory. You deploy a domain-based namespace when you want to ensure that the namespace remains available even if one or more of the servers hosting the namespace goes offline.
- **Standalone Namespace**   Standalone namespaces have namespace data stored in the registry of a single server and not in Active Directory as is the case with domain-based namespaces. You can have only a single namespace server with a standalone namespace. Should the server that hosts the namespace fail, the entire namespace is unavailable even if servers that host individual folder targets remain online.

To create a DFS namespace, perform the following steps:

1. In the DFS console, select the Namespaces node. In the **Action** menu, select **New Namespace**.

2. On the Namespace Server page, select a server that has the DFS Namespaces feature installed. You can install this feature with the following PowerShell cmdlet:

   ```
   Install-WindowsFeature FS-DFS-Namespace
   ```

3. On the Namespace Name and Settings page, provide a meaningful name for the namespace. This is located under the domain name. For example, if you added the name Schematics and you were installing DFS in the contoso.internal domain, the namespace would end up as \\contoso.internal\Schematics. By default, a shared folder is created on the namespace server, although you can edit settings on this page of the wizard and specify a separate location for the shared folder that hosts content you want to replicate.

4. On the Namespace Type page, you should generally select domain-based namespace as this gives you the greatest flexibility and provides you with the option of adding additional namespace servers later on for redundancy.

To add an additional namespace server to an existing namespace, ensure that the DFS Namespace role feature is installed on the server you want to add, and then perform the following steps:

1. In the DFS console, select the namespace to which you want to add the additional namespace server, and on the **Action** menu, select **Add Namespace Server**.

2. On the Add Namespace Server page, specify the name of the namespace server, or browse and query Active Directory to verify that the name is correct, and then select OK. This creates a shared folder on the new namespace server with the name of the namespace.

## DFS replication

A replica is a copy of a DFS folder. Replication is the process that ensures each replica is kept up to date. DFS uses block-level replication, which means that only blocks in a file that have changed are transmitted to other replicas during the replication process.

You install the DFS replication feature by running the following PowerShell command:

```
Install-WindowsFeature FS-DFS-Replication
```

In the event that the same file is being edited by different users on different replicas, DFS uses a "last writer wins" conflict-resolution model. In the unlikely event that two separate users create files with the same name in the same location on different replicas at approximately the same time, conflict resolution uses "earliest creator wins." When conflicts occur, files and folders that "lose" the conflict are moved to the Conflict and Deleted folder, located under the local path of the replicated folder in the DfsrPrivate\ConflictandDeleted directory.

### REPLICATED FOLDERS AND TARGETS

One of the big advantages of DFS is that you can create copies of folders across multiple servers that are automatically updated. Each copy of that replica is called a folder target. Only computers that have the DFS replication role feature installed can host *folder targets*. A replicated folder can have multiple folder targets. For example, you might have a replicated folder named \\contoso.com\Engineering that you have configured targets for in Sydney on \\SYD-FS1\Engineering, Melbourne on \\MEL-FS1\Engineering, and Auckland on \\AKL-FS1\Engineering.

### REPLICATION TOPOLOGY

A *replication group* is a collection of servers that host copies of a replicated folder. When configuring replication for a replication group, you choose a topology and a primary member. The topology dictates how data replicates between the folders that each server hosts. The primary member is the seed from where file and folder data is replicated.

When creating a replication group, you can specify the following topologies:

- **Hub and Spoke** This topology has hub members where data originates and spoke members to the location in which data is replicated. This topology also requires at least three members of the replication group. Choose this if you have a hub-and-spoke topology for your organizational WAN.

- **Full Mesh** In this topology, each member of the replication group can replicate with other members. This is the simplest form of replication group and is suitable when each member can directly communicate with the others.
- **No Topology** When you select this option, you can create a custom topology where you specify how each member replicates with others.

### REPLICATION SCHEDULES

You use replication schedules to determine how replication partners communicate with each other. You use a replication schedule to specify when replication partners communicate and whether replication traffic is throttled so that it doesn't flood the network.

You can configure replication to occur continuously and specify bandwidth utilization, with a minimum value of 16 Kbps and an upper value of 256 Mbps, with the option of setting it to Unlimited. If necessary, you can also set different bandwidth limitations for different periods of the day.

***EXAM TIP***

Remember how to block specific file types from being written to a file share.

# Skill 5.3: Configure Windows Server Storage

This objective deals with Windows Server storage technologies, from disks and volumes to file systems, and then how to increase the performance and resiliency of storage using Storage Spaces Direct.

**This skill covers how to:**
- Configure disks and volumes
- Configure and manage storage spaces
- Configure and manage Storage Replica
- Configure data deduplication
- Configure SMB Direct
- Configure Storage QoS
- Configure filesystems

## Configure disks and volumes

In Windows Server, a disk is a physical device, which can be traditional magnetic storage, solid-state, or persistent memory device (also termed storage class memory). There are two types of disks available to Windows Server: basic disks and dynamic disks.

## Basic disks

A *basic disk* is a disk that contains partitions that are generally formatted with a filesystem such as NTFS. Partitions are logical regions on a disk. A volume on a basic disk is a formatted partition. A basic disk using the Master Boot Record partition style can host as many as four partitions configured either as four primary partitions or three primary partitions and an extended partition. A basic disk formatted with the GUID Partition Table (GPT) style can have up to 128 primary partitions.

- **Primary partitions** Each primary partition has a single logical volume. This volume can be formatted with a filesystem such as NTFS or ReFS.
- **Extended partitions** Extended partitions are not formatted or assigned drive letters. Extended partitions can be divided into logical drives, which can in turn be used as formatted volumes.

You can perform the following operations on basic disks:

- Create and delete primary and extended partitions.
- Create and delete logical drives within an extended partition.
- Format a partition and set it as active.

## Dynamic disks

*Dynamic disks* allow you to create volumes that span multiple physical disks (as spanned and striped volumes) and to create fault-tolerant volumes (such as mirrored volumes and RAID-5 volumes). Dynamic disks support MBR and GPT partition styles. Dynamic disks were more commonly used in earlier versions of Windows Server, but most of the functionality of dynamic disks has been superseded by Storage Spaces, covered in a moment. The most common use case for dynamic disks in Windows Server 2022 is for mirrored boot volumes.

## Partition styles

Windows Server supports two partition styles: MBR, which has been available since the early 1980s, and GPT, which has been available since the late 1990s. In addition to supporting up to 128 primary partitions, disks that use the GPT partition type support partitions and volumes that exceed 2 terabytes.

# Configure and manage storage spaces

Storage spaces and storage pools were first introduced to Windows Server with the release of Windows Server 2012. A *storage pool* is a collection of storage devices that you can use to aggregate storage. You expand the capacity of a storage pool by adding storage devices to the pool. A *storage space* is a virtual disk that you create from the free space that is available in a storage pool. Depending on how you configure it, a storage space can be resilient to failure and have improved performance through storage tiering.

## Storage pools

A storage pool is a collection of storage devices, usually disks, but can also include items such as virtual hard disks, from which you can create one or more storage spaces. A storage space is a special type of virtual disk that has the following features:

- **Resilient storage**   Configure to use disk mirroring or parity in the structure of the underlying storage (if available). We discuss resilience in a moment.

- **Tiering**   Configure to leverage a combination of SSD and HDD disks to achieve maximum performance. Tiering is also discussed later in this chapter.

- **Continuous availability**   Storage spaces integrate with failover clustering, and you can cluster pools across separate nodes within a single failover cluster.

- **Write-back cache**   If a storage space includes SSDs, a write-back cache can be configured in the pool to buffer small random writes. These random writes are then later offloaded to SSDs or HDDs that make up the virtual disk in the pool.

- **Multitenancy**   You can configure access control lists on each storage pool. This allows you to configure isolation in multitenant scenarios.

## Storage space resiliency

When creating a virtual disk on a storage pool that has enough disks, you can choose among several storage layouts. These layout options provide the following benefits:

- **Mirror**   Multiple copies of data are written across separate disks in the pool. This protects the virtual disk from failure of the physical disks that constitute the storage pool. Mirroring can be used with storage tiering. Depending on the number of disks in the pool, storage spaces provide two-way or three-way mirroring. Two-way mirroring writes two copies of data, and three-way mirroring writes three copies of data. Three-way mirroring provides better redundancy, but it also consumes more disk space.

- **Parity**   Parity data is stored on disks in the array that are separate from where data is stored. Parity provides greater capacity than using the Mirror option, but it has the drawback of slower write performance. Windows Server provides two types of parity: Single Parity and Dual Parity. Single Parity provides protection against one failure at a time. Dual Parity provides protection against two failures at a time. You need to have a minimum of three disks for Single Parity and a minimum of seven disks for Dual Parity. You get the option to select between Single Parity and Dual Parity when configuring storage layout when there are more than seven disks.

- **Simple**   This option provides no resiliency for the storage, which means that if one of the disks in the storage pool fails, the data on any virtual hard disks built from that pool will also be lost.

If you configure disks in the storage pool that use the Hot Spare option, storage spaces will be able to automatically repair virtual disks that use the Mirror or Parity resiliency options. It's also possible for automatic repairs to occur if spare unallocated capacity exists within the pool.

## Storage space tiering

Storage space tiering allows you to create a special type of virtual disk from a pool of storage that is a combination of SSD and traditional HDD disks. Storage tiering provides the virtual disk with performance similar to that of an array built out of SSD disks, but without the cost of building a large capacity array comprised of SSD disks. It accomplishes this by moving frequently accessed files to faster physical disks within the pool, thus moving less frequently accessed files to slower storage media.

You can only configure storage tiers when creating a virtual disk if there is a mixture of physical disks with the HDD and the SSD disk type in the pool upon which you want to create the disk. Once the disk is created, you cannot undo storage tiering from a virtual disk. You configure storage tiering for a virtual disk by selecting the **Create Storage Tiers On This Virtual Disk** option during virtual disk creation.

One challenge when configuring storage tiering is ensuring that you have media marked as SSD and HDD in the pool. While media will usually be recognized correctly, in some cases you must specify that a disk is of the SSD type, which allows storage tiering to be configured.

You can specify the disk media type using the following PowerShell procedure:

1. First determine the storage using the `Get-StoragePool` cmdlet.

2. To view whether physical disks are configured as SSD or HDD, use the `Get-StoragePool` cmdlet and then pipe that cmdlet to the `Get-PhysicalDisk` cmdlet. For example, to view the identity and media type of physical disks in the storage pool named Example-Pool, issue the command:

   ```
   Get-StoragePool -FriendlyName ExamplePool | Get-PhysicalDisk | Select UniqueID,
   MediaType, Usage
   ```

3. Once you have determined the UniqueIDs of the disks that you want to configure as the SSD type, you can configure a disk to have the SSD type by using the `Set-PhysicalDisk` cmdlet with the `UniqueID` parameter and the `MediaType` parameter set to SSD. Similarly, you can change the type back to HDD by setting the `MediaType` parameter to HDD.

## Thin provisioning and trim

Thin provisioning allows you to create virtual disks where you specify a total size for the disk, but only the space that is actually used will be allocated. For example, with thin provisioning, you might create a virtual hard disk that can grow to 500 GB in size but is only currently 10 GB in size because only 10 GB of data is currently stored on the volumes hosted on the disk.

You can view the amount of space that has been allocated to a thin-provisioned virtual disk, and you can see the total capacity in the Virtual Disks area when the Storage Pools node is selected in the Server Manager console or in Windows Admin Center. When you create a virtual disk, the maximum disk size available is determined by the amount of free space on the physical disks that make up the storage pool, rather than the maximum capacity of the existing thin-provisioned disks. For example, if you have a storage pool with two 10 TB physical disks, you can create more than two thin-provisioned disks that have a maximum size of 10 TB. You can create thin-provisioned disks 10 TB in size as long as the actual allocated space on the storage pool doesn't exceed 10 out of the 20 available. It is possible to create thin-provisioned disks in such a way that the total thin-provisioned disk capacity exceeds the storage capacity of the underlying storage pool. If you do overallocate space, you'll need to monitor how much of the underlying storage pool capacity is consumed and add disks to the storage pool because that capacity is exhausted.

Trim is an automatic process that reclaims space when data is deleted from thin-provisioned disks. For example, if you have a 10 TB thin-provisioned virtual disk that stores 8 TB of data, 8 TB will be allocated from the storage pool that hosts that virtual disk. If you delete 2 TB of data from that thin-provisioned virtual disk, Trim ensures that the storage pool that hosts that virtual disk will be able to reclaim that unused space. The 10 TB thin-provisioned virtual disk will appear to be 10 TB in size, but after the trim process is complete, it will only consume 6 TB of space on the underlying storage pool. Trim is enabled by default.

> **NEED MORE REVIEW?** **THIN PROVISIONING AND TRIM STORAGE**
>
> You can learn more about think provisioning and trim storage at *https://docs.microsoft.com/ en-us/windows-hardware/drivers/storage/thin-provisioning.*

## Storage Spaces Direct

Storage Spaces Direct allows you to use Windows Server with locally attached storage to create highly available software-defined storage. Storage Spaces Direct (which uses the abbreviation S2D because the SSD abbreviation is already used for solid-state disks) provides a form of distributed, software-defined, shared-nothing storage that has similar characteristics to RAID in terms of performance and redundancy. S2D allows you to create volumes from a storage pool of physical drives that are attached to multiple nodes that participate in a Windows Server failover cluster. Storage Spaces Direct functions as a replacement for expensive large-scale hardware storage arrays.

Storage Spaces Direct has the following properties:

- You can scale out by adding additional nodes to the cluster.
- When you add a node to a cluster configured for Storage Spaces Direct, all eligible drives on the cluster node will be added to the Storage Spaces Direct pool.
- You can have between 2 and 16 nodes in a Storage Spaces Direct failover cluster.
- It requires each node to have at least two solid-state drives and at least four additional drives.
- A cluster can have more than 400 drives and can support more than 4 petabytes of storage.
- Storage Spaces Direct works with locally attached SATA, SAS, persistent memory, or NVMe drives.

- Cache is automatically built from SSD media. All writes up to 256 KB and all reads up to 64 KB will be cached. Writes are then de-staged to HDD storage in optimal order.

- Storage Spaces Direct volumes can be part mirror and part parity. To have a three-way mirror with dual parity, it is necessary to have four nodes in the Windows Server failover cluster that hosts Storage Spaces Direct.

- If a disk fails, the plug-and-play replacement will automatically be added to the storage spaces pool when connected to the original cluster node.

- A Storage Spaces Direct cluster can be configured with rack and chassis awareness as a way of further ensuring fault tolerance.

- Storage Spaces Direct clusters are not supported where nodes span multiple sites.

- While NTFS is supported for use with S2D clusters, ReFS is recommended.

S2D supports two deployment options:

- **Hyper-Converged**   With the Hyper-Converged deployment option, both storage and compute resources are deployed on the same cluster. This has the benefit of not requiring you to configure file server access and permissions and is most commonly used in small to medium-sized Hyper-V deployments.

- **Converged**   With the Converged (also known as disaggregated) deployment option, storage and compute resources are deployed in separate clusters. Often used with Hyper-V infrastructure-as-a-service (IaaS) deployments, a scale-out file server is deployed on S2D to provide network attached storage over SMB3 file shares. The compute resources for the IaaS virtual machines are located on a separate cluster from the S2D cluster.

Storage Spaces Direct in Windows Server supports nested resiliency. *Nested resiliency* is a capability designed for two-server S2D clusters that allows storage to remain available in the event of multiple hardware failures. When nested resiliency is configured, volumes can remain online and accessible even if one server goes offline and a drive fails. Nested resiliency only works when a cluster has two nodes. Nested resiliency requires a minimum of four capacity drives per server node and two cache drives per server node.

### S2D RESILIENCY TYPES

S2D resiliency options are dependent on how many fault domains are present, the failure tolerance required, and the storage efficiency that can be achieved. A fault domain is a collection of hardware, such as a rack of servers, where a single failure can affect every component in that collection.

Table 5-1 lists the different resiliency types, failure tolerances, storage efficiencies, and minimum fault domains.

**TABLE 5-1** S2D resiliency

| Resiliency | Failure tolerance | Storage efficiency | Minimum fault domains |
|---|---|---|---|
| Two-way mirror | 1 | 50.0% | 2 |
| Three-way mirror | 2 | 33.3% | 3 |
| Dual parity | 2 | 50.0%-80.0% | 4 |
| Mixed | 2 | 33.3%-80.0% | 4 |

### ADDING S2D CLUSTER NODES

Prior to adding a server to an existing S2D cluster, run the `Test-Cluster` validation cmdlet, while including current and existing nodes. For example, run this command to add the cluster node S2DN3 to a cluster that included nodes S2DN1 and S2DN2:

```
Test-Cluster -Name TestS2DCluster -node S2DN1,S2DN2,S2DN3 -Include "Storage Spaces
Direct", "Inventory", "Network", "System Configuration"
```

Once the validation has completed, run the `Add-Clusternode` cmdlet on one of the existing cluster nodes and specify the new cluster node name.

### S2D CLUSTER NODE MAINTENANCE

Before performing maintenance on a cluster node, you should pause and drain the node. You can do this with the `Suspend-ClusterNode` cmdlet with the `-Drain` parameter. Once the node is drained, which will also put it in a paused state, you can either shut the node down or perform other maintenance operations, such as restarting the node. When you have completed maintenance on the node, you can return it to operation by using the `Resume-Clusternode` cmdlet.

## Configure and manage Storage Replica

Storage Replica allows you to replicate volumes between servers, including clusters, for the purposes of disaster recovery. You can also use Storage Replica to configure asynchronous replication to provision failover clusters that span two geographically disparate sites, while all nodes remain synchronized.

You can configure Storage Replica to support the following types of replication:

- **Synchronous Replication**    Use this when you want to mirror data and you have very low latency between the source and the destination. This allows you to create crash-consistent volumes. Synchronous replication ensures zero data loss at the filesystem level should a failure occur.

- **Asynchronous Replication**    Asynchronous Storage Replica is suitable when you want to replicate storage across sites where you are experiencing higher latencies.

Storage Replica is available for single volumes under 2 TB in the standard edition of Windows Server. These limits do not apply to the datacenter edition of the operating system. Participant servers must be members of the same Active Directory Domain Services forest.

Storage Replica operates at the partition layer. This means that it replicates all VSS snapshots created by the Windows Server operating system or by backup software that leverages VSS snapshot functionality.

Storage Replica has the following features:

- **Zero data loss, block-level replication** When used with synchronous replication, there is no data loss. By leveraging block-level replication, even files that are locked will be replicated at the block level.

- **Guest and host** Storage Replica works when Windows Server is a virtualized guest or when it functions as a host operating system. It is possible to replicate from third-party virtualization solutions to IaaS virtual machines hosted in the public cloud as long as Windows Server functions as the source and target operating system.

- **Supports manual failover with zero data loss** You can perform manual failover when both the source and destination are online, or you can have failover occur automatically if the source storage fails.

- **Leverage SMB3** This allows Storage Replica to use multichannel, SMB Direct support on RoCE, iWARP, and InfiniBand RDMA network cards.

- **Encryption and authentication support** Storage Replica supports packet signing, AES-128-GCM full data encryption, support for Intel AES-NI encryption acceleration, and Kerberos AES 256 authentication.

- **Initial seeding** You can perform initial seeding by transferring data using a method other than Storage Replica between source and destination. This is especially useful when transferring large amounts of data between disparate sites where it may make more sense to use a courier to transport a high-capacity hard disk drive than it does to transmit data across a WAN link. The initial replication will then copy only blocks that have been changed since the replica data was exported from source to destination.

- **Consistency groups** Consistency groups implement write ordering guarantees. This ensures that applications such as Microsoft SQL Server, which may write data to multiple replicated volumes, will have that data replicated so that it remains replicated sequentially in a consistent way.

## Supported configurations

Storage Replica is supported in the following configurations:

- **Server-to-server** In this configuration, Storage Replica supports both synchronous and asynchronous replication between two standalone services. Local drives, storage spaces with shared SAS storage, SAN, and iSCSI-attached LUNs can be replicated. You can manage this configuration either using Server Manager or PowerShell. Failover can only be performed manually.

- **Cluster-to-cluster**  In this configuration, replication occurs between two separate clusters. The first cluster might use Storage Spaces Direct, storage spaces with shared SAS storage, SAN, and iSCSI-attached LUNs. You manage this configuration using PowerShell and Azure Site Recovery. Failover must be performed manually.

- **Stretch cluster**  A single cluster where nodes are located in geographically disparate sites. Some nodes share one set of asymmetric storage and other nodes share another set of asymmetric storage. Storage is replicated either synchronously or asynchronously, depending on bandwidth considerations. This scenario supports storage spaces with shared SAS storage, SAN, and iSCSI-attached LUNs. You manage this configuration using PowerShell and the Failover Cluster Manager GUI tool. This scenario allows for automated failover.

The following configurations are not supported on Windows Server, though they may be supported at some point in the future:

- Storage Replica only supports one-to-one replication in Windows Server. You cannot configure Storage Replica to support one-to-many replication or transitive replication. Transitive replication is where there is a replica of the replica server.

- Storage Replica on Windows Server does not support bringing a replicated volume online for read-only access in Windows Server 2016. In Windows Server 2019 and Windows Server 2022, you can perform a test failover and temporarily mount a snapshot of the replicated storage on an unused NTFS or ReFS formatted volume.

- Deploying scale-out file servers on stretch clusters participating in Storage Replica is not a supported configuration.

- Deploying Storage Spaces Direct in a stretch cluster with Storage Replica is not supported.

## Storage Replica requirements

Ensure that each server meets the following requirements:

- The servers have two volumes, one volume hosting the data that you want to replicate, the other hosting the replication logs.

- Ensure that both log and data disks are formatted as GPT and not MBR.

- Data volume on the source and destination servers must be the same size and use the same sector sizes.

- Log volume on the source and destination volumes should be the same size and use the same sector sizes. The log volume should be a minimum of 9 GB in size.

- Ensure that the data volume does not contain the system volume, page file, or dump files.

Use the Test-SRTopology cmdlet to verify that all Storage Replica requirements have been met. To do this, perform the following steps:

1.  Create a temp directory on the source server that will store the Storage Replica Topology Report.

2. Make a note of the drive letters of the source storage and log volumes and destination storage and log volumes.

When the test completes, view the TestSrTopologyReport.html file to verify that your configuration meets Storage Replica requirements. Once you have verified that the configuration does meet requirements, you can use the `New-SRPartnerShip` cmdlet to create a Storage Replica partnership.

You can check the status of Storage Replica replication by running the `Get-SRPartnership` and `Get-SRGroup` cmdlets. Once Storage Replica is active, you won't be able to access the replica storage device on the destination computer unless you reverse replication or remove replication. When you run this command, you will receive a warning that data loss may occur, and you will be asked whether you want to complete the operation.

By default, all replication when Storage Replica is configured is synchronous. You can switch between synchronous and asynchronous replication by using the `Set-SRPartnership` cmdlet with the `ReplicationMode` parameter.

Storage Replica uses the following ports:

- **445** Used for SMB, which is the replication transport protocol.
- **5985** Used for WSManHTTP, which is the management protocol for WMI/CIM/ PowerShell.
- **5445** Used for SMB with iWARP. This port is only required if using iWARP RDMA networking.

> **NEED MORE REVIEW?** **STORAGE REPLICA**
>
> You can learn more about Storage Replica at *https://docs.microsoft.com/en-us/windows-server/storage/storage-replica/storage-replica-overview*.

# Configure data deduplication

Deduplication works by analyzing files, locating the unique chunks of data that make up those files, and only storing one copy of each unique data chunk on the volume. (A *chunk* is a collection of storage blocks.) Deduplication can reduce the amount of storage consumed on the volume because when analyzed, it turns out that a substantial number of data chunks stored on a volume are identical. Rather than store multiple copies of the same identical chunk, deduplication ensures that one copy of the chunk is stored with placeholders in other locations pointing at the single copy of the chunk, rather than storing the chunk itself. Windows Server supports deduplication on both NTFS- and ReFS-formatted volumes. Before you can enable deduplication, you need to install the Data Deduplication role service.

When you configure deduplication, you choose from one of the following usage types:

- **General-Purpose File Server** Appropriate for general-purpose file servers, optimization is performed on the background on any file that is older than three days. Files that are in use and partial files are not optimized.

- **Virtual Desktop Infrastructure (VDI) Server**   Appropriate for VDI servers, optimization is performed in the background on any file that is older than three days, but files that are in use and partial files will also be optimized.
- **Virtualized Backup Server**   This usage type is suitable for backup applications such as System Center Data Protection Manager or an Azure Backup Server. Performs priority optimization on files of any age. It will optimize in-use files, but it will not optimize partial files.

When configuring deduplication settings, you can configure files to be excluded on the basis of file extension, or you can exclude entire folders from data deduplication. Deduplication involves running a series of jobs outlined in Table 5-2.

**TABLE 5-2** Deduplication jobs

| Name | Description | Schedule |
|------|-------------|----------|
| Optimization | Deduplicates and optimizes the volume. | Once per hour |
| Garbage collection | Reclaims disk space by removing unnecessary chunks. You may want to run this job manually after deleting a substantial amount of data in an attempt to reclaim space by using the Start-DedupeJob cmdlet with the Type parameter set to GarbageCollection. | Every Saturday at 2:35 a.m. |
| Integrity scrubbing | Identifies corruption in the chunk store and uses volume features where possible to repair and reconstruct corrupted data. | Every Saturday at 3:35 a.m. |
| Unoptimization | A special job that you run manually when you want to disable deduplication for a volume. | Run manually |

**NEED MORE REVIEW?**   **DEDUPLICATION**

You can learn more about deduplication at *https://docs.microsoft.com/en-us/windows-server/ storage/data-deduplication/overview*.

## Configure SMB Direct

SMB Direct allows you to use network adapters that have RDMA to improve the performance of file servers. RDMA allows the network adapter to mediate the transfer of large amounts of data rather than having that process managed by the computer's CPU. Windows Server 2022 and Windows 11 support SMB Encryption with SMB Direct. Previous versions of Windows Server and client offload encryption operations to the CPU, reducing traffic throughput. SMB Direct is enabled by default with Windows Server 2012 and later operating systems with compatible RDMA network adapters. Disabling SMB Multichannel functionality will also disable SMB Direct.

***NEED MORE REVIEW?*** **SMB DIRECT**

You can learn more about SMB Direct at *https://docs.microsoft.com/en-us/windows-server/ storage/file-server/smb-direct*.

## Configure Storage QoS

Storage Quality of Service (QoS) allows you to centrally manage and monitor the performance of storage used for virtual machines that leverage the Scale-Out File Server and Hyper-V roles. The Storage QoS feature will automatically ensure that access to storage resources is distributed equitably between virtual machines that use the same file server cluster. It allows you to configure minimum and maximum performance settings as policies in units of IOPS.

Storage QoS allows you to accomplish the following goals:

- **Reduce the impact of noisy neighbor VMs** A noisy neighbor VM is a virtual machine that is consuming a disproportionate amount of storage resources. Storage QoS allows you to limit the extent to which such a VM can consume storage bandwidth.

- **Monitor storage performance** When you deploy a virtual machine to a scale-out file server, you can review storage performance from a central location.

- **Allocate minimum and maximum available resources** Through Storage QoS policies, you can specify minimum and maximum resources available. This allows you to ensure that each VM has the minimum storage performance it requires to run reserved for it.

There are two types of Storage QoS policy:

- **Aggregated** An aggregated policy applies maximum and minimum values for a combined set of virtual hard disk files and virtual machines. For example, by creating an aggregated policy with a minimum of 150 IOPS and a maximum of 250 IOPS and applying it to three virtual hard disk files, you can ensure that the three virtual hard disk files will have a minimum of 150 IOPS between them when the system is under load and will consume a maximum of 250 IOPs when the virtual machines associated with those hard disks are heavily using storage.

- **Dedicated** A dedicated policy applies a minimum and a maximum value to each individual virtual hard disk. For example, if you apply a dedicated policy to each of three virtual hard disks that specify a minimum of 150 IOPS and a maximum of 250 IOPS, each virtual hard disk will individually be able to use up to 250 IOPS, while having a minimum of 150 IOPS reserved for use if the system is under pressure.

You create policies with the New-StorageQosPolicy cmdlet, which is specified by using the PolicyType parameter if the policy is Dedicated or Aggregated; also, you must specify the minimum and maximum IOPS. For example, run this command to create a new policy called Alpha of the Dedicated type that has a minimum of 150 IOPS and a maximum of 250 IOPS:

```
New-StorageQosPolicy -Name Alpha -PolicyType Dedicated -MinimumIops 150 -MaximumIops 250
```

Once you've created a policy, you can apply it to a virtual hard disk by using the `Set-VMHardDiskDrive` cmdlet.

> **NEED MORE REVIEW?** **STORAGE QUALITY OF SERVICE**
>
> You can learn more about Storage QoS at *https://docs.microsoft.com/en-us/windows-server/storage/storage-qos/storage-qos-overview*.

# Configure filesystems

Windows Server supports the following filesystems:

- NTFS
- ReFS
- FAT and FAT32

## NTFS

NTFS is a filesystem that has been present in Windows Server environments since the 1990s. The Windows Server Hybrid Administrator Associate certification doesn't concentrate on the specifics of NTFS other than as a point of comparison between it and ReFS. In most cases you'll use NTFS on a Windows Server system as it is the general-purpose filesystem and you'll only have to think about ReFS for circumstances such as when you have to deal with the sorts of large files used by virtual machine hard disks or databases. Boot volumes on Windows Server computers always use NTFS and cannot use ReFS.

NTFS supports volumes up to 16 terabytes using the default cluster size of 4 KB and up to 256 terabytes using the maximum cluster size of 64 KB. Most scenarios that require such large volumes will be better served by using ReFS. ReFS is engineered to address shortcomings that NTFS had with file and disk sizes that would have been incomprehensible when the filesystem was first made available.

NTFS has the following permissions that can be applied to files and folders:

- **Full Control** When applied to folders, allows the reading, writing, changing, and deletion of files and subfolders. When applied to a file, permits reading, writing, changing, and deletion of the file. Allows modification of permissions on files and folders.
- **Modify** When applied to folders, allows the reading, writing, changing, and deletion of files and subfolders. When applied to a file, permits reading, writing, changing, and deleting the file. Does not allow the modification of permissions on files and folders.
- **Read & Execute** When applied to folders, allows the content of the folders to be accessed and executed. When applied to a file, allows the file to be accessed and executed.
- **List Folder Contents** Can only be applied to folders. Allows the contents of the folder to be viewed.

- **Read** When applied to folders, allows content to be accessed. When applied to a file, allows the contents to be accessed. Differs from Read & Execute in that it does not allow files to be executed.

- **Write** When applied to folders, allows adding of files and subfolders. When applied to a file, allows a user to modify, but not delete, a file.

## ReFS

ReFS (Resilient File System) is a filesystem that is appropriate for very large workloads where you need to maximize data availability and integrity and ensure that the filesystem is resilient to corruption. The ReFS filesystem is suitable for hosting specific types of workloads such as virtual machines and SQL Server data, because it includes the following features that improve upon NTFS:

- **Integrity** ReFS uses checksums for both metadata and file data. This means that ReFS can detect data corruption.

- **Storage spaces integration** When integrated with storage spaces that are configured with Mirror or Parity options, ReFS has the ability to automatically detect and repair corruption using a secondary or tertiary copy of data stored by storage spaces. The repair occurs without downtime.

- **Proactive error correction** ReFS includes a data integrity scanner that scans the volume to identify latent corruption and proactively repair corrupted data.

- **Scalability** ReFS is specifically designed to support data sets in the petabyte range.

- **Advanced VM operations** ReFS includes functionality specifically to support virtual machine operations. Block cloning accelerates copy operations, which accelerate VM checkpoint merges. Sparse VDL allows ReFS to substantially reduce the amount of time required to create very large fixed-size virtual hard disks.

It is important to note that ReFS is suitable only for hosting specific types of workloads. It isn't suitable for many workloads used in small and medium enterprises that aren't hosting large VMs or huge SQL Server databases. On computers running Windows Server 2022, ReFS supports the following features available in NTFS:

- BitLocker encryption
- Data deduplication
- Cluster Shared Volume support
- Junctions/soft links
- Hard links
- Failover cluster support
- Access control lists
- USN journal (Update Sequence Number Journal)
- Changes notifications
- Junction points

- Mount points
- Reparse points
- Volume snapshots
- File IDs
- OpLock (opportunistic lock)
- Sparse files
- Named streams
- Thin provisioning
- Trim/Unmap

ReFS does not support File Server Resource Manager, file compression, file encryption, extended attributes, and quotas. ReFS does support block clone and file-level snapshots. ReFS volumes are also not bootable and cannot host the page file.

When used with Storage Spaces Direct, ReFS allows mirror-accelerated parity. Mirror-accelerated parity provides fault tolerance without impacting performance. To create a mirror-accelerated parity volume for use with Storage Spaces Direct, use the following PowerShell command:

```
New-Volume -FriendlyName "ExampleVolume" -filesystem CSVFS_ReFS -StoragePoolFriendlyName
"ExamplePool" -StorageTierFriendlyNames Performance, Capacity -StorageTierSizes 200GB,
800GB
```

You can use ReFSUtil, located in the %SystemRoot%\Windows\System32 folder, to recover data from ReFS volumes that have failed and are displayed as RAW in Disk Management. ReFS will identify files that can be recovered from a damaged ReFS volume and copy those files to another volume.

> **NEED MORE REVIEW?** **RESILIENT FILE SYSTEM**
>
> To learn more about ReFS, visit *https://docs.microsoft.com/en-us/windows-server/storage/refs/refs-overview.*

## FAT and FAT32

Windows Server does support creating volumes that use the FAT and FAT32 filesystems. There are few circumstances where you would need to create a volume that uses these filesystems, but many removable storage devices use FAT32 and sometimes the simplest way to get files on and off a recalcitrant server is to copy them onto a convenient USB stick.

> **EXAM TIP**
>
> Remember the minimum number of drives necessary for the various storage space resiliency options.

# Chapter summary

- Azure File Sync provides a method of replicating files between on-premises endpoints and an Azure File Share. Azure File Sync also provides storage tiering of files that have not been recently accessed and can ensure that a certain amount of space on a volume remains free.

- You can use DFS namespaces with Azure File Sync, with DFS namespaces pointing a client at the closest endpoint and Azure File Sync replacing DFS replication.

- File Server Resource Manager allows you to implement file screens, which can be used to block specific file types from being written to file shares.

- Using DFS, you can push a single shared folder structure out across an organization that has multiple branch offices.

- A storage pool is a collection of storage devices that you can use to aggregate storage. You expand the capacity of a storage pool by adding storage devices to the pool.

- A storage space is a virtual disk that you create from the free space that is available in a storage pool.

- Storage Replica allows you to replicate volumes between servers, including clusters, for the purposes of disaster recovery.

- Deduplication can reduce the amount of storage consumed on the volume because when analyzed, it turns out that a substantial number of data chunks stored on a volume are identical.

- SMB Direct allows you to use network adapters that have RDMA to improve the performance of file servers.

- Storage Quality of Service (QoS) allows you to centrally manage and monitor the performance of storage used for virtual machines that leverage the Scale-Out File Server and Hyper-V roles.

# Thought experiment

In this thought experiment, demonstrate your skills and knowledge of the topics covered in this chapter. You can find answers to this thought experiment in the next section.

You are responsible for managing several file servers for a university that has multiple branch locations spread across Australia. Files are presently replicated using Distributed File System (DFS) between each branch office. You want to replace DFS as a replication engine with Azure File Sync. Three separate sets of folders are replicated using DFS, with some DFS replicas present in some locations and not others. One of the DFS replicas is present in all locations. Another problem the university has is students storing unauthorized files in their personal directories. With this information in mind, answer the following questions:

1. How can you block students writing MP3 files to the file share?

2. How many cloud endpoints will you need to create when migrating from DFS to Azure File Sync?

3. What is the minimum number of storage sync service instances you'll need to deploy in Azure to support the migration from DFS to Azure File Sync?

# Thought experiment answers

This section contains the solution to the thought experiment. Each answer explains why the answer choice is correct.

1. You can use File Server Resource Manager to implement file screens to block students from writing MP3 files to the file shares.

2. You will need to create three cloud endpoints, one for each separate folder structure.

3. You will need to create only one storage sync service. This is because each server must replicate with the others and a server can only be associated with one storage sync service.

# Index

## A

## D

# Q-R

# S

# T

# Plug into learning at

# MicrosoftPressStore.com

**The Microsoft Press Store by Pearson offers:**

- Free U.S. shipping

- Buy an eBook, get three formats – Includes PDF, EPUB, and MOBI to use with your computer, tablet, and mobile devices

- Print & eBook Best Value Packs

- eBook Deal of the Week – Save up to 50% on featured title

- Newsletter – Be the first to hear about new releases, announcements, special offers, and more

- Register your book – Find companion files, errata, and product updates, plus receive a special coupon* to save on your next purchase

 Pearson

# Hear about
# it first.

Since 1984, Microsoft Press has helped IT professionals, developers, and home office users advance their technical skills and knowledge with books and learning resources.

**Sign up today to deliver exclusive offers directly to your inbox.**

- New products and announcements

- Free sample chapters

- Special promotions and discounts

- ... and more!

MicrosoftPressStore.com/newsletters

 Pearson